ST ANTONY'S/MACMILLAN SERIES

General Editors: Archie Brown (1978–85) and Rosemary Thorp (1985–   ), both
Fellows of St Antony's College, Oxford

Recent titles include:

Amatzia Baram CULTURE, HISTORY AND IDEOLOGY IN THE FORMATION
OF BA'THIST IRAQ, 1968–89
Gail Lee Bernstein and Haruhiro Fukui (editors) JAPAN AND THE WORLD
Archie Brown (editor) POLITICAL LEADERSHIP IN THE SOVIET UNION
Deborah Fahy Bryceson FOOD INSECURITY AND THE SOCIAL DIVISION OF
LABOUR IN TANZANIA, 1919–85
Victor Bulmer-Thomas STUDIES IN THE ECONOMICS OF CENTRAL AMERICA
Sir Alex Cairncross PLANNING IN WARTIME
Helen Callaway GENDER, CULTURE AND EMPIRE
Colin Clarke (editor) SOCIETY AND POLITICS IN THE CARIBBEAN
David Cleary ANATOMY OF THE AMAZON GOLD RUSH
Roger Cooter (editor) STUDIES IN THE HISTORY OF ALTERNATIVE
MEDICINE
Robert Desjardins THE SOVIET UNION THROUGH FRENCH EYES
Guido di Tella and Carlos Rodríguez Braun (editors) ARGENTINA, 1946–83: THE
ECONOMIC MINISTERS SPEAK
Guido di Tella and D. Cameron Watt (editors) ARGENTINA BETWEEN THE
GREAT POWERS, 1939–46
Guido di Tella and Rudiger Dornbusch (editors) THE POLITICAL ECONOMY OF
ARGENTINA, 1946–83
Saul Dubow RACIAL SEGREGATION AND THE ORIGINS OF APARTHEID
IN SOUTH AFRICA, 1919–36
Anne Lincoln Fitzpatrick THE GREAT RUSSIAN FAIR: NIZHNII NOVGOROD
Haruhiro Fukui, Peter H. Merkl, Mubertus Müller-Groeling and Akio Watanabe
(editors) THE POLITICS OF ECONOMIC CHANGE IN POSTWAR JAPAN
AND WEST GERMANY
Heather D. Gibson THE EUROCURRENCY MARKETS, DOMESTIC
FINANCIAL POLICY AND INTERNATIONAL INSTABILITY
David Hall-Cathala THE PEACE MOVEMENT IN ISRAEL, 1967–87
John B. Hattendorf and Robert S. Jordan (editors) MARITIME STRATEGY AND
THE BALANCE OF POWER
Linda Hitchcox (editor) VIETNAMESE REFUGEES IN SOUTHEAST ASIAN
CAMPS
Derek Hopwood STUDIES IN ARAB HISTORY
Amitzur Ilan BERNADOTTE IN PALESTINE, 1948
Derek Hopwood and Hiroshi Ishida SOCIAL MOBILITY IN CONTEMPORARY
JAPAN
J.R. Jennings SYNDICALISM IN FRANCE
A. Kemp-Welch THE BIRTH OF SOLIDARITY
Maria d'Alva G. Kinzo LEGAL OPPOSITION POLITICS UNDER
AUTHORITARIAN RULE IN BRAZIL
Bohdan Krawchenko SOCIAL CHANGE AND NATIONAL CONSCIOUSNESS
IN TWENTIETH-CENTURY UKRAINE

Robert H. McNeal STALIN: MAN AND RULER
Iftikhar H. Malik US–SOUTH ASIAN RELATIONS, 1940–47
Ziba Moshaver NUCLEAR WEAPONS PROLIFERATION IN THE INDIAN
SUBCONTINENT
Amii Omara-Otunnu POLITICS AND THE MILITARY IN UGANDA, 1890–1985
Ilan Pappé BRITAIN AND THE ARAB–ISRAELI CONFLICT, 1948–51
George Philip THE PRESIDENCY IN MEXICAN POLITICS
J.L. Porket WORK, EMPLOYMENT AND UNEMPLOYMENT IN THE SOVIET
UNION
Brian Powell KABUKI IN MODERN JAPAN
Laurie P. Salitan POLITICS AND NATIONALITY IN CONTEMPORARY
SOVIET–JEWISH EMIGRATION, 1968–89
Gregor Schöllgen A CONSERVATIVE AGAINST HITLER (*translated by Louise
Willmot*)
Pierre L. Siklos WAR FINANCE, RECONSTRUCTION, HYPERINFLATION
AND STABILIZATION IN HUNGARY, 1938–48
H. Gordon Skilling (*editor*) CZECHOSLOVAKIA, 1918–88
H. Gordon Skilling *SAMIZDAT* AND AN INDEPENDENT SOCIETY IN
CENTRAL AND EASTERN EUROPE
J.A.A. Stockwin, Alan Rix, Aurelia George, James Horne, Daichi Itô and Martin
Collick DYNAMIC AND IMMOBILIST POLITICS IN JAPAN
Verena Stolcke COFFEE PLANTERS, WORKERS AND WIVES
Jane E. Stromseth THE ORIGINS OF FLIXIBLE RESPONSE
Joseph S. Szyliowicz POLITICS, TECHNOLOGY AND DEVELOPMENT
Jane Watts BLACK WRITERS FROM SOUTH AFRICA
Philip J. Williams THE CATHOLIC CHURCH AND POLITICS IN NICARAGUA
AND COSTA RICA
Zhang Yongjin CHINA IN THE INTERNATIONAL SYSTEM, 1918–20

Series Standing Order

If you would like to receive future titles in this series as they are
published, you can make use of our standing order facility. To place a
standing order please contact your bookseller or, in case of difficulty,
write to us at the address below with your name and address and the
name of the series. Please state with which title you wish to begin your
standing order. (If you live outside the United Kingdom we may not
have the rights for your area, in which case we will forward your order
to the publisher concerned.)

Customer Services Department, Macmillan Distribution Ltd,
Houndmills, Basingstoke, Hampshire, RG21 2XS, England.

China, Britain and Businessmen

Political and Commercial Relations, 1949–57

Wenguang Shao

MACMILLAN

in association with
ST ANTONY'S COLLEGE
OXFORD

First published 1991

Published by
MACMILLAN ACADEMIC AND PROFESSIONAL LTD
Houndmills, Basingstoke, Hampshire RG21 2XS
and London
Companies and representatives
throughout the world

Printed in Hong Kong

British Library Cataloguing in Publication Data
Shao, Wenguang
China, Britain and businessmen: political and commercial relations, 1949–57. —
(St. Antony's/Macmillan series).
1. Great Britain. Foreign relations with China, history
2. China. Foreign relations with Great Britain, history
I. Title II. St Antony's College III. Series
327.41051
ISBN 0–333–53827–7

To Meisun and Xiaohai

Contents

List of Tables

List of Plates

The photographs in the plate section were made available by The 48 Group of British Traders with China. Every effort has been made to contact all the copyright-holders, but if any have been inadvertently overlooked the publishers will make the necessary arrangement at the first opportunity.

Preface

As China enters the 1990s with the rest of the world, the forty years she has traversed since the founding of the People's Republic of China on 1 October 1949 may stand as testimony to the beginning of a new era in which the Chinese nation comes to terms with her revolutionary legacy and her position in relation to the outside world.

This book hopes to contribute to the revaluation of past experience in a quest for better guidance for the reform process in the future. It examines the dynamic process of political and commercial relations between China and Britain from 1949 to 1957. One obvious point of departure is the belief that nobody could convincingly talk about the economic policies of the People's Republic towards capitalist Britain without looking at China's domestic politics and foreign relations. Nor could Britain's commercial exchanges with China stand unaffected by the atmosphere of the Cold War and the exigencies of Britain's alliance with the United States. The Sino–British commercial relationship of this period may best be viewed as a process of interaction between politics and business, between governments and business men, between ideology and common sense.

Naturally enough, one of the first points people tend to raise is: was there much trade between China and Britain at that time, given China's economic ties with the Soviet Union and Eastern Europe, and the Western embargoes and sanctions on China? An indirect answer to that question is that in spite of all that, trade never completely stopped between China and Britain; Hong Kong, a British colony with which mainland China has maintained extensive trade relations, also comes into the picture. But even without mentioning Hong Kong, and admitting the relative insignificance of Sino–British trade in terms of its share in each of the two countries' total foreign trade, one is still struck by the strength of commercial activities across the political boundaries, and above all the variety of commercial issues and problems that arose between China and Britain throughout the period, from before the outbreak of the Korean War to the eve of the Chinese campaign known as the 'Great Leap Forward'. Rather than focusing on comparative statistics and trade volumes, I was particularly drawn towards unravelling the underlying political problems as my main interest because they were created by a unique set of circumstances of the time, and also because some of them have hitherto been rarely understood.

At this point, an interested reader may ask: why choose the year 1957 with which to end the present analysis? Is it because something happened in that year which may signify a turning point? In fact my reason for doing this is twofold. First, the British government decided in May 1957 to come off the China Differential within the Western embargo regime against China in defiance of pressure from the United States. Many other COCOM–CHINCOM members followed suit, as did a number of Commonwealth nations. This was not only an important political move in itself; it also removed a major stumbling block to the expansion of economic relations between China and Britain. A more practical reason for the choice is that, when I began this project as part of my doctoral studies at Oxford, the British government's Thirty Year Rule in releasing official documents for public use unabled me to read the hitherto classified files right up to 1957–8. I thought it was rather convenient for my purpose. Afterwards, when I revised my D Phil thesis and developed it into the present book, I did not wish to extend the period, having already gathered more than enough material to put into a single volume.

When the Chinese Communist Party took power in 1949, the new government began to eliminate all vestiges of Western economic domination. This policy served the twin objectives of national assertion and State socialism. The events in mainland China clashed fiercely with the perceptions of the Western governments, who participated to a greater or lesser extent in the US-inspired strategy of containment, and pressurised Beijing through tactics of diplomatic isolation and economic hardship. The PRC's alliance with the Soviet Union and the massive aid she received enabled the country to stand on her feet after the ruins of the war, and to undertake an ambitious programme of industrialisation and social welfare. Part of the cost China had to pay for the political polarisation and tension in East Asia was the Korean war, which admittedly was not of China's making, but which created circumstances compelling her to defend herself in the face of the wrath and war-making capabilities of almost the entire Western world.

These were among the major forces at work, which set the conditions in which Sino–British relations evolved from 1949 onwards. Bearing these in mind, one can then proceed to untie the knots in the political and commercial interchanges between China and Britain in the 1950s. It is striking that although Britain was the first Western government to recognise the PRC in January 1950, this did not lead to formal diplomatic relations between Beijing and London. Instead they stumbled on issues on which neither side was prepared to compromise. As a result of the diplomatic impasse, the British presence in China was stripped of its political legitimacy, and Britain's official representation on behalf of her nationals was rendered largely ineffective. Even after diplomatic representation was upgraded to the level of Chargé d'Affaires in 1954, official relations remained cold throughout the 1950s and 1960s.

The British government's China policy was no more than one of waiting it out and keeping a foot in the door. Both the stability of Hong Kong and Britain's economic interests in China required that it should maintain contact and, better still, a working relationship with China. Its hope of weaning China away from the Soviet-dominated socialist camp was fading, but it never evaporated completely. However the many inconsistencies which troubled this policy appeared to be rooted in a confusion of priorities, and in Britain's unwillingness to distance herself from American objectives in the Far East. Nor did this appear entirely unavoidable after hostility broke out in Korea in the summer of 1950. Where trade became a political weapon, and where commercial activity was heavily burdened with security objectives, expansion of business with China was in reality not as important as No. 10 Downing Street at times declared it to be.

Although Britain contributed a contingent to the UN forces in Korea, China and Britain were never formally at war. One would have thought that the British commercial interests in China could still count on the Chinese government's recognition that, at least during the transitional period in China's economic rehabilitation, British capital and expertise would be put to good use. While the CCP challenged the old, semi-colonial pattern of foreign commerce and investment on the basis of its notions of sovereignty and independence, its actions did not strike the West as absolute and devoid of logic and common sense. Many in the foreign business community may also have hoped that the local population might be willing to appreciate the Westerners' role in helping them build a strong China, and to forgive and forget the unpleasant encounters and humiliation in the past. That did not prove easy in reality.

But the principal dilemma lay in the CCP's new policy of utilisation, restriction and transformation with respect to the country's private capital during the transition. How would such a policy, then,

be applied to foreign commercial interests in China without antagonising Western public opinion? What form would the transformed
foreign capital take, short of either complete integration or outright
expropriation? The events which kept unfolding outside China's
borders generated so much pressure on her policy at home that
Beijing was never given the chance to think through these questions
and their consequences in connection with foreign interests in Chinese
territory, just as a financially weakened Britain was never given the
chance to think through the question of what role British capital
could usefully play in a revolution-inspired host country – other than
one based on sheer opportunism and business expediency. In the
event, British firms were soon confronted with the dire necessity of
cutting losses and pulling out from China.

As a new pattern of trade gradually took shape, London initially
responded by signalling to Beijing that it would endorse trade only
through the Old China Hands, to the possible exclusion of new
trading groups sympathetic to China. This complicated any coordinated British effort for better business with China and, more significantly, it may have reinforced China's doubts about the wisdom of
substantial commercial involvement with a politically hostile system.
Much as they desired to trade with each other, Chinese trade organisations and British firms could not free themselves from the ideological bias and political exigencies of the time.

Most British firms had left China by the end of 1952. What
happened to these firms and individuals through the unsettled years
of the 1950s must have been a unique experience for those concerned, but when synthesised and examined will provide material for
analysing the kind of problems that firms of a capital-exporting
country are likely to encounter under radically changed circumstances in the host country. Without a mutual consensus on applicable commercial rules, supervised by bilateral policy coordination at
the official level, China, ill-prepared, was largely left to do what she
saw fit with the foreign investors during the socialist transition of
ownership and production. The Chinese authorities managed to
accomplish a gradual disposal of most foreign interests short of direct
confiscation. But the process nonetheless provided the West with a
classic case of 'politics of hostage capitalism' and 'creeping nationalisation', to the extent that the stigma continued to bother China in the
international capital market for years afterwards.[1]

Writings on this period have hitherto tended to emphasise either
historical legacy, or individual events, or transboundary perceptions

as determinants of China's policy towards the West. It is evident to this author that only a comprehensive approach embracing all these factors, and probably more, can fully explain the logic and complex dynamism of New China's early relationship with Britain. Previous difficulties in examining its commercial aspects may be explained by a general apathy on the part of governments towards this less glamorous side of the Cold War, the propensity of private businessmen to neglect past balance sheets in favour of present and future opportunities, the daunting technicality associated with trade control regimes often shrouded in secrecy, and probably a sense of guilt shared by those directly responsible for what had been done or undone in the past.

Above all, this is a vast field; there is no way to unravel all the unknown at one go. Instead this book aims to present a survey, to give a sense of the flow of events, and to fill in many a factual gap along the way. I can only hope that it has made a useful start. It is encouraging that the exercise has benefited from a greater willingness amongst the Chinese to talk and write about these things as they reflect upon historical lessons and take a fresh, honest look at the outside world. It is my earnest hope that this rethinking will continue.

This book has been developed from a D Phil thesis I wrote at St Antony's College, Oxford. I wish to take this opportunity to acknowledge my deep gratitude to Dr Paul M. Hayes of Keble College, who supervised my studies with wisdom and precision, and to Professor Adam Roberts, of Balliol College, for his encouragement and confidence in me. My appreciation also goes to Michael Kaser of St Antony's College, Oxford, and Brian Hook of Leeds University, both of whom gave me invaluable comments and criticism as my thesis examiners and kindly recommended the present work to the publishers. Mr Kaser graciously agreed to handle copy-editing queries on my behalf, for which I am very grateful.

I should like to thank the librarians and archivists at St Antony's College, the Bodleian Library, the Rhodes House Library, the British Public Record Office, the SOAS Library, as well various people at the '48' Group, the Sino–British Trade Council, the China Association, the Hongkong Bank Group Archives, the Swire Group, and the Shanghai Academy of Social Sciences, without whose permission to use their records and other assistance this research would not have been possible.

I wish to recall, in particular, the extensive interviews given me by Huan Xiang (who had led me by the hand in this and other professional undertakings and whose death early in 1989 deeply saddened me), by Huang Hua, by S. Gordon Sloan (whose death in 1989 was a great loss to the cause of Sino–British trade), and by numerous other individuals in governmental and private institutions in Beijing, Shanghai, Hong Kong and England. I could never thank them enough for the insights and knowledge they shared with me on arguably some of the most significant dimensions of New China's early relations with the outside world.

My research in the United States and England was made possible by the generous grant of scholarship from the Tangkakji Trust, to whose Board of Trustees I express my deep gratitude and appreciation. I was also a recipient of an ORS Award while at Oxford, which I gratefully acknowledge to the ORS Committee, and to the University of Oxford who nominated me.

W.S.

Note

1. See T.N. Thompson, *China's Nationalization of Foreign Firms: The Politics of Hostage Capitalism, 1949–57*, Baltimore: University of Maryland School of Law, 1979; Paucras, Nagy, Jr., *Country Risk*, London: Euromoney Publishers, 1984.

List of Abbreviations

ABCC	Association of British Chambers of Commerce
APC	Asiatic Petroleum Co. (Shell)
BAT	British-American Tobacco Co.
BCC	British Chamber of Commerce
BCPIT	British Council for the Promotion of International Trade
BoC	Bank of China
BoT	Board of Trade
CA	China Association
CAAC	Civil Aviation Administration of China
CATC	Central Air Transportation Corporation
CBI	Confederation of British Industries
CCP	Chinese Communist Party
CCPIT	China Council for the Promotion of International Trade
CPG	Central People's Government
CNIEC	China National Import and Export Corporation
CNAC	China National Aviation Corporation
CO	Colonial Office
CRO	Commonwealth Relations Office
ECA	Economic Cooperation Administration
ECGD	Export Credits Guarantees Department
EPC	Economic Policy Committee
FAB	Foreign Affairs Bureau
FBI	Federation of British Industries
FES	Command in Chief, Far East Station (Royal Navy)
FO	Foreign Office
HSBC	Hongkong & Shanghai Banking Corporation
IC/DV	Import Certificate-Delivery Verification
ICC	International Chamber of Commerce
ICI	Imperial Chemical Industries
IL	International Lists
KMA	Kailan Mining Administration
LCC	London Chamber of Commerce
LEC	London Export Corporation
MCC	Military Control Commission
MFA	Ministry of Foreign Affairs

MFT	Ministry of Foreign Trade
MoD	Ministry of Defence
MoF	Ministry of Food
MoS	Ministry of Supply
MoT	Ministry of Transport (& Civil Aviation)
NUM	National Union of Manufacturers
OEEC	Organization of European Economic Cooperation
PLA	People's Liberation Army
PRC	People's Republic of China
SASS	Shanghai Academy of Social Sciences
SBTC	Sino–British Trade Committee (1954)
	Sino–British Trade Council (1957)
SECWP	Security Export Control Working Party
SFTC	Shanghai Foreign Trade Corporation
SOAS	School of Oriental and African Studies, University of London
TAC	Transit Authorization Certificates scheme
YTT	Yee Tsoong Tabacco Co. (BAT)

Key to Notes

The books are cited in the footnotes without their publishers, but are listed in full in the Bibliography. Official communications cited with a number (no.) are telegrams, the rest being letters or notes.

BT	Board of Trade Files
CA: M & C	China Association: Minutes & Circulars
CA: Bull.	China Association: Bulletins
CAB	Cabinet Papers
CMD	Command Papers
CHC	*Cambridge History of China*
Cresta	China Association: *Foreign Office Correspondence Jan. 1950 – July 1956*
CMSNA	Archives of the China Merchant Steam Navigation Co., Shanghai
DEFE	Ministry of Defence Files
FEER	*Far East Economic Review*
FO	British Foreign Office Files
FRUS	*Foreign Relations of the United States*
HKBGA	Hongkong Bank Group Archives, HK
JSS	The Papers of John Swire & Sons Ltd.
LCM	The '48' Group: Liaison Committee Minutes
NCNA	New China News Agency
PD	*Parliamentary Debates (Hansard)*, House of Commons
PREM	Prime Minister's Office File
RMRB	*Ren Min Ri Bao* (The People's Daily)
SBTC	Sino–British Trade Council: Working Committee Agenda & Minutes
SJZS	*Shi Jie Zhi Shi* (World Knowledge)
SW	*Selective Works of Mao Zedong*
XHYB	*Xin Hua Yue Bao* (New China Monthly)

1 China and Britain: A Theme of National Liberation

Sweep the house clean, and then invite the guests in.

Mao Zedong

Change, indeed, is painful, yet ever needful; and if memory has its force and worth, so also has hope.

Thomas Carlyle

Western influences have dominated China's international relations since the second half of the 19th century. For the British at least, the golden era of the China trade and diplomacy came to a close upon the outbreak of the Pacific War in 1941. The CCP-led victory of the civil war in 1949 hastened the pace of the national revolution through which the remainder of Western influences were swept away.

This chapter discusses the major issues relating to the institutional structures of British commercial interests in China during the years prior to 1949, events which directly affected their legal status under the Guomindang, and the situation in which British firms found themselves when China's political power changed hands. An analysis of the concept of 'national liberation' postulated by the CCP leadership will be followed by a general survey of the new governmental measures designed to sweep away the vestiges of the country's colonial past. These specifically relate to the British experience, and will encompass the issue of the PRC's attitude towards old treaty obligations and bonded debts. The preservation of Hong Kong's status quo as a British colony after 1949 is an exception to the application of national liberation. It serves as an example of how nationalism cannot by itself fully explain the events which took place in post-1949 China.

SPECIAL PRIVILEGES AND INFLUENCES

For good or ill, the British commercial activities overseas which have been most vividly remembered are probably those relating to the

1

special status and privileges enjoyed by British subjects in the old China. For some it was but a part of the Empire's glory and supremacy. As the most industrialised and powerful nation in the world, Britain took the lead in forcing open China's door to expanded foreign contacts. After the Treaty of Nanking was signed in 1842 to end the Opium War, foreign nationals were lodged in five 'Treaty Ports'. The number of treaty ports eventually increased to 74, in addition to 17 ports voluntarily opened by the Chinese government. Foreign settlements and concessions existed in 19 cities at various dates between 1843 and 1943.[1] According to Chinese statistics, British subjects residing in China numbered 2402 in 1882, 8966 in 1913, and 15 377 in 1936 (excluding the northeast). British-owned firms increased from 298 in 1882 to 590 in 1913, and to 1027 in 1930.[2] These figures are of course insignificant by present standards.

To make their life easier, British nationals in foreign concessions or settlements had their own courts, municipal councils, and police protection. Latter-day writings on the history of the foreign settlements reveal legal ambiguities and sometimes blatant illegal practices from the early period until the Japanese occupation of 1941.[3] Foreigners, by dint of their political advantages and extra-territorial rights, exercised substantial control over many aspects of Chinese life. Britain and other Western powers kept garrisons in Chinese cities and their warships plied Chinese waters. Foreign consuls gave permission for their ships to enter or leave a port, while foreign-controlled customs gave port clearance.[4] Consuls assumed jurisdiction over ships and crew in both civil and criminal matters. They also took it upon themselves to carve out the best located waterfronts for their nationals.[5]

From 1859 to the Second World War the post of Inspector-General of the Chinese Imperial Maritime Customs was held by British nationals, this having been agreed by Chinese authorities and reaffirmed by the Boxer Indemnity Protocol of 1901.[6] Early loan agreements stipulated that until these loans were paid back, foreign control of the maritime customs would remain unchanged. The customs, kept under foreign inspectorate, were biased in favour of importers. One of their methods was to keep the basis of valuation below prevailing market prices. In addition customs authorities retained 15 per cent of the gross revenues, allegedly in payment for operating the revenue side of the service. The actual use of the money, as well as revenues from tonnage dues and fines, was however never publicly accounted for. China eventually restored tariff autonomy between 1929 and 1931, by way of international agreements and promulgation of uniform schedules of customs duties, but certain goods either imported from abroad or manufactured in foreign-owned factories in China for export were treated in the same way at customs as Chinese native products.[7]

The old Chinese authorities allowed British merchant shipping to operate along the China coast as well as in the internal waterway system, controlled by means of registration and reporting procedures. There was an intense cut-throat rivalry between major British and American shipping firms on the China coast in the late 19th century, bearing a strong similarity to scrambles for riparian and littoral commercial navigation in Africa and elsewhere.[8]

BRITISH INVESTMENT IN CHINA

Foreigners enjoyed national treatment in their business undertakings in China. Britain remained the most important investor in China at least up until 1936, both in absolute amounts of investment and in the relative share among foreign countries. British investment consisted primarily of direct investment, although loans to the Chinese government figured very importantly in the last century. According to Hou, direct investment formed respectively 58 per cent, 66 per cent and 81 per cent of the total British investment for 1902, 1914 and 1930, while loans to the Chinese government constituted 42 per cent, 34 per cent and 19 per cent respectively for the same years. Of the direct investment in 1931, half was in areas directly associated with trade: import, export, and general trading, 25 per cent; banking and finance, 12 per cent; and transportation (predominantly shipping), 14 per cent. The remaining half was distributed amongst real estate, 21 per cent; mining, 2 per cent; and miscellaneous, 3 per cent. 77 per cent of British investment in China in 1939 was located in Shanghai, 9 per cent in Hong Kong, and 14 per cent in the rest of China.[9]

Most critics of Sino–Western commercial relations in the 19th and 20th centuries focus their attention on the Western Powers' unequal and privileged position vis-à-vis China, and the alleged lack of fair competition resulting from it. Political and diplomatic support aside, it would seem that in the nature of things world capital, when given a free rein, would move into whichever markets and sectors held out the best prospect of maximum return at minimum risk.[10] On the other hand foreigners' economic power was undoubtedly strengthened by the privileges and facilities they enjoyed in China. On top of that, China's political misfortunes and the weakness of government tended to free foreigners from moral restraints on their economic intrusions and political importunities.

There is almost no doubt that British investment in China prior to the second world war was highly profitable, particularly in textiles, the tobacco industry and landed property.[11] It is suggested that the infusion of foreign capital into the Chinese economy, together with modern technology and management skills, served as necessary fuel to get the modern Chinese economic vehicle on the road. The debating point is whether harmful effects, if any, outweighed the benefits. There is at one end of the spectrum the view that countries most heavily indebted to the British rarely found in their reliance upon foreign capitalists a source of irritation or a matter for regret.[12] At the other end is the Marxist assertion that the history of modern China is a history of imperialist aggression, of imperialist opposition to China's independence and to her development of capitalism.[13] Other viewpoints range from the notion of a 'high-level equilibrium trap' obstructive to incentives for capitalism in China, to blaming Chinese bureaucracy's lack of cooperation with Western firms' efforts to initiate changes in the traditional economy.[14] It is also argued that China's foreign trade did not link effectively with developments in various sectors of China's economy, nor did a major portion of foreign investment in China result from a net inflow of capital from capital-exporting countries, other than funds secured through various commercial operations inside China.[15]

It is generally agreed that the Western impact undermined the self-confidence and prestige of the Chinese Confucian tradition and engendered in nearly all politically conscious Chinese a sense of frustrating and infuriating helplessness. While it is valid to point out that the nature of China's old-fashioned economic institutions, as well as the superficial resistance of the officialdom to Western influences and the absence of a consistent national policy, retarded the modernisation of China's economy, and while many Chinese were convinced that their country badly needed economic modernisation and social revolution, the physical reality of foreign penetration equally convinced many Chinese that in modern times China had been deeply wronged by the imperialist powers by virtue of the latter's material strength and aggressive instinct.

To many Chinese the question of whether or not the activities of foreign capital had actually brought about benefits and progress to their country, and whether or not the Chinese government was capable of balancing one foreign firm against another in competitive business, was of little importance as long as it was understood that the interests and progress of China did not figure in the considerations of foreign investors. To them the crucial question was – knowing (or perceiving on account of their experience) that the foreigners were primarily motivated to make fortunes – should the Chinese be willing and prepared to let the foreigners have their way, even at the expense of the Chinese people's livelihood and dignity, in the hope that their personal difficulties and losses would in the long run be compensated for by the fact that China would be enabled to industrialise and move slowly up the scale of 'European civilisation'? For the majority of the politically conscious, the answer was inevitably 'no'. It was the negative consequences that they feared most, and they did not as yet possess the effective tools, political and economic, with which to exercise some kind of preventive control. Rejecting Western influences did not in itself solve China's problems, but it was felt preferable for the Chinese people to handle their problems their own way, even if this took a long time and produced other forms of suffering.

BRITISH COMMERCIAL INTERESTS IN CHINA: 1945–9

Britain's commercial activities greatly contracted after the second world war, partly because its special privileges in China were greatly reduced by the Sino–British treaty of January 1943, and partly owing to its weakened economic and financial position in the world in general, and in the Far East in particular. Under the 1943 Treaty, Britain relinquished extra-territoriality in China as well as its rights in the international settlements in Shanghai and Xiamen. The treaty also provided for the surrender of Britain's concessions in Tianjin and Guangzhou, the relinquishment of its right to claim the appointment of a British subject as inspector-general of Chinese customs, and its right to inland shipping and cabotage in Chinese waters. Rights normally enjoyed by vessels of one country in the waters and ports of another were in principle substituted. However an annex stipulated that the abolition of the system of treaty ports would not affect existing property rights, British and Chinese nationals being entitled to 'the right to acquire and hold real property throughout' each other's territories.[16]

One of the main reasons for the treaty's quick conclusion was that China was then occupied by Japan and the Japanese, on 1 January 1943, had informed the puppet regime of Wang Jingwei of their own 'surrender' of extra-territorial privileges so as to show 'the solidarity of the Asian peoples'. The subsequent declaration by others to abolish their extra-territorial rights thus became a matter of gesture forced upon the Western Powers by events obviously beyond their control; a mere *de jure* recognition of a reality existing *de facto*.[17] Just the same, the treaty was viewed among the British community in China as their Government's unconditional surrender of assets and a 'one-sided bargain'.[18]

The Sino–Japanese conflict, paradoxically, also strengthened Guomindang's control of the national economy. The government had since 1938 been directly controlling major exports and imports. When private foreign merchants tried to re-establish themselves after the war they found their sphere very restricted, while official trade corporations enjoyed priority and competitive advantage. Nor was the British government able to make any progress in getting the Guomindang government to resume service of the pre-war loans. This subject, as well as that of Britain's inland shipping rights, was raised during the course of negotiations for a commercial treaty, like the one concluded between China and the US in 1946, to be established. After nearly a year's foot-dragging, deadlock was reached and the talks broke down in October 1947.[19]

Britain's economic strength experienced a general decline in China, and her investment in China greatly contracted in the postwar period. After the war most of the more important British properties, including those of nearly all the big firms, were returned by the Chinese government to British control, but some British private owners continued to have difficulty in establishing title to their properties. In early 1946 the authorities took steps to legislate a new company law aimed at subjecting foreigners to the Chinese legal system.

Except for some cases in which British shipping companies were allowed to carry relief materials under special permission, the Guomindang authorities put a general ban on foreign inland shipping after strong pressure from Chinese shipping interests,[20] which greatly dismayed British business and political circles.[21] Related was the question of foreign pilotage in coastal ports. In principle this was given up by Britain (and the United States) under the treaties of 1943 as a special right, but for a few years the service in Shanghai was kept as part of the Maritime Customs, then under L.K. Little as Inspector-General. In January 1948 the service was taken over by the navigation administration bureau of the Kuomintang government in Shanghai; as a compromise, foreign pilots were allowed to remain in service for ten more years, with an arrangement for their pay cheques to be drawn in New York.[22]

The contraction of British commercial interests in China was also attributable to a general decline of Britain's economic power in the Far East after the war. The British had by 1936 lost their predominance due to competition from Japan and other powers trading with China. Once that privileged monopoly was lost it was difficult for British firms to stage a comeback. After the abrogation of the treaties of extra-territoriality, many British firms trading in China chose to base themselves in Hong Kong rather than Shanghai. The drastic change in the balance of power between Britain and the United States was only too obvious when viewed from the perspective of their comparative postwar economic presence in China.

In late 1946, the Treasury of the British government asked the Board of Trade to survey British interests in China, and to assess how much the United Kingdom would have to spend in order to rehabilitate existing British undertakings, before the Treasury would commit itself to extending further credits to China for new commercial ventures. Investments abroad would only be considered if either they were necessary, or if they would bring in substantial and immediate advantage to the United kingdom.[23] The survey estimated the total amount of expenditure required for rehabilitation to be over £20 million, of which perhaps no more than £10–12 million would need to be found from UK funds if Chinese authorities could be persuaded to provide foreign exchange against other British money available locally.[24] Given the priorities of the British government and the investment environment in China, neither the Treasury nor the Board of Trade was in favour of new investment in China's war-torn economy (except for special cases). Attempts by some firms at early restoration and expansion of business in China met with government discouragement.[25] The British government also decided not to encourage exports to China while trade was more profitable in other (hard currency) areas, and not until Britain's own hard currency position became better.[26]

ASSETS AND VALUES

The official British estimates in 1947 of their assets in China have often been cited by Western writers.[27] According to their figures, the total value in 1941 of direct British business investment in China represented by actual property was approximately £124 million (excluding the value of coastal and inland waterway shipping). Of this sum £110 million represented the value of immovable property and consisted almost entirely of land and buildings, and £14.2 million represented movable property such as stocks, machinery, equipment and personal belongings. Annual remittances to the United Kingdom out of the yield from this investment were probably no less than £3.75 million. Estimated losses sustained by those actual assets as a result of the war totalled £13.7 million, of which possibly £9.4 million represented the value of materials, which might have been replaced by 1947 by purchases from the UK. Roughly 75 per cent of the total movable property was believed to have been destroyed or removed, and the comparative smallness of this estimated loss (£10.7 million) was due to depleted stocks of most British merchants as a result of the European war and the Sino–Japanese conflict.[28]

It was felt that the capital represented by Chinese government and railway bonds quoted in London – amounting to £53–5 million – should also be added.[29] The value of all kinds of property owned by British shipping companies was later estimated by the British government at something between £15–20 million.[30] That would make the total British business investment worth £134–9 million, excluding the bonded debt. It may be noted that Chinese estimates of the total British business investment in China, including enterprise investment and real estate, appear to be higher, at £189 916 290 and £177 547 150 for 1941 and 1948 respectively.[31]

British companies were trying hard to preserve and make the best use of their shore facilities on the coast and on the Yangtze. Their efforts included the carriage of Chinese government, cargo, which allowed some limited transport of goods and passengers for commercial purposes.[32] Both Butterfield and Swire and the Jardines managed to enter into joint ventures with Chinese shipping interests, with a view to keeping a profile in the shipping business and preserving their waterfront facilities.[33] The wharves, godowns and port facilities of China's ports varied from 20 to 40 per cent of British ownership, with large shares being taken by Butterfield and Swire, Jardine Matheson and Co. and the Kailan Mining Administration (KMA).[34] Besides

Butterfield and Swire and the Jardines, British shipping companies operating ocean-going transport to and from China included Mackinnon, Mackenzie and Co., Bank Line (China) Ltd, Harrisons King and Irvin Ltd, Dodwell, and Mollers (China) Ltd.[35] While China tried to protect her navigation rights in her territorial waters, overseas shipping was still almost exclusively in the hands of foreign firms. Foreign cargo surveyors, sworn measurers, analysts and inspectors of produce at various ports were also mostly foreigners. Contracts for insuring sea-borne cargoes often stipulated that only the agents of British insurance firms were qualified to inspect the goods to be shipped out to Britain.

The Maritime Customs, manned by Chinese and foreign staff, retained considerable Guomindang trust despite some reports of corruption and graft, so much so that at the end of 1948 some 80 tons of gold bars and 120 tons of silver were shipped to Taiwan not in naval gunboats but in the Customs' lighter vessels. Lester Knox Little, the Inspector General of US nationality, eventually left for Taipei with the service itself when the Guomindang government fled the mainland in 1949.[36]

Despite the various setbacks for British interests, many industrial properties resumed activity on a small scale after the war. Other firms also tried hard to maintain activity where conditions were more favourable to foreign business. The extent of geographical concentration of foreign-related economic activities was evident from the fact that the foreign trade of Shanghai equalled that of all China's other ports put together. In Shanghai a number of large firms, such as Jardine Matheson, Butterfield and Swire and the Sassoons, as well as the subsidiaries of such transnational corporations as Shell, BAT, ICI and Lever Brothers, dominated the economic scene. According to a 1948 estimate, these seven giants alone engaged 60 per cent of the capital, 53 per cent of the staff and 58 per cent of the land holdings of the British business community in Shanghai.[37]

To resume their activities, three British banks applied for formal registration with the Ministry of Finance under the new regulations of the Chinese government. Foreign banks were advised to fix their local capital at a nominal figure of CNC ¥10 million, irrespective of the number of branch offices a bank might have in China or of the capital investment in offices and residences in the country.[38] It was also reported that Shanghai's foreign banks lost their most important source of income – from exchange dealings and arbitrage.

Paradoxically one result of the 1943 treaty on extra-territoriality was that foreign land holdings would not henceforth be confined to the former concessions. The authorities also introduced a new measure under which foreigners' right to leases 'in perpetuity' was changed into their right to 'land ownership', evidenced by the new issue in some cities of a Land Ownership Certificate in lieu of the old 'estate for years' deeds. This caused a good deal of confusion and disquiet among government officials. It is estimated that the value share of the British capital as represented in landed property in China increased from US $219 504 000 (£54 467 494) in 1941 to $321 763 000 (£79 841 936) in 1948.[39]

The British were not at all happy with their post-war position in China, and they blamed the Guomindang for their difficulties. There is no question about British aversion to the Guomindang regime, both in government and commercial circles. They believed that Chiang Kai-shek's government shamefully exploited the slogan of 'China's sovereign rights' to expel British interests, in connivance with Chinese vested interests whose motives were hardly benevolent. It was also suggested that government regulations for economic control decayed into instruments for organised 'rackets' by minor, if not senior, officials.[40] Britain was also annoyed by Chiang's discrimination in favour of the United States, be it in the field of shipping, import trade, land holdings or in respect of other extra-territorial rights.[41] It was believed that the government's nationalistic feelings were by no means directed at all foreign powers in China. Its predominant policy posture and the sentiments of the elite were decisively pro-American. It was American money that propped up the government forces in the test of strength with the Communists.[42]

CCP: A THEME OF NATIONAL REVOLUTION

The theoretical framework of the Chinese revolution was formulated by CCP leaders in the late 1920s and was firmly established within the party by 1935. Mao Zedong initially identified two major targets against which the revolution should be directed: imperialism and feudalism. Later he added the 'compradore big bourgeoisie', who were the chief beneficiaries of bureaucratic capitalism, as another principal target.[43] To Mao, China always seemed to be on the verge of *wang-guo*, that is, the catastrophic loss of total nationhood to foreign powers. The experience of the Revolution of 1911 and subsequent events further stiffened his resolve to fight for the cause of China's independence and equality. During the early republican period, feudal warlords – themselves guardians of the big landlord class – and the various imperialist powers were seen to have banded together to impose a twofold oppression of the Chinese people. The compradore class in the cities, dallying with foreign interests, acted as a linkage between feudal gentry in the rural areas and foreign interests in the treaty ports. Mao saw the main tasks of the Chinese revolution as being to strike at the twin heads of the hydra by carrying out a national revolution to overthrow foreign imperialist oppression, and a democratic revolution to overthrow feudal land-lord oppression.[44]

This does not mean that Mao did not recognise the positive impact of the West on the Chinese society. Penetration by foreign capitalism in China accelerated the growth of a commodity economy in town and country, and gave rise to possibilities for the development of capitalist production and the birth of national capitalism in China. On the other hand, the invasion of foreign capitalism and the gradual growth of capitalist elements in Chinese society changed the country by degrees into a semi-colonial and semi-feudal society. Out of the enterprises directly operated by foreigners, and with the advent of national capitalism in China, emerged and grew a new social class, the Chinese proletariat, which was eventually to lead the Chinese people in toppling the rule of imperialism, the feudal landed gentry and the 'compradore big bourgeoisie'. A weakened traditional power hierarchy enabled the revolutionary forces to grow in strength and eventually bring about a revolution.[45]

Mao rejected the proposition that China should first industrialise herself and establish a capitalist society under the leadership of the bourgeoisie and with the assistance of the West. In the first place, international capitalism wanted nothing of the kind. Indeed foreign Powers were the first to violate China's independence and oppose her development of capitalism. Mao wrote: 'It is certainly not the purpose of the imperialist powers invading China to transform feudal China into capitalist China. On the contrary, their purpose is to transform China into their own semi-colony or colony.' Towards this end they colluded with Chinese feudal forces both to arrest the growth of capitalism in China through domination of the market; and to strangle earlier revolutions, through their support to the suppression by Chinese rulers of peasant rebellions, and the Western Powers' alliance with individual warlords in different regions of China in a bid for spheres of influence. To crown it all, foreign territorial concessions and military occupation were seen as blatant attempts to colonise China. For Mao and the Chinese Communist Party, the political objective of driving out the imperialists came first, especially when China was under foreign invasion, because 'national oppression by imperialism is the more onerous'.[46]

Secondly, and this has a stronger ideological tone, the development of a capitalist society in China would be anachronistic as it would be against the tide of the world revolution for socialism. Mao wrote:

The world today is in a new era of wars and revolutions, an era in which capitalism is unquestionably dying and socialism is unquestionably prospering. In these circumstances, would it not be sheer fantasy to desire the establishment in China of a capitalist society under bourgeois dictatorship after the defeat of imperialism and feudalism?[47]

Thus Mao views the cause of democratic revolution in China in a larger world context of communism fighting and eventually triumphing over capitalism. This was developed from his Marxist beliefs and his identification of China's national salvation with the world revolution championed by the Soviet Union.

Mao's statements on imperialism were doubtlessly powerful in simplicity and logic. Unlike his class analysis of domestic forces within Chinese society for the purpose of democratic revolution, he did not see a theoretical necessity for distinguishing between Western business communities in China and their governments' policies and actions with respect to China. Nor did his conceptual framework contain specific analysis of such issues as foreign loans and bonded debts, or foreign industrial activities and landholdings in China. One might have expected these to constitute crucial test cases for theoretical conceptualisation so that a judgment could be made as to whether, by allowing these, China's sovereignty would necessarily have been compromised.

The CCP leadership saw Western activities over one hundred years of China's modern history as having had adverse effects on China's political status and on the control over the country's social wealth and state revenues. They spoke about 'evils' associated with Western activities in China and grouped them together under the rubric of 'imperialist oppression'. In this respect the doctrine of imperialism had its function as an ideology in giving China's colonial past a focal point and in eliminating any illusion in ordinary people's minds about China's contact with the outside world.

POLICY CONSIDERATIONS

The clearest indication of the Communist notion of how the new-democratic economic structure would bear on foreign economic interests was given in Mao's 'On New Democracy', written in January 1940. Mao postulated that when the republic was established, it would control the big banks and large industrial and commercial enterprises, whether Chinese-owned or foreign-owned. In particular he cited a policy statement to that effect from the Manifesto of the Kuomintang's First National Congress of 1924, a document which had actually been drafted by the Communist Party itself and tabled by the two parties as a joint political platform during the brief period of CCP-Guomindang cooperation.[48] Presumably foreign enterprises and capital of a monopolistic character would not be able to operate in China independently of government intervention, and there is reason to believe that at one point Mao had in mind the possibility of nationalisation.[49] However there is no evidence to suggest that nationalisation of foreign enterprises was actually being planned prior to the CCP takeover in 1948–9.

Subsequent CCP documentation suggests that the Party contemplated that an independent China would welcome foreign investment.[50] In the course of the civil war, the CCP once again emphasised that the policy for foreign residents and their interests would not be one of expulsion or expropriation, no matter whether or not they were of an imperialist nature.[51] The Party gave detailed instructions on such matters in early 1949:

We shall not accord formal legal recognition to the special economic privileges, industrial and commercial enterprises, and investments of governments and private individuals of capitalist countries in China. However, to give hasty indications about any prohibition, restoration or expropriation is equally uncalled for. Only with regard to those cases where either the people's livelihood is most seriously harmed, such as in the case of financial speculation, or where the state sovereignty is most seriously encroached upon, such as in the case of inland navigation, should an order be issued to impose an immediate ban. With regard to other matters such as those relating to foreign banks, it is necessary not hastily to order them to close-down, but first of all to request them to report their capital, accounts and operations, on the basis of which verification and other measures may be undertaken. In particular, we should not act in a hurry to deal with the insurance companies, especially maritime carriage insurance companies.[52]

In March 1949 Mao made an important report to the Second Session of the Seventh CCP Central Committee in which he enunciated the Party's future foreign policies. There he reaffirmed the Party's policy of refusing to recognise the legal status of any foreign diplomatic establishments and personnel of the Guomindang period, of refusing to recognise all the treasonable treaties of that period, of abolishing all imperialist propaganda agencies in China, and their intention of taking immediate control of foreign trade and reforming the customs system. The remaining Western economic and cultural establishments would be allowed to exist for the time being, subject to government supervision and control. 'As for ordinary foreign nationals, their legitimate interests will be protected and not encroached upon.'[53] He did not however say on this occasion whether there would be any formal acknowledgement or denial of the legitimacy of foreign economic interests in China (in contrast to diplomatic institutions), but the overwhelming impression from these pronouncements was that their legitimacy was very much in doubt, and even if legal recognition was a possibility, consideration of this matter would be postponed until a later date. Meanwhile there would be 'supervision and control'.

By the time the People's Republic of China was proclaimed in 1949, the new authorities had already begun to institute a series of legislative and administrative changes to restore China's control over a number of areas where national sovereignty and prestige were affected. Foreign businesses were allowed to carry on for the time being, provided that they abide by the laws and regulations of the land, and that they did not insist upon the special privileges they had enjoyed in the past. Some functions which had hitherto been performed by foreign nationals would as a matter of sovereign right be taken over by state organisations.

Foreign Garrison Compounds

Foreign garrisons had been emptied of troops since the end of the war, with the exception of US marines who withdrew in 1947. From January to September 1950, CCP authorities took formal steps to take over the garrison compounds and buildings of the United States, France, the Netherlands, Britain and the Soviet Union in Beijing, Tianjin and Shanghai. It was implied that compensation would be paid for the requisitioned buildings on the compounds. This government move had been expected by Britain since the cities were put under CCP control, so it did not come as a surprise. Only the United States protested that its title to the land had been confirmed in perpetuity by the Treaty of 1943, which set US–Chinese relations on a new and 'equal' basis. The new Chinese government rejected the notion of residual foreign privileges claimed from the treaty.[54]

Port Pilotage and Inland Shipping

Foreign pilotage and inland shipping had long been held by the Chinese to be an encroachment upon the sovereign rights of the country. CCP authorities, as soon as they assumed control over such ports as Tianjin, Shanghai and Guangzhou, took measures to put these back under Chinese control. Foreign pilots were relieved from their posts and given a pension. Where foreign ships used to come in without bothering about pilotage, the new government now insisted on compulsory pilotage by virtue of newly promulgated regulations. These regulations also covered such matters as application for entry and departure of foreign vessels, inspection on board, and berthing. Often this was part of an overall reorganisation of the Maritime Customs. Thus ships in port had to anchor at designated moorings, the lists of seamen and passengers on board would have to be checked by the Navigation Bureau before a ship could leave Shanghai, and foreign ships in port were not allowed to send out wireless messages through their own stations.[55]

Considerable agitation was aroused when Butterfield and Swire's ship *Hanyang* was not permitted to unload at Tianjin because the master refused to lower the Union Jack and fly the house flags only. She was consequently forced to unload at Tanggu, the seaport outside Tianjin. Later the Chinese authorities relaxed the rule.[56] The Tianjin port was reported to be under very tight control; Customs and other officials observed strict discipline, even to the extent of declining any offer of tea on board. This drove home the point to foreign seamen that the change-over was revolutionary and complete. In Shanghai the control was at first not very effective and ex-Nationalist soldiers in their hundreds forced their way on board foreign vessels leaving port.[57]

Foreign vessels were in principle not allowed to sail into China's inland waterways. British shipping companies such as the Swire group's Tientsin Lighter Company were refused permission to operate their fleet.[58] Exceptions were made for inland shipping when it was clear that a rigid conformity with the rules would cause significant economic losses. In 1950 Chinese foreign trade organisations were allowed to charter foreign vessels to sail on the Yangtze, provided that they flew Chinese flags and strictly followed official instructions with regard to routing.

Maritime Customs

From 1949 to 1950 eighteen principal maritime customs offices and their branches were taken over by CCP Military Control Commissions. Arrangements were made to gradually phase out foreign staff and all documents were required to be prepared in Chinese.[59] A series of major changes were introduced when the General Administration of Maritime Customs of the Central People's Government was established in late November 1949. These related to new tariffs and regulations for goods inspection. Finally in 1951 the Chinese Government was able to produce its first national maritime customs code and tariff regulations.[60]

With regard to cargo surveys and measurements, the process of takeover was also a gradual one. The Tianjin Bureau of Inspection and Testing of Commodities was established in April 1949. A year later the People's Municipal Government issued an order to the effect that all private firms of adjusters, Chinese and foreign alike, must cease operation, and that the functions of inspection and marine measurement of commodities must henceforth be performed exclusively by the Government Bureau. Two British firms were affected, but a Swiss firm of analysts, despite press reports to the contrary, was informed by the Bureau that they would be permitted to continue their activities privately.

To follow up this action, the People's Bank sent notification to the British banks instructing them to advise head offices and agents of the requested revision of clauses in Letters of Credit following examination by the Government Bureau. British shippers were also required to apply to the Bureau for cargo inspection. In Shanghai British inspection firms were not ordered to cease operations until August 1951.[61] Trading concerns in Britain, Canada and the Netherlands for some time refused to accept the contract clauses specifying certification by Chinese commodity inspection offices. There were also complaints about delays in getting the goods passed through and, in view of the possibility of coming into conflict with foreign buyers, that being forbidden to arrange their own inspection or sampling would expose them to inadequate coverage against loss.[62]

Foreign Exchange Controls

When business activities were resumed, the authorities published regulations for the control of foreign exchange. This was aimed at protecting China's foreign exchange reserve and preventing market instability as a result of speculation. The government designated appointed banks for handling foreign exchange transactions exclusively. In Tianjin three foreign banks – the Hongkong and Shanghai Banking Corporation, the Chartered Bank and the Banque Belge – were so designated, together with seven Chinese banks. In Shanghai both British banks were designated, together with seven other foreign banks, twelve Chinese owned private banks and four banks owned by overseas Chinese capital.[63] Meanwhile, both the Hongkong Bank and the Chartered Bank were approached by the Bank of China to act as their collection agents abroad.[64]

There was no question that the People's Bank was to dominate the scene. New regulations stipulated that when a foreign firm received remittance from abroad, the appointed bank handling the draft should deposit the foreign exchange through the People's Bank into the Bank of China. The firm, when notified of the receipt of the sum by the bank and issued with a certificate of receipt, would apply to the Bank of China for permission to draw cash against this remittance for whatever purpose the money was sent. This was also the case for importers, except that their certificate of receipt would have to be purchased with their licences for the imports. All remittances, especially inter-city ones, had to be cleared first by the People's Bank.[65]

In accordance with the terms of the Provisional Regulations Governing the Control over Foreign Exchange, all foreign exchange items transacted through the appointed banks were to be cleared daily with the Bank of China. These applied to money transfers and items withdrawn, including, on the one hand, payments of ordered export goods and consignment goods, overseas remittances, receipts from commercial transactions, receipts of appointed banks themselves, foreign currency notes converted and deposited, and other inward remittances and, on the other hand, payments of import–export goods, shipping charges, insurance and commission on export goods, expenses of students studying abroad, government expenditures, expenses of families or other personnel going abroad, expenses of appointed banks, and other outward remittances.[66] Moreover, whereas Surrender Certificates could formerly be negotiated on the open market, they now had to be passed through the appointed banks for settlement in the Bank of China's foreign exchange clearing house. All this, plus arrangements for giving loans, represented a comprehensive plan of foreign exchange and credit control and was intended to give the central bank wide powers of supervision over larger firms, with the ultimate intention of using state banks as organs of general control over production and trade.[67]

Related to this control was the decision of the government to fix daily the exchange rate between the People's Currency and foreign currencies. This was part of the effort to stabilise the local currency, control commodity prices and quote realistic rates. This however did not prevent devaluation of the new currency owing to inflation. Inflation was particularly rampant during 1949, when there were acute shortages of essential supplies and floods in central China.[68] Chinese wages were mostly based on the so-called 'parity units', which was the average ongoing monetary value of a basket containing a fixed quantity of essential commodities, which had been rising steadily in terms of hard currency.

One effect of the devaluation of the new currency and the 'linkage' device was that British firms had to pay an increasing amount for their overheads in terms of pound sterling. The official exchange rate for foreign currencies tended to get out of line with the prevalent black market rate and with the cross rates among foreign currencies, such as between the pound sterling and the US dollar.[69] Firms which were compelled to rely on remittances to fill in the gap between income and cost were confronted with the fact that the value of the remitted money was often greatly reduced when converted at the official rate. Especially important was the fact that wage increases were kept in line with the rise in commodity prices; thus the drawings of British firms to cover administrative overheads and wages caused no small drain on the resources of their head offices. The problem was partly redressed when certificates of receipt for foreign exchange deposited in the People's Bank were made negotiable in the authorised open market at a rate to be fixed by mutual consultation between the buyer and the seller on the basis of supply and demand. However, owing to inflation and exchange rate disparity, British firms found that attempts to equalise matters by enhancing their prices to buyers abroad often made sales very difficult. In the end this drain on their sterling resources contributed to a considerable extent to the decision of the head offices to discontinue remittances and resign themselves to a complete withdrawal of their China operations, even after the Chinese government succeeded in bringing inflation largely under control.[70]

It was not until July 1950 that the Bank of China was able to establish a single unified foreign exchange rate for the whole nation; the next year Shanghai's foreign exchange was abolished, and foreign currencies as well as gold were removed from the sphere of free transaction. By 1955, with the exception of three banks owned by overseas Chinese capital and two British banks (the Hongkong Bank and the Chartered Bank) which were appointed banks, the entire foreign exchange operation was handled by the Bank of China, embracing both state and joint private Chinese capital.[71]

British Financial Claims

Following the conclusion in 1946 of a Treaty of Friendship, Commerce and Navigation between the Guomindang and the US, in February 1947 the CCP authorities took the formal step of issuing a statement in which they declared null and void all international agreements negotiated by Guomindang since 10 January 1946 without the consent of other political parties. Nor would the future government recognise any existing foreign loans, treaties which disgraced the country, or diplomatic negotiations of the same character. This position was reiterated in early 1949.

China had started to borrow foreign capital as far back as 1874. Between that year and 1887 small loans were contracted with foreign institutions – mostly British – secured on the general resources of the country at a time when China was relatively free of internal as well as external obligations. Between 1894 and 1898 China found herself obliged to apply to foreign powers for huge loans in order to finance her war with Japan and to pay the 230 million-*tael* indemnity claimed by Japan (the Anglo–German Gold Loans of 1896 and 1898). Then came the Boxer Indemnity fixed at 450 million *taels* by the Protocol of

1901, which would be paid out on the security of China's customs revenues. As a consequence of those events, foreign powers succeeded in securing railway concessions for their nationals; most of the loans for railway construction were also secured on customs, salt and other revenues, which in turn lent a large measure of control over China's financial and fiscal policies to foreign powers.[72]

It was suggested that China's Sterling Loans could be classified according to their securities. Another way of classification was based on the purpose for which a loan was made.[73] According to one estimate, China owed to Britain US$109.4 million in 1902, US$195.7 million in 1914, and US$150.1 million in 1936.[74] By 1939, as the Japanese invasion spread southwards, the whole of China's foreign debt service fell into default, with the exception of the Imperial Railway Loan 1899 (Peking–Mukden Line), which was serviced until February 1942 by the Japanese.

It was argued that China had to pay higher interest for the railway loans than the rate prevailing in world financial markets.[75] The counter-argument pointed to the lack of any adequate financial system or regulation in China, the great investment risks related to the possible financial breakdown of the central government or defaults, and a need to compare the terms of China loans with those for countries like Argentina, rather than with Europe, North America or Japan.[76] It was also reported that the Guomindang regime under Chiang made £7–8 million worth of bond issues between 1927 and 1938, nominally for projects such as roads or railways, but possibly also to pay for his campaign to annihilate Chinese Communists.[77]

In 1948 the British claimed that on 31 March 1947 the amount of principal and interest in arrears with respect to outstanding loans amounted to some £42 million (out of a total of approximately £55 million excluding Skoda Loans). The total figure of the bonded debt was subsequently claimed by Britain to be £60.9 million.[78] The British government also claimed that the Chinese government incurred liabilities, under the 1943 treaty, concurrent with the takeover of assets in the Municipal Councils of the foreign settlements in Shanghai and Tianjin, including the service and liquidation of the debenture issues, and settlement of compensation, superannuation and pension claims of foreign ex-employees. It claimed that it had advanced nearly £1.5 million as the ultimate caretaker of the interests of the British subjects concerned, but that these sums were never recovered from the Guomindang authorities.[79] The British government declared in later years that it ultimately paid out £7.5 million over the years, and a claim of £2.5 million was tabled to the Chinese government.

At least twice during the Second World War (in 1941 and 1944) the British government provided official credit loans to the Guomindang government, presumably for the purpose of relieving the war front in Burma. The Guomindang authorities paid the annual instalments up until 1949, whereas final payment was scheduled for the 1960s.[80] On top of that might be added the 1939–53 China 5 per cent Sterling Bonds (issue £2 859 000) guaranteed by BoT, under an agreement made on 18 August 1939.[81] The British government tried to get the PRC government to restore interest and redemption payment on these loans in 1950 after officially recognising Beijing, although it refrained from making it a precondition for such recognition. While the British government recognised that the general external debt had been in suspense since 1939 and that resumption of its service would involve full discussion between China and the British Council of Foreign Bondholders, it deemed the government loans as never having been in default and therefore not *in pari materia* with the general debt.[82]

The official position of the PRC is not to recognise foreign debts incurred by previous governments. Specifically it refuses to undertake any obligation to pay back the old bonded debt and government loans, the liabilities to pensioners who had worked for the previous governments or in foreign settlements, nor is it prepared to compensate foreign nationals for their previous private land holdings (other than buildings) in China. It was agreed between China and Britain in the 1980s that after both sides signed a lump-sum agreement, each party was free to distribute the money to their nationals in conformity with their own principles of compensation. Such agreement was concluded on 5 June 1987, under which Britain would pay China US$3.8 million (£2.33 million) to settle the entirety of China's claims against Britain, whereas China would pay Britain £23.5 million in return.[83]

THE QUESTION OF HONG KONG

The three treaties which Britain concluded with China in the 19th century defined the geographical framework of the Crown Colony of Hong Kong and have sustained its legal existence: the 1842 Treaty of Nanking under which Hong Kong was to be ceded in perpetuity to

Britain; the 1860 Convention of Peking which resulted in Stonecutters Island and the Kowloon Peninsula being ceded in perpetuity to Britain; and the 1898 Convention Respecting an Extension of the Hong Kong Territory under which the area known as the New Territories was leased to the Crown for a 99-year term ending on 1 July 1997.[84]

Neither the PRC government nor any other Chinese government since the Revolution of 1911 have recognised the validity of the three unequal treaties. Whereas the CCP authorities insisted that the three locations remained Chinese territory, they handled the question of Hong Kong with great care and sensitivity. Leading CCP figures indicated privately in November 1948 and 1949 that the CCP did not intend taking back the colony by force but would treat it as a diplomatic issue.[85] The CCP Central Committee later took a decision that the question of Hong Kong should not be settled at once but that a long-term view would be adopted. When the PRC Ministry of Foreign Affairs was constituted in late 1949 it did not contain a separate office for Hong Kong affairs – the issue was handled by the Department of Western Europe and Africa, though under the direct control of the CCP Central Committee.[86]

Insofar as Hong Kong comes into the theme of national liberation, a perceived tacit recognition of the colony's status quo by Beijing upon the founding of the People's Republic may appear to have been a *contretemps*. It is apparent that the new government did not wish to confront Britain politically over the status of Hong Kong when the main target for its diplomatic offensive was the United States. Moreover Hong Kong was useful to China both as a centre for her foreign trade and in terms of overseas remittances from or via Hong Kong. The colony thus played an important role in Sino–British commercial relations for many years to come, not least during the period after the outbreak of the Korean conflict in June 1950. Throughout the PRC period, the Beijing authorities always assumed moral responsibility over Hong Kong's Chinese residents, and there have been numerous official communications with the British and Hong Kong authorities over their welfare.

In 1963 the Beijing government stated publicly for the first time that both Hong Kong and Macao were Chinese territories, and should be restored to Chinese sovereignty through peaceful negotiations when conditions were right. It subsequently ruled out the possibility of Hong Kong and Macao being treated as colonies awaiting independence.[87] China and Britain eventually signed and ratified a Sino–British Joint Declaration on the Question of Hong Kong, under which the entire Hong Kong region is to be restored to China in 1997. A similar agreement was concluded between China and Portugal in 1987, under which Macao is to be returned to China in 1999.[88]

2 New China: Diplomacy and Trade

The Cathedral was packed to the doors, with people standing in all the aisles. Capt. Cazalet, in spite of the shrapnel in his hip, read one lesson, Urquhart the other. We had about 300 Navy present, and the service was broadcast to the people outside who could not get into the Cathedral. Alas the Navy left us the following Wednesday, and we wonder when we shall see them again. We had a collection for the Amethyst fund and realized £400 in seven different currencies.

Trivett (Dean of the Cathedral in Shanghai)

But a fuller and fairer symbol of Taxation, both in its possible good and evil effects, is to be found in the evaporation of waters from the surface of the planet. The sun may draw up the moisture from the river, the morass, and the ocean, to be given back in genial showers to the cornfield; but it may likewise force away the moisture from the fields of tillage, to drop it on the stagnant pool, saturated swamp, or the unprofitable sand-waste.

S.T. Coleridge

While the new Chinese government was making foreign policy pronouncements and introducing institutional changes for direct control of customs and foreign exchange operations, it was also moving into the area of foreign-controlled industry and trade. The latter however was affected by two other considerations insofar as they were related to Western commercial interests in China. One was the need to strike a balance between utilising them for economic recovery and controlling them for the purpose of socialist reform; the other was a decision on their future status.

The shape of the new political relationship between China and Britain gradually emerged out of the initial confusion and ambiguity as CCP forces swept across the country. The political events which brought the two authorities into direct contact with each other, and the political issues which separated them, directly affected the basic attitude of the new government towards British commercial interests in China and crystalised into the question of their legitimacy. It is

24

suggested here that whatever assumptions the British had made about the new China, and no matter how much they tried to use British economic presence to influence the orientation of the revolutionary regime, CCP policy makers were prepared to accept Western commercial presence only to the extent to which the country's political relations with the West and its socialist programme would allow.[1]

A NEW POLICY ON BRITAIN IN THE MAKING

By March 1949 the CCP leadership had decided on the broad lines of foreign policy adjustments for the new government. New China would establish diplomatic relations and trade with socialist countries, but relations with Western countries would need a general overhaul on the basis of new principles and new realities. Mao stated that the new government would refuse to recognise the legal status of any foreign diplomatic establishments and personnel of the Guomindang period, and would refuse to automatically recognise the validity of previous treaties. These were later summed up in the two principles of 'making a fresh start' and 'sweeping clean the house before inviting guests in'.[2]

Thus, pending the founding of the PRC and the *negotiated* establishment of diplomatic relations, a situation of non-recognition and reluctant contact developed at the political–diplomatic level. British and other consuls in Shenyang and other cities were officially ignored after the CCP takeover. Letters were not answered and interviews evaded.[3] Sometimes letters were returned with a stamped notification to the effect that official letters could not be accepted as diplomatic relations had not been established.[4] This frustrated the British, who later blamed Chinese for the *Amethyst* incident by attributing it to a deliberate Chinese policy of non-communication with British diplomatic officials.[5] Only at a later stage of this uncertain period did the directors of the Foreign Affairs Bureaux at Nanjing and Shanghai agree to receive foreign diplomatic representatives – with the usual rider that the talks would be on a strictly personal and unofficial basis.[6]

The British believed that the CCP personnel either found such contacts psychologically repugnant or were stalling for fear of compromising themselves in the face of unreasonable demands. They soon found that the authorities had never directly stated that they regarded the consulates as closed and that they probably did not wish to commit themselves either way.[7] Where a reply was expected to foreign official communications, Chinese officials would indicate that their contents had been duly noted and passed on to higher authorities. This seemed to indicate that the Communist Party was following a considered foreign policy decision, rather than simply being pettily aggressive or pathetically taking advantage of foreign diplomats for national self-assertion so as 'to impress the Chinese population.'[8]

In effect the CCP was determined to start with a clean slate. Mao more than once referred to the need to draw lessons from Dr Sun Yat-sen's government in dealing with foreign powers after the 1911 revolution. To win recognition from Western powers Sun and those who succeeded him were compelled to agree to maintain existing diplomatic ties, together with the old obligations and institutions, which in effect made an independent foreign policy impossible.[9] Recalling these experiences Mao stated that the new government should not be in a hurry to settle the question of recognition by the imperialist countries 'even for a fairly long period'.[10] Relationships with foreign powers were to be started anew, and the terms of the new relationship were to be *negotiated* between the Chinese government and the foreign government on the basis of equality, mutual benefit and mutual respect for each other's territorial sovereignty. 'China's affairs must be decided and run by the Chinese people themselves, and no further interference, not even the slightest, will be tolerated from any imperialist country.'[11]

The Amethyst Incident

Drawn by an innate logic of history, the very first round of contacts with the CCP during the *Amethyst* incident proved to be disastrous to the British government, which was desperately trying to impress upon the new Chinese authorities that its attitude was anything but one of hostility, intervention or contempt. The one hundred days of abortive negotiations after the incident brought to a sharp focus the conflict in each other's perceptions of how future official relations were to be conducted. It was also herald to the stirring summer in which the Communist Party's grand plan in the East–West relations was to be formulated.

The British frigate *Amethyst*, under the Royal Navy's Far East Command, sailed from Shanghai to Nanjing on 19 April 1949 in order to relieve another British frigate, the *Consort*. Before moving the seat of government to southern China, the Guomindang authorities had requested that all foreign vessels withdraw from the Yangtze in view of the risk of incidents with PLA forces. The *Amethyst*'s ill-timed journey up river coincided with the end of a temporary truce and the anticipated crossing of PLA forces to capture the capital city of Nanjing. Even if the *Amethyst* had had time to reach Nanjing before the PLA crossing, there certainly would have been little time left for the *Consort* to sail through to Shanghai without being caught in the crossfire over the Yangtze.

As it happened, the *Amethyst* came under heavy fire from PLA batteries at Sanjiangyin near Rose Island at about 9.30 a.m. on the 20th of April. The frigate returned fire before being grounded on a nearby mudbank, and suffered a toll of 13 killed and 15 wounded. The *Consort*, which later came to her rescue, also exchanged full fire with PLA batteries. The *Consort* then met with the frigate *Black Swan* and a cruiser *London* (which had sailed from Shanghai to the scene) at Jiangyin that evening – which must have seemed a dramatic show of combativeness to anybody watching from the shore. The next day these ships, under Deputy Commander-in-Chief of the Far East Station A.C.G. Madden, endeavoured to approach the *Amethyst* in spite of the PLA's warning salvos. The flotilla fired heavy rounds at the PLA batteries and provoked fierce PLA bombardments, then abandoned the operation and sailed back to Shanghai. Massive numbers of the Communist Second and Third Field Armies soon crossed the Yangtze, and Nanjing – the focal point of the Chinese civil war – fell on the 23rd of April. But the *Amethyst*, later re-floated, was not allowed to leave. The PLA General Headquarters spokesman issued a statement denouncing the invasion by British warships of Chinese waters.[12]

The British government stressed the peaceful nature of the *Amethyst*'s mission, and rejected the notion that a foreign naval presence could be seen by PLA as a menace. They also argued that had CCP authorities objected in the past to the British naval presence, it would always have been open to them to raise the matter through British consular authorities in North China.[13] In London however the government was criticised in the House of Commons for its lack of judgment. There it was pointed out that the British government had presented a number of warships to the Guomindang in the previous few months, and that for more than a hundred years British gunboats had been involved in events in China, causing resentment on all sides.[14]

There is some *prima facie* evidence to suggest that the CCP sincerely believed that the *Amethyst* had fired at their batteries first.[15] The likelihood of the parties misjudging each other's intentions could well have been reinforced by the explosive nature of the situation, by the poor visibility of the ship's identity through a fog on the river, and by both sides' failure to understand each other's signals.[16] In particular, as a PLA officer later recalled, his troops had first fired warning shots from the Low Island battery, requesting the British warship to stop. The British claimed that the frigate had responded by exposing 'additional flags to emphasize the peaceful nature of the mission', had refrained from firing back at first because she herself had not been hit, and had then sailed on.[17]

The CCP authorities argued that the British misdemeanour had resulted from their failure to obtain permission to sail up river through a war area.[18] The British argued that other than the Guomindang government, 'there was no other properly constituted authority to whom His Majesty's Government were under an obligation to notify [the *Amethyst*'s] movements even had they been in a position to do so.'[19] The Chinese pointed to a CCP Central Committee proclamation of 14 February 1947 to the effect that any agreement between the Guomindang and foreigners concerning movements in Chinese territorial waters was null and void. This the British refused to recognise as valid in the circumstances.[20]

Even more serious to the British was the PLA's demand that the British admit to them their 'basic fault' of intruding into Chinese territorial waters. The British admitted that their ship had entered the zone without the PLA's concurrence, but implied that this was but one of the causes of the misunderstanding. They insisted that both sides might have been responsible, that the PLA had no right to detain the *Amethyst*, and that the present negotiation should not prejudice the merits of the case.[21] The PLA deemed this unacceptable for the ship's release.

The ostensible reason for this British position was that the overall question of responsibility was a matter for discussion on a higher diplomatic level because it involved issues of international relations. The *Amethyst*'s Lieutenant Commander J.S. Kerans was instructed to confine his talks to obtaining safe conduct for the ship.[22] This put the Chinese in a dilemma. On the one hand, they did not want to talk to the British at a higher political level lest their position on future relationships with Britain be compromised. On the other hand, they wanted Britain to admit responsibility for the incident through an exchange of notes at local level, for which the British naval commanders claimed they were not authorised and never would be.[23] The British then accused the Chinese of moving away from their position of a speedy settlement of the ship's release, whereas the Chinese questioned British sincerity for their guilty conduct in twisting responsibilities and quibbling over the question of authorisation.

While the Chinese had ample common sense to realise that the ship could not be detained indefinitely, they felt that they could not very well mortgage a verdict over the present political event to future uncertainties and certainly not to the bad faith of the British. They were dismayed that the British were so amoral as to refuse to say anything for fear it might later implicate them and thereby weaken their bargaining position.[24] The upshot of this unhappy event was the *Amethyst*'s escape on the night of the 30th of July, blessed by a rare set of circumstances.[25]

The CCP authorities had initially decided that the shooting event had happened by accident.[26] But eleven rounds of negotiations over a hundred days failed to reach the just settlement they had expected. Nevertheless they used the opportunity to make a political statement against the British 'gunboat diplomacy', and to confront the perceived Western challenge against the CCP's claim to legitimacy. The manifest resentment from both sides, generated by the conflict which had broken out so early between them, made an unpropitious beginning to relations not yet officially started. It also highlighted the sensitive issue of official representation, and thus gave a foretaste of the difficulties over legal status and recognition which haunted the bilateral relations for years to come.

'Leaning on One Side'

While negotiations were bogged down over the *Amethyst*'s release, on 1 July 1949 Mao Zedong formally announced the Party's decision to lean to the side of the Soviet Union.[27] It signified the CCP's choice for its major strategic alliance in East–West relations. Other than the shared ideology, the CCP justified its decision for a one-sided national alliance on two grounds. First, it would lead to a recognition by international Marxist orthodoxy of the CCP's status in the world communist movement. Secondly, China would be able to count on economic assistance from within the socialist camp. The Soviet leadership under Stalin satisfied the CCP's two major needs by way of prompt recognition and a subsequent aid programme under a mutual alliance treaty with the PRC.[28] Soviet industrial supplies and technicians assumed a highly visible significance in China's economic recovery and industrialisation, in spite of latter-day expressions of doubt about Soviet generosity.[29]

Weighing on the other side of the balance was possible reconciliation with the West. To the CCP leadership, the United States, Britain and France stood out altogether differently from the rest of the Western bloc for new China's international relations, both on account of their role in the century-long history of modern China, and because of their foreign policy postures in the Far East after the war.[30] Of the three the United States was the most conspicuous. During the war the United States received special attention from the CCP leadership, on such occasions as Patrick Hurley's mission in Yenan in November 1944 and the American mediation in the civil war up to mid-1947. The CCP failed however to prevent the US from giving massive military support to the Guomindang blockade following Shanghai's fall, which finally sealed the party's decision to break with these leading Western powers.

It emerged that in the course of some secret contacts, Washington had instructed US Ambassador John Leighton Stuart to deliver an official message to the CCP, through the director of Nanjing's Foreign Nationals Affairs Bureau Huang Hua, stating that if the CCP would go for industrialisation instead of 'communization', the United States would give the new government a $3–5000 million loan, an amount close to what India would have received over 15 years.[31] Huang urged the United States to stop aid and sever relations with the Guomindang as conditions for new Sino–US relations, but Stuart insisted that only when a new Chinese government was formed could foreign powers judge whether it fulfilled the necessary conditions for international recognition.[32] This probably precipitated the decision by the CCP leadership that however badly they needed external assistance, they should not accept it from a country like the US, which they believed lacked sincerity for developing equal relations with China. Even on pure economic terms, Mao saw no possibility of China accepting Western countries' loans on their terms.[33]

It also became clear that neither Britain nor the United States was prepared to take any action other than paper protests to the Guomindang for their blockade outside Shanghai and other parts of the coast. The People's Government firmly believed that America supported this blockade.[34] Britain was seen to have added its support to the blockade by threatening the 'closure' of all British-owned firms in

Shanghai and 'withdrawal' of all British business men from China.[35] The CCP leadership thus concluded that China's campaign for political legitimacy was closely connected with a struggle for economic independence, and that on neither count could the Western powers be expected to refrain from attempts to frustrate China's legitimate aspirations. As Mao wrote, 'Internationally we belong to the side of an anti-imperialist front headed by the Soviet Union, and so we can turn only to this side for genuine and friendly help, not to the side of the imperialist front.'[36]

The CCP's 'lean-to-one-side' policy, the *Amethyst* incident, the CCP–Stuart contacts, and the economic blockade (later turned into a Western embargo) together marked a turning point in China's relations with Britain, both for reasons associated with the British government itself and on account of Britain's special relationship with the United States. In a general context, it was suggested that Britain had not had dealings with the CCP on a footing of amicable equality. She had made protestations of neutrality during the civil war but she had been the CCP's tacit enemy for years and had not yet been able to give the Communists any convincing contrary indication.[37]

RECOGNITION: PERSPECTIVES AND ISSUES

Britain was the first Western government to recognise the PRC – on 6 January 1950. However subsequent negotiations made little progress towards the establishment of diplomatic relations. The two governments finally decided at the Geneva conference in 1954 to have a low-level representation by exchanging *chargés d'affaires ad interim*. Full diplomatic relations were established in March 1972.

Britain: 'Keeping a Foot in the Door'

British foreign policy towards China under the CCP was based on the following considerations: (1) anti-communism and the drive to prevent communist expansion in the world; (2) a special relationship with the United States in the context of NATO and the cold war against the Soviet Union, with an emphasis on the security of Western Europe; (3) the legacy of the British Empire and the politics of a Commonwealth common front; (4) economic interests in mainland China and Hong Kong.

The British government abandoned its 'wait-and-see' position on

China at the end of 1948 when communist victory in China was imminent. It was suggested that a communist-dominated China would almost certainly tilt the East–West balance of power in favour of communism worldwide, and would conceivably pose a real threat to British strategic interests in the Far East. A paramount concern was to wean China away from the Soviet Union, with economic benefits if possible, with threats of Western sanctions when necessary. On the other hand, the Far East was not vital to Britain's survival compared with a West European commitment.[38]

There was some concern over the position of Hong Kong in the face of possible communist attack, with greater implications for Southeast Asia as a whole. The Crown Colony was valuable to Britain as an important centre of trade and capital. It was estimated that 'every month Hong Kong handles about £20 000 000 worth of goods', and that 'the total value of capital invested in Hong Kong is probably of the order of £350 million'.[39] But since Hong Kong was ultimately indefensible against serious communist attacks, the aim of British policy should be to find a basis on which a communist Government of China could acquiesce to Britain continuing to hold Hong Kong. Prime Minister Clement Attlee said, 'If we made it a point of prestige that we should retain Hong Kong as a British possession, it might become a matter of prestige for the communists to force us to withdraw from it.'[40]

British commercial interests inside China, though at a lower priority than either Britain's global objective or the preservation of Hong Kong, were by no means taken lightly. The total value of British commercial property and investments in China of £300 million, as assessed in 1941, was less than in Hong Kong, and during the early post-war period exports to China did not receive top priority. But a defeatist China policy would not only cause substantial material loss of capital, it would also damage Britain's long-term prospect of increased trade with China and of getting a foothold in the potentially great Chinese market. On the contrary, Western commercial and financial interests should endeavour to maintain themselves in China for as long as possible so that they would be available when the necessity for trade, in order to overcome economic difficulties, prompted Chinese communists to approach private concerns for normal commercial relations.[41]

More importantly from the British government's point of view, the presence of British interests in China would have appreciable political value. It would be part of a calculated tactic to prevent China from falling into the arms of the Soviet Union by giving the new regime time 'to realise both the necessity of Western help in overcoming its economic difficulties, and the natural incompatibility of Soviet imperialism with Chinese national interests.'[42] It was against this background that the British government's China policy of keeping a foot in the door was formulated. Its aim was to keep the option of Western contacts open to the Chinese, which in turn would help drive a wedge in the Sino–Soviet alliance. The implication of the metaphor was clearly its transitional posture, as the foot could keep the door open for an eventual full presence inside, or it could withdraw completely if needs be. From the day when it was approved by Cabinet in late 1948 until after the outbreak of the Korean war, this policy and its underlying assumptions changed but little.[43] It was mainly to implement this policy that Britain decided to recognise the PRC early in 1950.

The British government originally thought it should state unilaterally its assumption that the new Chinese government accepted China's existing international obligations. These would include an acknowledgement of the previous Chinese governments' loans and bonded debts, British nationals' existing rights of property and of free movement in China, and Britain's rights in respect of shipping and consular representation derived from the Sino–British Treaty of 1943. Indeed, Foreign Secretary Ernest Bevin went on record on this point in his address to the UN General Assembly on 28 September 1949. On other occasions he also alluded to the treatment of British nationals in China, as well as the new government's general attitude towards Britain as conditions for British recognition. However the British government later decided that if conditions were attached to the recognition, it would lead to a laborious and unpromising series of negotiations, thereby hampering an early establishment of diplomatic relations. Moreover any delay might seriously prejudice British commercial interests 'without compensating advantages being obtained'. The Cabinet decided on 15 December 1949 that the UK should accord *de jure* recognition to the Central Government of China at an early date. Bevin sent a recognition telegram to Chinese Premier cum Foreign Minister Zhou Enlai on 6 January 1950, in which John Hutchison was officially designated as the British representative to secure normal diplomatic relations.[44]

The British government did realise that the Chinese would probably raise issues of substance as pre-conditions. Hutchison was so warned, and was given strict instructions to limit discussions to procedural matters before formal relations were established. It was stated that, 'What we must guard against is an attempt to impose conditions unfavourable to us as the price for the establishment of normal relations'. It looked as if the two sides were going to repeat the *Amethyst* negotiations all over again.[45]

China: 'Negotiations First'

The Chinese government decided that in its relations with Britain substantial issues would take precedence over the procedural matter of establishing diplomatic relations. Thus, upon Britain's notification of recognition, Mao Zedong brushed aside counsels of accommodation from his colleagues and instructed that there should be a delay in responding to the British. As a result of this deliberate gesture the British officials were kept in the dark for almost two months. In a curious case of mirror-imagery, some British officials appeared to have anticipated this Chinese move by expressing the same sentiments earlier.[46] The Chinese government suggested the need for negotiations, the British accepted it, and talks began in Beijing in March.[47]

The key issue for China was whether the British government was prepared to demonstrate its sincerity by way of unconditional recognition, in both bilateral and multilateral diplomacy, of Beijing as the sole legitimate government of China, coupled with a severance of previous relations with the Guomindang. This was used as a yardstick to be applied universally, with the ultimate purpose of establishing the PRC's legitimacy in the world. From this legitimacy would flow all the legal consequences: UN representation, territorial jurisdiction, and property rights. The Chinese civil war never officially ceased, the legitimacy of government was thus in dispute between the two parties, and this inevitably spilled over into areas of China's foreign relations, with long-term political implications.[48]

The effectiveness of the British recognition of the PRC was compromised by moves and ambiguities over substantive issues, which led the Chinese to question British sincerity. One of these was Britain's official decision for 'an extensive propaganda campaign to explain that policy of opposition to Communism still holds.' It was stated that British recognition did not mean approval of the policies of the recognised government, citing Britain's recognition of the Franco regime in Spain.[49] The move was probably designed to placate American public opinion or to ward off domestic opposition, but it alerted the Chinese to Britain's anti-communist stand and the possibility of British insincerity and ulterior motive.[50]

Another ambiguity stemmed from Britain's attitude on the status of Taiwan. One position held that the Guomindang still exercised *de facto* control over Taiwan and that 'in law Formosa was still part of Japan'. This confusion was probably responsible for the decision to maintain a British consulate in Tamsui, as well as for British abstention in a vote in the UN Security Council on 13 January 1950 on a Soviet proposal that China should be represented by the government in Beijing.[51]

Lastly the British position on Chinese national properties in British territories – notably some 70 aircraft in Hong Kong – clashed with that of the Chinese government. The British government argued that the only solution to the disputes between and PRC and the Guomindang over China's properties would be to have the disputes settled in the courts. Internally it was suggested in the Cabinet that 'the main issue for decision was not a question of law but the political question of whether the Government's action should be directed to placating the United States Government or the Chinese People's Government'.[52] Thus it was decided that the Hong Kong and British authorities would continue to use measures to prevent the aircraft from being flown out of Hong Kong. The Chinese protested against Hong Kong authorities' moves and the Privy Council's issuance of an Order-in-Council for the detention of the aircraft, pointing to Britain's lack of respect of China's property and to an unfriendly gesture to the new republic.

The British government's actions over these issues may have been taken in deference to the possible reaction of the United States, but they in effect qualified the recognition it purported to accord to the PRC. Trevelyan later suggested that the strength of Anglo–American alliance was of much greater importance to Britain than her relatively small interests in China, and that she was not going to abandon the American alliance in favour of a neutralist position.[53] Although the British decision-making process on the recognition of the PRC appears to have been wracked by conflicts of interests and impossible dilemmas, when viewed in perspective these were definitely of low intrinsic value and urgency to Britain in terms of her survival and global objective. This seemed to be one of the reasons why lack of progress in negotiations with the Chinese did not cause too much concern to the British. When the Korean war eventually broke out, their China policy of keeping a foot in the door further dwindled in significance.

Britain's recognition of the PRC was not completely in vain. A diplomatic outpost was maintained throughout the 1950s and 60s, and official contact never ceased completely. As China insisted, negotiating with Britain outside the traditional framework of diplomatic relations represented as much of a 'direct relationship' as negotiating within it. It was the substance that should matter, not the form. To Britain however, this kind of 'relationship' was not very effective as far as legal consequences were concerned, such as the legal status of British interests in China and official representation on their behalf.

BRITISH INTERESTS: THE QUESTION OF LEGITIMACY

When PLA forces first captured cities from the Guomindang, they issued declarations to give guarantees of protection for foreign nationals and their property. The military takeover of various cities and areas was generally an orderly affair, with PLA troops 'polite and courteous' and respectful of properties owned by the British.[54]

From early 1949 to mid-1950, British businesses in China faced grave difficulties which came from three directions. First, a serious shortage as a result of the CCP's war efforts, and of economic dislocations in general, imposed upon them heavy financial burdens. Secondly, as the result of an organisational shake-up, the government instituted tight controls over trade, industry and finance. Lastly, the Guomindang blockade along the coast and outside Shanghai from June 1949 onwards effectively closed the channels of trade and shipping for British businesses. The 'farcical and dangerous' coastal siege, during which British ships were bombed or harassed at sea, prevented crucial supplies of raw materials, petroleum and machine parts from reaching the ports.[55]

During the first few months of confusion and uncertainty in 1949, the biggest worry for the British community was their loss of political identity. Not unlike the British diplomatic personnel, British businessmen found CCP officials most reluctant to respond to foreigners' attempts at contact. Officially they were requested to approach only the Foreign Affairs Bureau of the Military Control Commission in a city or region, but not the MCC itself. This arrangement hampered ways of speedily solving their specific difficulties, even when other responsible departments were already in place. This gave rise to the complaint that 'the new regime is operating a preconceived plan of non-cooperation'.[56] Anxiety appeared to be all the greater since historically it had always been important for British companies to keep in close touch with Chinese governments in power. They now felt depressed by the lack of official sympathy, their enforced business inactivity, and their inability to estimate what conditions were going to be in the future.[57]

Over months the general psychological suspense about the CCP's policies on private industry and trade was eventually overcome, as the government's constitutional structure and nation-building programme gradually took shape. There were signs that the new authorities wanted to treat foreign enterprises as part of a solution to the economic depression rather than as a political problem. The general manager of KMA obtained an interview with Yao Yilin, then Minister of Industries and Commerce of the People's Government of North China, and received official promises for flexible price policies and better financial and transport facilities. General Chen Yi, Mayor of Shanghai, and Zhang Hanfu, FAB Director at Shanghai, received John Keswick, Chairman of the British Chamber of Commerce at Shanghai, to hear his complaints on behalf of the British business.[58]

Prior to the establishment of diplomatic relations between China and Britain, the situation with regard to the legitimacy of British commercial activities in China was none the less blurred. Thus Yao Yilin originally agreed to receive a proposed deputation in Beijing from the British Chamber of Commerce at Shanghai for consultation, but after the proclamation of the People's Republic, the issue was deferred pending political talks between the two governments.[59] It was likely that one of the reasons for the CCP's non-recognition of the legal status of Western economic interests was that the CCP refused to recognise the treaty obligations of previous governments. The Guomindang undertook under the 1943 treaty to allow British interests to remain, which in the absence of a commercial treaty between the Guomindang and Britain was probably the only peg on which the British government could hang any legal argument for the protection of the British businessmen in China.

While negotiations after Britain's recognition ran into an impasse, British commercial interests seemed to have fallen in a legal and political vacuum. Short of previous extra-territorial rights and deprived of effective official representation by the British government, British firms felt more exposed than ever before to local economic requirements and regulations. They might also have been disturbed by manifestations of Chinese nationalism.[60] Whatever legitimacy might have been expected by British businesses had by now become largely residual insofar as it was determined by their usefulness to China's economic recovery and by their compatibility with the mode of China's social transformation.

SINO–BRITISH TRADE IN CHINA

When peace was first restored in an area, affairs were put under the charge of a Military Control Commission pending the establishment of civilian administration. The new authorities took over all state-owned mines and factories from the previous regime. The war had done great damage to the country's industry and commerce, so the government took urgent measures to get the economy going lest the population lapse into a dejected state of prostration or into anarchy. Armies were used to restore and control communication lines, and specialised offices were set up within the MCC to supervise production and civilian life. State trading agencies were formed to coordinate the supply and distribution of basic commodities across country and town. Other measures included a greater control over the flow and distribution of basic necessities and raw materials, and taxation. Government actions in these areas inevitably had a restrictive effect on the businesses of British firms.

Structural Overhaul in Foreign Trade

In the scheme of economic reconstruction, trade was essentially subordinate to economic policy. Foreign trade policy needed to be coordinated with production, and had to fit into the general programme of the national economy. The government initially allowed the operation of private capital in foreign trade. As the national economy became increasingly centralised, it brought individual trade operations as well as other economic activities under greater control and planning. During the transition to full socialism, the CCP decided that its policy towards private capital in the fields of trade, production and banking should be one of utilisation, restriction and transformation.[61]

Many British trading firms agreed that the new government had every reason to carry out a general house-cleaning in the foreign trade system in China, in view of the reckless speculation, widespread corruption and inefficiency in foreign trade under the Guomindang rule.[62] On the other hand China undoubtedly needed foreign trade for her economic recovery and development. Industrially, pre-1949 China was working with her bare hands. What relatively few industries there were had only been established in fairly recent years, and these were devoted mainly to the manufacture of consumer goods such as cotton textiles, flour, vegetable oil, light machinery, and miscellaneous electric supplies. China was almost wholly dependent upon the outside world for fuel oil, gasoline and lubricants, as well as industrial supplies and machine tools. All these China had to exchange with exports of her agricultural and native products.

The new pattern of China's foreign trade developed from the regulations governing external trade in liberated areas such as Shandong, devised to 'safeguard import–export trade, promote production, and support the war'. Most of the exportable products were divided into categories according to their relative scarcity, and were exchanged for essential supplies from imports. On top of these categories was a list of luxury goods, the import of which was prohibited. For both imports and exports, a series of formalities would need to be gone through and discriminative tariffs were applied where relevant. When the North China People's Government published its regulations governing the control of foreign trade in the region, the barter element of earlier regulations was retained, and goods designated for marketing in bulk were to be transacted only by state-operated foreign trading companies.[63] This was soon followed by other liberated areas.

At national level was a Ministry of Trade under the State Financial and Economic Commission, which enabled the central government to integrate exports and imports into its national economic programme. From the outset, the new government's guiding principle was to promote exports while limiting imports, and to use exports as a means of financing essential import supplies. In September 1952 a separate Ministry of Foreign Trade was founded. State trading companies were consolidated into fifteen specialised import–export corporations. But the entire import–export trade with non-socialist countries was in effect under the charge of a national corporation, the China National Import and Export Corporation (CNIEC).

To enable British and other foreign trading firms to participate in China's external trade, the government specially required that they should apply to the foreign trade control bureau for a business licence, upon recommendation by the FAB. They were obliged to tender their accounts for auditing, and the final decision on their application rested with the Ministry of Trade (later the Ministry of Foreign Trade). Of the 1621 private firms re-registered in Shanghai, 376 were foreign firms, of which more than two-thirds were British-owned. It was understood that firms which did not do any business during a specified period were liable to have their trade permits cancelled, as indeed was the case with a number of Chinese and foreign firms over time.[64]

While conditions varied from city to city, the common complaint from British as well as private Chinese merchants appeared to be that Government monopolies embracing bulk commodities, which constituted a large proportion of China's normal export trade, took away business opportunities from private firms.[65] It appeared that exporters were allowed to charge a handling commission, payable in local currency, of no more than two per cent, and had to submit firm bids for consideration by the state export companies responsible for particular commodities. Should a bid be accepted, a letter of credit would be established, either direct or assigned to them.[66] British firms were faced with strong competition from private Chinese firms, both for business and for government financial facilities. Coordination among the Chinese firms seemed to enable them to avoid a cutthroat price war when selling Chinese goods abroad and to strengthen their bargaining position when importing foreign goods.

Basic Supplies and Raw Materials

State trading agencies purchased basic supplies and raw materials for the government-run enterprises, which constituted the backbone of the economy. By the end of 1949 70 per cent of coal, 60 per cent of salt, 30 per cent of cotton yarn and 50 per cent of cloth in the country were produced by state-owned enterprises and were handled by state agencies. The entire railway transport system was also in government hands, plus 25 million tons of commodity grain in reserve. With these supplies and facilities secured for key production and consumption policy support, the government was able to ensure its new currency against inflation, implement its war and relief programmes, and build up popular confidence in the new regime. On the other hand it meant a drain on the raw materials for the private mills, including British ones, which had previously been supplied through their traditional collecting network, and compelled the private sector to rely increasingly on government allocations for processing flour, manufacturing textile products or collecting stocks for exports. Private firms which processed raw materials mainly for domestic consumption had to sell their products solely to state trading agencies rather than through their own retail networks.

A typical example was the British American Tobacco Company (China) Ltd, which had factories in Harbin, Shenyang, Yingkou, Tianjin, Qingdao, Shanghai and Hankou, and had over the years built up its own network of purchasing and selling organisations penetrating deep into the interior. Their supply line was effectively cut off when the government gradually monopolised the direct purchase of tobacco leaves from the growers, and the company was requested by the government to sell its cigarettes to state trading organisations.[67]

Although state trading companies operated on a large scale in most types of export goods, there was little evidence in the early days that they were actually selling direct in foreign markets (apart from Hong Kong). Private traders not only acted as selling agents for the Government, but were allowed to trade independently in numerous articles, with the exception of soya beans, bristles and minerals, which were Government monopolies.[68]

Import Trade in China

The imports of both British and Chinese firms were controlled through foreign exchange allocations. Prior to 1949 foreign exchange was granted to general importers, and to private and public industries for payment of purchases from abroad. Approvals were given as and when the applications were received, and no careful check was made of the end use of the articles requested for import, resulting in misuse of foreign currency resources by speculators, and in abuse by firms and factories who bought for resale at higher local prices.

The post-1949 policy was based on a planned economy, aiming at conserving foreign exchange for use only for more important and immediate requirements, and at procuring the highest returns for China's exports.[69] Even though government organisations accepting offers of supply were principally responsible for arranging direct finance for British suppliers, the latter often found themselves compelled to answer questions concerning a given application and the proposed use of foreign exchange. British importers found the system difficult to grasp since it entailed considerable advance planning on their part, followed by negotiations with the departments concerned on what prices they were allowed to pay for imports, and in what quantities, before finance could be arranged. The potential for mis-understanding was great indeed, especially in view of the existence of significant cultural boundaries. Things were sometimes made difficult by the lack of coordination between Chinese departments. For in-stance one government organisation might want to place an emerg-ency order for some urgently needed material but could not obtain the foreign exchange, even though the amount involved might be quite small.[70] (This seemed to be a constant feature of China's import trade over many years, which was forever troubled by the shortage of hard currency, both before foreign trading firms withdrew and after they came back in the late 1970s.)

Trade *in* China Versus Trade *with* China

The distinction between trade in China and trade with China as it was traditionally understood was drawn between industrialists, real estate and hotel businesses on the one hand, who derived their profits from economic operations in China, and on the other hand, importers, exporters, and shipping companies, who directly traded with China in goods and services even though they also had business premises in China. Banks and insurance appeared to come into both categories. This was gradually replaced by a new interpretation based on a narrower definition of 'trade'. The line was then drawn between those trading firms who operated inside China and those who di-rected their trading transactions with China from offshore, such as from Hong Kong and Britain. Especially after the outbreak of the Korean War, when most trading firms withdrew their staff from China, trade in China no longer seemed practicable. To maintain their business between Britain and China trading firms began to put greater emphasis on trading with China.[71] The following discussion is based on the latter narrower sense of the term.

In both export and import business, larger British firms trading in China appeared to manage better than smaller firms, in spite of the allegation that the government favoured Chinese export firms and discriminated against foreign firms. In imports, large British firms used centralised buying to boost their business, resulting in substantial orders for forward sales, much to the dismay of small Chinese firms.[72]

Smaller trading firms owned by British nationals were more con-cerned about their business prospects, especially in view of the decreasing numbers of lines of business open to them and 'the aggravated competition and intensified battle for existence amongst the starving colleagues of trade'.[73] They also saw an official inclination to circumvent the middle men, brokers and agents so as to cheapen the costs of imports. Since almost the entire amount of the Government's foreign exchange was initially devoted to the purchase of urgently required materials for reconstruction, some of the business was placed with direct producers abroad, and much of it through their buying agencies in Hong Kong, working through the representatives of producers.[74]

By the second half of 1950 it was clear that the Chinese government's trading was well represented in Hong Kong. There were trading, banking and other corporations which the new government took over from the old regime, along with their stock and personnel. Later it also established entirely new firms as branches of Beijing, Tianjin, Shanghai and Guangzhou organisations. Some firms were founded as Hong Kong companies, with or without direct or overt official connections. It appeared that these new organisations had made themselves successfully known and many European firms preferred to deal with them rather than continue with old contacts. It was through these more or less official trading organisations that China–Hong Kong trade was arranged, while private British merchants, both in Hong Kong and mainland China, participated within this framework.[75]

British Shipping Trade in China

During the first half of 1949, irregular shipping connections between North China and ports further south were confined to KMA's barter of coal for flour between Qinhuangdao and Shanghai, and to export to Hong Kong, South Korea and Japan for foreign exchange.[76] Sometimes chartered by private Chinese firms, British companies undertaking China coast runs included Dodwell and Co., Butterfield and Swire, Jardine and Matheson, Wheelock and Marden, and Wallem and Co., exchanging petrol, gunny sacks and industrial equipment for Chinese vegetable oils, vermicelli and Shandong silk.[77] In Tianjin the reception and clearance of vessels, whilst not as smooth, simple and efficient as desired, was not found unduly difficult. Since the Tientsin Lighter Co. Ltd was not permitted to resume business, all lighterage in Tianjin was handled by the China Merchants Shipping Navigation Co. and the Po Hai Navigation Co., both Chinese owned.[78]

With the imposition of the Guomindang blockade, shipping on the China coast, especially with regard to Shanghai, was at risk of being slowly strangled. British blockade runners were frequently intercepted by the Guomindang navy, but the incentive for blockade running was high. It was reported that because of the risk and bonus payments to crews the Chinese were paying from three to four times the appropriate market price of materials. During the four months following the declaration of the blockade, a total volume of 200 000 gross tons were traded with the liberated areas on the coast; against that total figure, more than 80 000 gross tons were shipped during November alone, breaking all previous records. For some time Tianjin and Yingkou were said to have received more than 80 per cent of the blockade running ships. In Yingkou the foreign trade authorities of the Northeast People's Government presumably followed the standard procedure of making deals in bulk with British ships as they came into port, inadvertently allowing them a profit margin of 25 to 30 per cent for whatever goods they happened to carry.[79]

The situation improved during the last months of 1949 as PLA military advances pushed back the blockade southwards. While Panamanian, Norwegian and Soviet registries appeared to be dominant, the number of ships under British registry also increased, amounting to almost 50 per cent, averaging one British-flag ship per day each way from Hong Kong to North China. British shipping now had access – with varying degrees of risk, delay and damage – to Yingkou, Dalian, Qinhuangdao, Tianjin, Qingdao, Shitao, Shanghai, Shantou, and Xiamen. In places where British ships were bombed during daylight, the authorities arranged with the charterers to have their cargoes loaded during the night.[80]

In 1950 a great menace to shipping came from mines deployed by the Guomindang at the mouth of the Yangtze, which resulted in the loss of four vessels and serious damage to a fifth. This contrived to deter the regular ocean lines from visiting Shanghai. Miscellaneous coastal vessels however were fortunate enough to be able to enter and leave the port safely when guided through by craft of the People's Navy. Nonetheless the effects on Shanghai's industry and commerce were immediate and crippling. Other potential deterrents, quite apart from the blockade, came from pilotage regulations in Wusong as well as other restrictions imposed by Shanghai's navigation bureau, which were said to have caused increasing resentment among foreign companies.[81]

China itself did not seem to have sufficient tonnage to sustain regular runs between its ports and Hong Kong. To counter the blockade and make up for the deficiency in shipping, the Chinese government set out to do three things: (1) to make greater efforts to enhance railway carriage of goods; (2) to expand the operations of vessel chartering and term leasing through local and Hong Kong based agencies so as to ensure regular runs between Northern ports and Hong Kong; and (3) to develop ocean shipping lines in cooperation with the Soviet Union and other East European countries such as Poland and Czechoslovakia. Not until 1953 was China able to revive its own coastal shipping.

TAXATION

Taxation policy was not standardised in the initial period of the PRC, nor was there as yet any exact policy or coordination at national level. The shortage of funds and the absence of inter-regional revenue-sharing meant that local authorities had to rely on taxation to a large extent to raise money for their public expenditure. In Tianjin, for instance, several kinds of dues were imposed:

(1) *Business tax*, subdivided into an industrial tax and a commercial tax, its amount being pegged to the price of cornflour. The industrial tax (also known as the special tax) was applied to importers, manufacturing concerns, banks, insurance companies, trust companies and to shipping, aviation and bus companies. Tax was at the rate of 1.5 per cent of turnover or 4 per cent of gross profits, except in the case of manufacturing concerns which would pay 0.75 per cent of turnover. The tax was made retroactive to 1 October 1948. The commercial tax (also known as the ordinary tax) was applied to trading concerns dealing both in exports and imports, and to hospitals (sale of drugs only) and shops. It was levied at the rate of 3 per cent of turnover or 6 per cent of gross profits, and was made retroactive to 1 July 1948.[82]

(2) *Income tax*, based on a sliding scale with the majority of employees of large firms paying up to 4 per cent on the basis of the cornflour standard, collected as of 1 February, 1949. Foreign staff were required to submit returns pertaining to their locally drawn income, and the amount of tax involved was not regarded as unreasonable. It seemed that the tax on landed property also fell into this category, although its calculation was more frequently based on

the value of the property rather than the actual earnings derived therefrom. Also at one point there seemed to be a discrepancy between Tianjin and Beijing, the latter's income tax scale ranging from 4 to 15 per cent.

(3) *Revenue Stamp tax* (also known as commodity tax or excise duty). This was collected from consumers not only of finished products, but also of semi-finished products for further processing.[83] This presumably applied also to imported goods; for industrial concerns using them as materials, there was always a risk of double taxation embracing both customs duties and subsequent excise duties.

Together these almost certainly increased total business costs to above the previous level. The retroactive income tax and the levy on property seem to have caused heavy losses to both British and Chinese firms. Moreover British firms complained that taxation hit them unfairly because local authorities often refused to believe that foreign firms did not follow the old Chinese practice of keeping one set of books for the tax authorities and another set for their own use. Lastly, payment delays led to heavy penalties and to an official threat of 'withdrawal of protection, refusal of registration and expropriation of properties'. In any case authorities stated that whatever injustice might be involved, 'the firms must pay first and appeal afterwards'.[84]

In Shanghai the tax scales first announced by the authorities appeared to be reasonable. A business tax of 0.5 per cent was levied on manufacturing industries, export firms, transport and other service industries, 0.75 per cent on public utilities, and 1–4 per cent on other businesses.[85] It appeared that real estate and other property agency business fell into this last category and was independent of income tax. Some of the sums demanded were said to be out of proportion to the nature and value of the property (such as motor vehicles, cathedrals and business premises), and that they were invariably much higher than any property taxes paid hitherto. On the other hand, the tax on rent seemed to be an income tax, but it was raised substantially above what had previously been charged, and bore little relationship to the revenue actually collected.[86] The authorities were in many ways 'as efficient as its predecessor was inefficient', and taxation was administered 'more heavily and more efficiently than ever before in the experience of foreign traders'.[87] The Shanghai government was said to have taken a realistic view of the land tax and allowed a delay in payment.

In April 1950 the Central People's Government modified its financial management system, leaving local governments some discretionary power over their revenues in order to accomodate their needs. Thus revenues derived from public utilities, house rent, and land tax, as well as tonnage dues, port dues and other minor collections, were allowed to be retained by local governments for social and public expenditure. Ironically this gave local governments a greater incentive to formulate their own taxation policies and lean more heavily on property holders. The national tax schedules set a standard for local governments, but they could not prevent local authorities from charging more or less to suit their purposes.[88]

As a result of national tax consolidation in early 1950, the rate of tax on industrial concerns remained more or less at the same level, from 1–2 per cent on gross profits; in some cases, taxes decreased. There was a visible increase in commercial tax on financial services, warehouse operations, leasing, and other commercial services (5 per cent), and an even higher rate on real estate, commodity exchanges, dental professions, and property conveyancing (now 6 per cent). There was also an increase in excise duties on high consumer goods and materials such as cigarettes, textile fibres and yarns (up to 15 per cent), wines and liquor (up to 120 per cent), and cosmetics (up to 80 per cent). Income tax also widened its range (up to 30 per cent).[89] During the same period the Central Government issued a huge volume of People's Victory Parity Bonds in the hope of raising further revenue from various regions and industries. This met with strong resistance from British firms as they claimed that they were compelled to purchase these involuntarily, which added further hardship to their already serious financial situation.[90]

By mid-1950 it had become apparent to the authorities that heavy taxation, austerity measures and the rapid development of state enterprises, if unmodified, would soon lead to the paralysis of all private industry and to a general depression. A national conference was held to design better coordination between public and private businesses. Consequently pressure was relaxed with respect to payment of some arbitrary taxes and for enforced subscriptions to Victory Bonds. There was also a reduction in property taxes of 36 per cent for business premises, 10 per cent for residential premises, and 20 per cent for land tax. The burden of taxation was eased for manufacturers. In particular manufacturers who used their own materials and goods were exempt from excise duties. On top of that excise duties on 238 items were given an exemption and those on another 149 items were abolished.[91]

It is evident that the central government tried to come to terms with the increasing financial burden on cities caused by taxation. While taxation was indeed used by certain local authorities to control private capitalism in the country, the dire needs of the economy tended to help strengthen the case for those within the CCP leadership who advocated a high-tax policy. As long as the tax revenue was used for legitimate and justified purposes, went the argument, the people who had been taxed would sooner or later receive the induced benefits in return. S.T. Coleridge was quoted in order to drive home the point, and attention was drawn to the need to revive production by using the revenue collected through taxation, which would benefit all taxpayers.[92]

It was agreed among the British that during this period business taxes generally bore relation to the turnover, and that the actual percentage could not be described as 'crippling'.[93] On the other hand, until the reduction in land and property tax was introduced, many firms paid heavily on their fixed assets. This conformed with the Party's stated intention that commercial activities should be taxed more heavily than industrial activities, and that speculative commercial activities should be taxed more heavily than general commercial business.[94]

The difficulty of British firms and property holders was aggravated in those cases where the authorities withheld permission for the businesses concerned to close down, even though other decrees dictated that such businesses, by the nature of things, could not continue. Thus the authorities levied land tax, almost as if in revenge, on British race courses and gambling businesses even though there was no income. Hotels, restaurants and clubs fell into the category of special consumption tax (which was levied on the customers) introduced nationwide in 1950 as part of the government's austerity measure. It was partly abolished and partly modified in 1953.[95]

LABOUR–MANAGEMENT RELATIONS

One of the problems constantly cited in British Foreign Office and private correspondence from China related to the militancy of labour and government discouragement of retrenchment by British firms. Labour unrest had occurred in private foreign firms well before the Communist takeover. Such outbreaks were naturally perceived by the CCP as part of the workers' revolution against capitalist exploitation and oppression. After 1949 the new government did not feel able to intervene effectively on behalf of the management with respect to labour demands. The problem was not confined to foreign firms alone. As CCP personnel were sent to industrial sectors of various cities for political mobilisation, poorly briefed cadres backed the workers against management without reserve, with the result that many factories did not function properly owing to industrial strife.[96]

In Tianjin British shipping firms had trouble dealing with Bund labourers and their service stations, who demanded 'exorbitant rates' when in fact the level of pay for the wharf labourers prevailing at the time was still very low. Where the management proved adamant, employees in some firms were said to have taken extreme measures in enforcing their demands, ranging from verbal abuse and physical lock-ins of British employers, to strikes. It was also reported that Shanghai labour union leaders and workers, acting without union approval, indulged in a rampage of wage increase and other demands.[97]

The CCP leadership quickly recognised the disruptive effects of excessive demands by industrial workers, and Liu Shaoqi, Vice-Chairman of the Party, first intervened in Tianjin in April 1949 by criticising the excessive demands for wage increases, the lack of discipline and the general leftist radicalism among the staff. Liu's Tianjin démarche was followed by authorities elsewhere, underlying the Party's intention to mollify national capitalist interests and compel workers to make short-term sacrifices in the interest of long-term gains.[98] In August 1949 the authorities in Shanghai issued two sets of regulations, which laid down detailed procedures for settling labour disputes in private enterprises through mediation by the Shanghai Labour Bureau (and if this failed through the People's Court), penalties for strikers and obstructers of production, and procedures for retrenchment and severance payments.[99]

The Party's intervention helped British firms to secure labour concessions. Direct bargaining between labour and management was also gradually institutionalised, such as in the case of BAT's Yee Tsoong facilities, leading to workers' voluntary reductions in wages and in the number of shifts.[100] In other cases however, it was asserted that attempts at wage reduction was ineffectual, because labour would only agree to a token reduction provided that 'a much larger percentage was deducted from more highly paid expert and loyal workers'.[101]

One of the difficulties that British firms continued to experience in facing wage requirements arose from the government's policy of linking wages with a weighted index of increases in the basic commodity prices as a way of protecting wage-earners against inflation. Even when the exchange rate was adjusted, the continuing increase in the cost of living forced the unions to submit wage increase demands. To minimise any social disruptiveness from unemployment, the new government adopted the policy of retaining on the existing pay roll practically the entire labour force of state enterprises and ex-government employees. It also introduced allowance schemes for the unemployed.[102] The government was extremely reluctant to see private firms dismiss workers or close down and thus increase the number of those on the welfare. For British firms and catering services, it meant compulsory payment of wages when no work was available and very high severance payments in cases where dismissal of staff was permitted.

BRITISH INTERESTS AND SOCIAL TRANSFORMATION

The initial CCP position on foreign economic presence as a whole was one of restriction and utilisation, not of squeezing out or nationalisation. The majority position of the Party was that the matter should be handled prudently and without rush.[103] CCP leaders made it clear that they regarded the question of allowing Western economic presence as a matter of expediency. As a result the policy of utilisation was carried out wherever appropriate, even after Mao's July speech on 'leaning to one side'.

After a series of internal discussions on how best to use the services of foreign businesses in China, in early 1950 the government set up a Foreign Enterprises Administration Bureau under the directorship of Dr Ji Chaoding. Work was initiated to draft a set of regulations governing the registration and supervision of foreign-owned enterprises, as well as procedures for review and approval of foreign investments, including detailed provisions on the ratio of capital holdings by Chinese and foreign partners in joint ventures. There were plans for introducing the necessary legislation.[104] The Bureau never accomplished the task due to the outbreak of the Korean War. Until that time, there is no evidence to show that a decision had been made to eliminate all foreign firms. Indeed, new businesses were started by Western investors in Tianjin in the first half of 1950. One of the officials who was personally involved in the drafting work was Wu Chengming. The Bureau was later reorganised into a division in charge of foreign properties (*Wai Zi Chu*) within the Bureau for the Administration of Industry and Commerce, with Wu as head of the division. Wu later used its transliterated derivative (modified by his Shanghai accent) as a nom-de-plume when publishing a few works on British commercial interests in China, as well as publishing books under his real name.[105]

Government intentions to regulate foreign economic presence, however, did not in any way make foreign businesses immune from the tide of social transformation. When the government tried to bring down inflation and balance its budget through high taxation in 1949 and the first half of 1950, British firms, like all private firms owned by foreigners and Chinese alike, had to bear the brunt and suffered financial losses. When the government tried to expand the public sector and control the economic activities of the private sector, the state trading companies were given access to government subsidies, transport facilities and favourable exchange rates. When the People's Bank began assuming the role of a major foreign trade financier, it took away a good deal of business which had previously been in the hands of Western banking institutions. The Chinese People's Insurance Company, not surprisingly, insured all the business of the Chinese state trading corporations. By May 1950 the total number of foreign insurance companies operating in China was reduced from some 70 to 27, including 20 British and 3 American companies.[106]

When labour unrest threatened to get out of hand, British firms had to count on the goodwill of local authorities and judicial organs for reaching fair and equitable settlements.[107] When the government introduced adjustment measures in the spring of 1950 to allow the private sector greater leeway in expanding businesses and increasing productivity, British firms had to compete with their Chinese counterparts for government facilities and contracts.[108] Private firms which were given contracts by state trading monopolies were permitted only a small profit margin. When the government set out to organise export and import associations, each specialising in a particular commodity, British firms never joined but chose to rely on their own expertise and overseas connections. Occasionally there were reports of official discrimination against British firms.[109] Viewed in a larger perspective, discrimination may well have been an unavoidable element built into the system, since British firms were at odds in almost every possible way with the business conditions and political environment in which they had to operate.

The hasty expansion of the public sector in foreign trade affected the entire private sector, British and Chinese alike. In 1950 China's foreign trade transacted by state companies amounted to 66 per cent of the national total. It reached 93 per cent by 1952, 98.3 per cent by 1954, and 99.2 per cent by 1955. In 1956 the government finally brought the whole of industry and commerce under its control by buying off private assets and paying a fixed interest on private shares over a period of time.[110] The number of private Chinese import and export firms in Shanghai decreased steadily from 1621 in 1949 to 902 in 1951. After the 'Five Antis' Movement in 1952, there were 785 left. These were subsequently organised into several specialised associations, which were by 1956 incorporated into seven giant joint-stock trading companies owned by public and private capital. In 1957, through the 'buying-off' policy, the government accomplished the complete transfer to public ownership of this sector. The private shares of stock from which the shareholders in Shanghai earned a fixed interest of 5 per cent amounted to ¥1.2 billion (the new currency), which was 50 per cent of the national total.[111]

In retrospect the transformation of the private sector of the Chinese economy, which was as thorough and complete as the planners had wished, was carried out in probably the most peaceful and smooth manner possible under the circumstances. Not only did the CCP leadership have to go out of their way to defend their moderate course of action to the Soviets, they also had to convince the radical rank-and-file members within the Party that the policy of gradual restriction and buying-off, instead of outright nationalisation, was the best way to ensure a smooth transition from state capitalism to socialism. Indeed since 1948 Mao and his colleagues had been fighting against leftist radicalism at various levels of Party leadership, manifested in destructive industrial and commercial taxes in some liberated areas, and in confiscation of properties of petty shop-keepers and other private assets, described as 'a policy of suicide'.[112] Again in 1950, when the government's austerity measures and expansion of state ownership led to a general depression in the private sector, Mao initiated a relaxation of tension with the national bourgeoisie by means of readjustments in industry and commerce by reducing taxation and stimulating production.[113] This led to a period of general relaxation and economic growth, later described by some Western commentators as 'Mao's honeymoon with private Chinese capitalists'.[114]

This in effect discredited the 'squeezing out' policy advocated by some within the Party and even practised in some areas. Liu argued that nationalisation, which would be inconsistent with the Party's stated position, would cause political damage. He also rejected the policy of 'squeezing out' as a disguised form of nationalisation, characterised by refusing to place any orders with private enterprises or giving them any raw materials and business opportunities. Should that happen, he argued, the government would have to face the unpleasant consequence of diverting additional resources for relief to capitalists deprived of their livelihood, in addition to the task of turning them into labourers through ideological education. The running of production would presumably also be affected because of the abrupt change in management. Thus, among the three ways of realising ownership by the whole people, the 'buying off' policy appeared to be the least traumatic.[115] When economic recovery, political campaigns and state planning had paved the way for the eventuality in the mid-1950s, Mao seized the opportunity to bring about a shift in emphasis more decisively to the side of transformation.[116]

The economic disincentive of early nationalisation would seem to apply in the same way in the case of British firms, all the more so because such a course of action would precipitously commit the government to a policy of antagonising the Western governments concerned. However, given the relatively decentralised form of government at the time, certain difficulties suffered by British firms may well be attributed to the radical tendency at some levels of leadership to 'squeeze out' the Western capitalists as part of eliminating the private sector. The disadvantages of a 'squeezing out' policy, for all practical purposes, did not appear to local authorities to be as formidable when applied to foreign firms as was the case with Chinese ones. Those who did benefit from the CCP's readjustment measures in industry and commerce in mid-1950 included many British trading firms, who began to receive an increasing number of government orders for massive imports as tension in Korea mounted. But by the time tens of thousands of Chinese military forces had crossed the Yalu River in October 1950, it was clear that the momentum of the Chinese government's initiative with regard to Western commercial presence would soon be lost, together with all the possibilities still on the drawing board.

3 The Korean War Period

The British have always been realistic, but if they do a thing of which they have reason to be ashamed, they like to wrap it up in a legal covering.

Sir Alexander Grantham (Governor of Hong Kong)

When at times we have feared that the Bureau had been driving us too hard, we have taken comfort in the saying that 'Whom the Lord loveth he chasteneth'. We cannot of course hope that the Bureau loves us: but we do hope that it realises our desire to co-operate with the Powers that be in the interests of the People.

J. Gadsby (Shanghai Gas Co.)

The outbreak of the Korean war in the summer of 1950 brought Sino–British relations into a period of freeze and precipitated the withering away of British commercial presence in China. Not only did the sudden halt in bilateral trade undermine the *raison d'être* of commercial ties for China, the war also decidedly tipped the precarious balance in China's government policy on Western capital investments within her territory, which had hitherto been judiciously maintained, towards a position in favour of their forfeiture.

THE POLITICAL SITUATION 1950–52

The bilateral negotiations between China and Britain on the establishment of formal diplomatic relations, launched in March 1950, never quite got off the ground owing to the irreconcilable position of both sides over a number of issues. While there was ample speculation in the press about the possible concessions that the Chinese government would be prepared to make, the British made it known that they were not in the mood to meet the Chinese half way.[1] Thus Foreign Secretary Ernest Bevin declared in the House of Commons, 'The Chinese are attempting to find little things which may be annoying and irritating to a country of this character. To that we have no intention of submitting'.[2]

The Start of the War

On 25 June 1950, war broke out in Korea and North Korean troops crossed the 38th Parallel. According to Khrushchev's memoirs, the North Korean leader Kim Il-sung conceived the attack and proposed the plan to Stalin for his agreement. Stalin was said to have then consulted Chairman Mao Zedong.[3] Both the Chinese and the Soviets seemed to agree with the North Koreans that the United States was not likely to intervene since the Americans had recently withdrawn their occupation forces from South Korea, and a series of statements made by US officials, including Secretary of State Dean Acheson, had perhaps indicated that the Americans did not regard South Korea as vital to their own security interests.[4] A private Chinese view denied that genuine consultations took place between Mao and Stalin, but held that Stalin, proceeding from his assumption of paramount leadership within the Socialist bloc, merely notified the CCP leadership of the decision to attack. Tito was said to have made the remark that the attack could never have been made without an order from the Kremlin.[5] Mao himself probably believed that whatever happened between North and South Korea was only an 'internal matter' for the Koreans. He certainly stressed this point at a meeting of the Central People's Government on 28 June, accusing the United States of interfering in Korea's internal affairs.[6]

The US government quickly sent in its Seventh Fleet to seal off the Taiwan Straits, ostensibly to prevent any resumption of hostility between the Chinese Communists and the Guomindang regime in Taiwan complicating US military campaign in Korea. This by implication brought the Chinese into conflict with the Americans and gave rise to the PRC's concern that her legitimate status and rights were now being openly challenged by an international 'gendarme', particularly China's sovereignty over Taiwan. Chinese Premier Zhou Enlai declared that the object of American military action in support of South Korea was 'to make a pretext for American aggression against Taiwan, Korea, Vietnam and the Philippines'.[7] China was further aggrieved over the fact that Zhou Enlai's telegraphed request that the PRC be represented at UN discussions on the Korean–Taiwan issue did not seem likely to elicit an early response; nor were Soviet and Indian efforts to have Chinese diplomats invited to the UN any more successful. The Chinese were genuinely alarmed by the sudden change of the military situation following General Douglas MacArthur's successful Inchon landings on 15 September, which opened the way for South Korean and Allied forces to cross the 38th Parallel in the name of the United Nations and to advance to the Yalu on the Chinese border.

While MacArthur was skillful in using the UN's 'unification' theme to justify his military actions, the British government was instrumental in the Western sanction of his forces crossing the 38th Parallel. The British Chiefs of Staff agreed to an American plan for Mac-Arthur to initially use South Korean forces in an advance to the Yalu, while Prime Minister Attlee convinced himself that 'China would not be so sorry if Russian influence was eliminated from Korea, provided that the new regime was a real United Nations Organization trustee-ship for the eventual freeing of the Koreans'.[8] The phrasing of the proposed resolution which recommended that 'all necessary steps be taken to ensure conditions of enduring peace throughout the whole of Korea' is said to have been drawn up by a member of the British delegation.[9] It was in essence a call for a military solution of the Korean question and ignored the 38th parallel, 'which has never been internationally recognised as a frontier'. The British mission pushed the point and got the approval of the Cabinet. The resolution, sponsored by Britain, passed the General Assembly on 7 October and reaffirmed the declared objective of the United Nations (in accordance with the Assembly resolution of 1948) to establish a 'unified' Korea, but brushed aside the political reality of North Korea.[10]

By the end of September it was clear to the Chinese that the situation in Korea had reached crisis point. Mao in particular saw a neighbouring Korea under US occupation as a direct threat to China's security and stability and a source of protracted tension, to which China would be forced to indefinitely commit the entire Northeast industry and defence resources. Indeed American bombers were already devastating territories on the Chinese side of the border.[11]

China's warnings in early October, related by Indian Ambassador K.M. Pannikar, were ignored by British and US leaders as pure bluff. Bevin also suggested that the President of the UN General Assembly issue a further appeal to the North Korean's to abandon active resistance.[12] The Western illusion was soon dispelled when Chinese forces intervened on 25 October, which dismayed the British. The Chiefs of Staff Committee admitted, 'It was no longer practicable, without risking major war, to attain the original objective of occupying the whole of North Korea . . . '. The Cabinet agreed that the West had judged badly: 'We [in Britain] had fully supported the proposal that the UN forces should advance beyond the 38th Parallel, despite India's warning that this would provoke Chinese intervention. We, as well as the Americans, had taken the risk of proceeding on the assumption that the Chinese would not in fact fulfil their threat'.[13]

With the massive Chinese forces fighting on the side of the North Koreans the military situation soon turned, reaching a climax when the combined forces retook Pyongyang on 6 December 1950 and Seoul on 4 January 1951. In its diplomatic communications with the UN, China linked the question of ceasefire to an end to the US military intervention in Korea and Taiwan, and to China's representation in UN discussions. Rejecting a General Assembly resolution on 22 December 1950, China demanded that a negotiated settlement be based on the withdrawal of all foreign troops from Korea, and refused to enter into contact with a three-man Cease Fire Group (composed of the President of the General Assembly and representatives of India and Canada), appointed under a resolution which China said had been adopted without its consent.[14]

After China had rejected the Cease Fire Group's new proposals on the same 'linkage' grounds on 17 January 1951, the way was wide open for the US to push its condemnatory resolution through the United Nations, with Britain duly voting in favour when it passed the General Assembly on 1 February. Branded an 'aggressor' by the UN, China was greatly embittered at the political ostracism from international organisations which was to last for the next two decades.[15] In retaliation for its military losses, the US also imposed a comprehensive embargo on China trade and shipping and froze the assets of the Chinese government in the United States, as well as US bank deposits of British firms in connection with business transactions with China. Britain joined with other Western governments in imposing economic sanctions against China, a subject to which we will return later in the book.

Diplomatic Stand-Off

Throughout this period Sino–British bilateral diplomatic contact in Beijing was reduced to a minimum. Hutchison ended his mission in Beijing early in 1951 and his final report on Chinese communism as a political force separate from Soviet-type orthodoxy gave rise to anxious debates within the British government, especially with regard to its implications on British policies towards China.[16] The majority opinion in London seemed to be resigned to the inevitability of clashes between Chinese and British interests over Korea, Taiwan and the UN, whatever form Chinese communism might take. Others suggested that the Chinese were either themselves actively concerned in the formulation of North Korea's plans for the war, or at least they acquiesced with Soviet plans, taking orders as a Soviet satellite.[17]

John Hutchison was replaced by Lionel H. Lamb (later Sir Lionel), who spent the next two years in Beijing with little accomplishment. Almost from the start his efforts to obtain interviews with Chinese Ministry of Foreign Affairs (MFA) officials were said to have been 'consistently, and evidently deliberately, ignored or side-tracked'. Also, 'Written communications have likewise been cavalierly treated'. It turned into a virtual stand-off after Winston Churchill became Prime Minister in October 1951. According to Lamb's count, between 1 January and 27 June 1952, British diplomats addressed 134 communications to MFA, dealing with a whole range of administrative and politically significant issues. Of these, 60 concerning routine matters of local administration – such as travel permits for Queen's Messenger and for Lamb himself, the import of necessary stores and the issue of identity cards – were not answered in writing, but nevertheless all facilities thus requested were forthcoming. Six chiefly concerned exit permits for British and American citizens, which were not answered but apparently elicited appropriate action. Another 50 concerned matters of major importance, such as the protection of UK, Commonwealth and American nationals, British trade, entry permits for Lamb's staff and care of British government property in China. No answer was received to these communications, nor was it apparent that the Chinese authorities had taken the requested actions. There were further 18 communications which required no answer and elicited none. While this state of affairs embittered Lamb, the British government felt that it was important to retain the link – admittedly tenuous – with China.[18]

It is apparent that the Chinese government deliberately cold-shouldered the British representatives in order to convey their resentment of Britain's 'two-China' policy, Churchill's open support of American hostility towards China, and a series of issues in Hong Kong and elsewhere. Sino–British relations deteriorated greatly following the Hong Kong authorities' deportation of trade union leaders and other pro-China activists, their punitive action against Hong Kong newspapers for their reporting of a riot which followed a fire in the walled city of Kowloon, the enforced registration of Xin Hua

News Agency on threat of closure, the *Ta Kung Pao* trial, and numerous border incidents in the Hong Kong–Macao area.[19] Nor did the Chinese government ever recognise Leo Lamb's claim to represent the interests of the US and a number of Commonwealth governments as well as those of their respective nationals in China, hence there was no response to those communications from Lamb concerning these matters. The British reduced the number of their consulates in China to two – in Beijing and Shanghai, all the others having been closed over a period of two years – to the great dismay of the British commercial community in various cities.[20] The official foothold in the door dwindled to insignificance.

BILATERAL TRADE DURING THE KOREAN WAR

The Import Offensive

The Chinese government's relaxation of trading conditions in the summer of 1950 anticipated the outbreak of the Korean War and increasing tension in the Far East. There is reason to believe that Beijing had sensed the imminence of a crisis in China's national security over Korea and was giving urgent priority to stockpiling import materials for war.

There began a marked improvement in the position of local importing houses – British and Chinese alike – from about the middle of 1950, evidenced by the authorities' new foreign exchange policies. Exchange allotments to registered private importers steadily increased, both for 'factory quota' business and for covering imports of a range of essential goods for ex-stock sales. In the meantime, CNIEC – the official purchasing organisation of the government – had become very heavy enquirers, and in the summer and autumn of the year finalised, through registered importers, substantial contracts for the supply of essential materials, principally metals, cotton, transportation and electric goods. Many of these contracts went to British manufacturers, who were at an advantage due to tighter American export restrictions.[21] As opportunities were offered to private importers to utilise their foreign connections to provide essential materials to China, an increasing number of importers were reportedly well on the way towards balancing their budgets, and even making local profits.

One case in point was the British-owned China Engineers Co.

Ltd, whose trade department received orders for purchases ranging from power plant and machinery, spindle worsted plant, underground cable for power plant, and cotton spinning plant, with a total value of import licenses reaching £260 000 in October and November.[22] The same company's experience also provides an extraordinary insight into the length to which a government purchasing organisation was prepared to go to meet its contingency procurement targets. The China Engineers Ltd entered into a contract on 6 September with CNIEC's East China Regional Office to import 5000 bales of Pakistan cotton; the Pakistani government twice raised the export duty during the course of this contract, first from 120 to 360 Rupees per candy, then from 360 to 600 Rupees per candy. There was no provision in the contract to enable the British company to make a claim for the increase in export duty, the price of cotton having been fixed by the contract. CNIEC quickly agreed to make a concession in both cases, incurring correspondingly £65 000 and approximately $36 000 in additional expenses.[23]

Curiously the outbreak of the war in Korea caused a general rise in world market prices, and resulted in an increased demand for Chinese products and for many essential materials in general. The demand gained strength, and the last three months of 1950 saw a boom in China's exports. So much so that the Chinese authorities found it necessary to regulate the trade flow by imposing a system of export licenses during September, under which no export could be made without the approval of local foreign trade control bureaux.[24]

A marked improvement in the government's mobilisation and movement of export goods from the interior was made possible by restored water, road and rail networks across the width and breadth of the country. The British-owned International Export Corporation (Tientsin) Ltd and Jardine, Matheson and Co. Ltd agreed with the China Egg Produce Co. (a Chinese state-operated organisation) to pack and export to Britain 20 000 tons of frozen hen eggs during 1950, and Jardine also undertook to export 35 000 tons of soya beans in return for the supply of a wide range of commodities to China. The last set of contracts that Jardine's John Keswick was known to have negotiated with China in 1950 included the export of cereals from the Northeast to a value of £7 million. In return, China ordered from the United Kingdom supplies of industrial equipment, including all materials for 1000 kilometres of railway. The increased volume of China's exports provided her with much needed foreign exchange with which to purchase essential industrial materials from the West.

It was even suggested that the Chinese government had overspent during the period between July and November in a terrific 'buying spree'.[25]

Emergency Stop and Barter Trade

Already there was a sense of unease in the air, against the background of rumbling artillery explosions and battle cries of an escalated war in Korea. In November 1950 it was reported that the Bank of China had been transferring US dollars to Switzerland since July, estimated to be anywhere from US$200 to $1200 million, mostly, it was believed, through Chekiang Industrial Bank and Crédit Suisse. BoC officials expressed the fear that the United States might freeze their dollar holdings in a crisis; by transferring the money to Switzerland they would prevent losses and would still be able to obtain supplies from Europe.[26] In November–December the government also ceased the issue of exchange allocations (except in very special cases). Ordering for forward deliveries was drastically reduced in November, and in many cases existing contracts were reported to have been cancelled, although cancellations seemed to have affected American orders more than those from Europe. Where new contracts had to be signed, they specified much earlier delivery than usual. Local purchases had also become slack, the main reason cited being the Chinese fear that owing to their intervention in Korea goods en route might be seized.[27]

On 16 December 1950 the US government announced the freezing of Chinese assets in the US. The Chinese central authorities quickly responded by ceasing the issue of export licences to US dollar trade and ordering dollar cancellation of letters of credit. Importers were urged to negotiate with sellers so that cargoes already ordered could be shipped in by certain deadlines: cargoes bought with US dollars by 17 January 1951, other cargoes by the end of January, and cargoes from the UK by the end of February.[28] For American orders in particular it was a frantic race against time. Emergency centres were quickly set up to have shipments of imports diverted to neutral ports or transferred to vessels operated by East European shippers. In exceptional cases, foreign exchange allotments were approved to private importers so that they could ship back whatever residual amounts of goods and materials were stranded in Hong Kong.

In spite of Chinese anticipation of the worst, the freezing of Chinese assets in the US, and the virtual imposition of economic sanctions by not allowing any goods for China to be shipped on American vessels or to pass through American ports, was said to have been a great shock to the Chinese economy. These actions had also aroused fears that similar steps might be taken by Britain. It was thus alerted:

> The fear of sanctions by the UK has had precisely the same effect as though sanctions were actually imposed. The Chinese government will not consent to open any Letters of Credit save in exceptional cases where the goods are ready for immediate shipments. Similarly, they will not allow exports because the sale of exports will result in building up foreign currency which might run the risk of being frozen.[29]

To preempt this eventuality, the Chinese government announced that in future all trade would be conducted on a barter basis. The actual form of such trade would include: (a) cargo for cargo; (b) export against import account; (c) link system; and (d) exchange of letters of credit subject to the approval of the Ministry of Trade and to cancel by order of that Ministry. To make doubly sure, they stipulated that imported goods should arrive in China first, and only afterwards could exports be released.[30] It soon emerged that as far as exports from China were concerned, the situation had deteriorated very rapidly. In Tianjin the government was no longer prepared to permit the export of cargo in respect of which export licences had previously been granted, unless the full value of the goods was deposited with the BoC office in London to the order of the BoC in Tianjin. This position was maintained in spite of telegrams from London saying that importers were prepared to deposit money to be paid against shipping documents. As no permission for shipping goods would be granted them until the purchase money had been deposited in China by telegraphic transfer (TT), British importers feared that they might not be able to claim *force majeure*.[31]

It was understood that this new ruling was not only being enforced in respect of future business, but it also affected contracts which had been made before 19 December 1950. In most cases importers had furnished irrevocable letters of credit. Especially, importers in Britain who had already contracted with Chinese shippers found themselves in an invidious position, as in many cases they had contracted for on-delivery of goods to their own customers within a specified time. Buyers were not prepared to remit money to China on the terms demanded, since there was no guarantee that either the goods would be shipped or, in the event of non-fulfilment of the contract, that the deposit would be refunded. Nor was the British government prepared to enable British importers, if compelled to make advance remittances to China, to cover this political risk through the Export Credits Guarantee Department.

Things were not much brighter on the export side. Chinese government trading organisations initially agreed to provide 100 per cent advance deposits in the UK covering British exports to China, but later, especially after the UN adopted the embargo resolution in May 1951, adopted the use of letters of guarantee, which were promises on the part of the Bank of China to pay for imports only after they had been unloaded and inspected in a Chinese port.[32]

As a result of the US freeze and Chinese counteractions, a breakdown in the world supply position occurred. By early 1951 British merchants were said to have completed old contracts for goods not covered by the embargo, and for a while no new business appeared to be forthcoming. The conditions of fixed prices and delivery which the government insisted upon proved to be almost impossible for trade in spite of increasing enquiries. No importer would willingly take the risk involved by this procedure, which was further complicated by the fact that ordered goods, as a general rule, could not be obtained in less than three or four months. Also the People's Government was becoming more and more selective in the commodities they wished to import, probably owing to decreased foreign exchange earnings from corresponding exports.[33]

The Effects of the Embargo

British firms engaging in trade with China were finding it increasingly difficult to carry on as a result of the embargoes against China. Ostensibly the British government for a while did not impose formal restrictions on goods for China at the same level of severity as those introduced by the American government; however it aimed to achieve roughly the same result through informal and discreet administrative means, such as advice from government production departments.

One complexity that arose out of this kind of informal arrangement between the British government and British trading firms related to the letter's inability to produce certificates of *force majeure* or other adequate evidence of inability to supply, when they were unable to

Table 1   Value of China's trade with the UK, 1949–57 (in million pounds sterling)

	Import	Re-export	Export	Total	Annual % change in turnover
1949	3.62	0.15	3.18	6.95	–
1950	10.32	0.004	3.59	13.914	+100.20
1951	7.67	0.02	2.70	10.39	– 25.32
1952	3.01	0.04	4.58	7.63	– 26.56
1953	10.22	0.11	6.27	16.60	+117.56
1954	8.96	0.09	6.92	15.97	– 3.80
1955	12.30	0.08	7.95	20.33	+ 27.30
1956	12.55	–	10.78	23.33	+ 14.76
1957	14.22	–	12.20	26.42	+ 13.24

Source: *Annual Statement of The Trade of the United Kingdom*, vol. I, 1949–1957 (London: HMSO).

fulfil contracts with the Chinese government buying agencies in Hong Kong. The Chinese side complained in their legal actions that in some cases goods contracted for had arrived in Hong Kong but had been diverted to other purchasers. The China Association suggested to the Board of Trade the British government should give *force majeure* certificates in those cases where it could be shown that British exporters had withheld shipments at the request of the British government, forcing them into renunciation of contracts. While the British government and British mercantile concerns were likely to be shown in an unfavourable light if the story was ventilated in the Courts, the China Association believed it reasonable for British merchants to demand that, as their difficulties arose solely from patriotic acquiescence in government suggestions on the part of suppliers in the UK, they were entitled to government support in helping them defend themselves.[34]

The level of trade between China and Britain roller-coasted from 1949 to 1952, as shown in Table 1. The total value of trade was some £7 million in 1949. It shot up to almost £14 million in 1950, but fell to just over £10 million in 1951, and fell further to £7.6 million in 1952 – slightly better than the 1949 level. The reduction largely came from imports from Britain, from over £10 million in 1950 to some £3 million in 1952, whereas exports from China increased slightly over the period, from £3.6 million in 1950 to £4.58 million in 1952. It may be pointed out that, because UK exports were ineluctably cut before imports, turnover (the sum of imports and exports) between the UK and China was less obviously affected. The figures for 1953–5 show some varying increases, especially in China's imports from Britain, owing largely to the end of the Korean war and the relaxation of tension between China and Britain.

As can be seen from Tables 2 and 3 showing the composition of China's export and import trade with Britain, over the years China steadily increased her export to Britain of raw materials and manufactured goods over and above Class I goods, whereas her imports from Britain had a preponderance of manufactured goods and, later, raw materials and resources including petroleum.

China's trade with Hong Kong declined significantly from the latter part of 1951, although its sheer volume was far greater than trade between China and Britain.[35] China's exports to Hong Kong amounted to HK$858 million in value (approximately £54.3 million) in 1950, whereas her imports from Hong Kong were worth HK$1461.1 million (£92.5 million) for the same year. The total value of China–Hong Kong trade during the first half of 1951 amounted to HK$1607 million, but that figure was halved for the latter part of the year, reaching only just over HK$860 million. Hong Kong's exports (re-exports) to mainland China declined by some 67.6 per cent in 1952, when the embargo and shipping restrictions went full swing in the colony. Indeed the 1951 figure represented a peak in China–Hong

Table 2 Summary of the value of merchandise consigned from China, 1949–57 (in thousand pounds sterling)

	Class I *(food, drink and tobacco)*	*Class II* *(raw materials and articles mainly unmanu- factured)*	*Class III* *(articles wholly or mainly manufactured)*	*Total* *(including miscellaneous items)*
1949	2202.6	1269.9	146.1	3,622.3
1950	7111.3	2208.3	1004.3	10,324.3
1951	3464.2	3163.1	1042.4	7,669.8
1952	2068.5	655.3	287.9	3,011.9
1953	4801.5	4919.2	501.4	10,222.2
1954	3139.6	4447.9	1371.1	8,958.7
1955	2755.7	6787.2	2759.1	12,302.1
1956	2320.0	7051.5	3177.8	12,549.3
1957	3608.5	6826.2	4329.8	14,224.5

Source: *Annual Statement of The Trade of the United Kingdom*, vol. I, 1949–57 (London: HMSO).

Table 3 Summary of the value of the total exports of merchandise to China, 1949–57 (in thousand pounds sterling)

	Class I (food, drink and tobacco)	Class II (raw materials and articles mainly unmanu- factured)	Class III (articles wholly or mainly manufactured)	Total (including miscellaneous items)
1949	18.8	266.5	2884.9	3,178.7
1950	5.6	9.9	3575.5	3,591.0
1951	0.7	22.3	2673.5	2,696.5
1952	0.6	66.2	4514.2	4,581.0
1953	22.4	522.5	5721.6	6,266.6
1954	22.5	3617.0	3279.5	6,919.0
1955	33.5	5262.5	2650.5	7,946.5
1956	4.9	5137.7	5638.1	10,781.9
1957	1395.1	4255.6	6542.0	12,195.4

Source: *Annual Statement of The Trade of the United Kingdom*, vol. I, 1949–57 (London: HMSO).

Table 4 Hong Kong's trade with China, 1949–57 (in millions of Hong Kong Dollars)

	Imports from China	Exports to China	Total
1949	593.5	584.6	1178.1
1950	858.0	1461.1	2319.1
1951	863.1	1603.8	2466.9
1952	830.2	520.0	1350.2
1953	857.1	540.3	1397.4
1954	691.8	390.8	1082.6
1955	897.6	181.6	1079.2
1956	1038.3	136.0	1174.3
1957	1131.1	123.4	1254.5

Source: *Hong Kong Annual Reports*, 1949–57, (Hong Kong Government).

Kong trade, which was not to be exceeded until 1965. As can be seen from table 4, Hong Kong's trade surplus with China was HK$603.1 million in 1950, which increased to HK$7.4 million in 1951, but turned into a deficit of HK$310.2 million in 1952.[36]

Table 5 shows China's visible trade with Britain and other major capitalist partners, excluding the Hong Kong–Macao region, over the

Table 5   China's trade with capitalist partners (in ten thousand US Dollars)

	Total	Exports from China	Imports to China	Total	Exports from China	Imports to China
	West Germany			France		
1950	1 942	875	1 067	591	208	383
1951	1 752	200	1 552	472	36	436
1952	707	231	476	242	165	77
1953	3 207	322	2 885	2 392	618	1774
1954	2 037	751	1 322	1 517	561	956
1955	1 925	899	1 026	2 349	951	1398
1956	3 088	1172	1 916	3 839	1845	1993
1957	5 745	1152	4 593	3 672	1103	2569
1958	18 627	3010	15 524	3 442	1550	1892
	Britain			Italy		
1950	7 351	3260	4 091	1 040	904	136
1951	3 507	1552	1 955	322	262	60
1952	2 581	1215	1 366	373	244	129
1953	9 704	2985	6 719	969	517	452
1954	7 068	2459	4 609	805	307	498
1955	10 463	4007	6 456	994	442	552
1956	11 250	4916	6 334	1 925	1003	922
1957	10 228	4393	5 835	1 512	463	1094
1958	20 395	7573	12 822	3 910	810	3100
	United States			Canada		
1950	23 812	9549	14 263	653	399	254
1951	799	8	791	55	39	16
1952	5.3	0.3	5	109	105	4
1953	0.2	0.2		127	124	3
1954				110	110	
1955				326	263	63
1956				537	323	214
1957				576	285	291
1958				1 073	420	653
	Australia			Japan		
1950	462	125	337	4 719	2105	2614
1951	292	95	197	1 290	95	1195
1952	61	30	31	440	332	108
1953	319	72	247	992	680	312
1954	385	105	280	3 517	2057	1460
1955	758	149	609	8 331	5817	2514
1956	1 137	170	967	12 840	6474	6366
1957	2 179	311	1 868	11 473	5966	5507
1958	3 590	472	3 118	8 065	3252	4813

Source: *Almanac of China's Economy*, 1982.[37]

period 1950–8. It may be noted that Chinese official trade statistics are based on customs documents, and may vary from those recorded by those trading partners concerned.

China's Trade with the USSR and Eastern Europe

While China's trade with the UK steadily decreased, her trade with the Soviet Union and other East European countries increased considerably. Especially during the 1949–53 period, it coincided with the drive among the socialist countries towards the so-called 'intra-bloc trade' under the influence of Stalin's 'two parallel world markets' doctrine.[38] Both before 1937 and between 1945 and 1949, the Soviet Union and Eastern Europe accounted for less than 1 per cent of China's foreign trade. In 1950 it was 26 per cent, in 1951, 61 per cent, in 1952, 72 per cent, in 1953, 75 per cent, in 1954, 80.55 per cent.[39] The annual volume of Sino–Soviet trade increased from 1.4 billion (old) rubles in 1950 to 5.4 billion rubles in 1957, accounting for over half of China's total foreign trade. China obtained from the Soviet Union all kinds of machinery, petrol, chemicals, tractors and motor vehicles, which were the principal items China had traditionally imported from the UK but which largely came into the embargo. China also became an important market for engineering and machinery exports from the German Democratic Republic and Czechoslovakia, the two most industrially advanced countries in Eastern Europe. Already in 1950, owing to long delivery dates offered by UK manufacturers, China had placed substantial orders of railway material with the USSR through the Skoda Works, Czechoslovakia, plus some others with Japanese manufacturers.[40]

Trade with Poland was also considerable; Polish deliveries consisted chiefly of machine tools, mining and farm machinery, iron and steel products and non-ferrous metals. Hungary supplied various types of equipment, machine tools, locomotives and lorries, while trade contacts were made with Romania (which supplied oil-drilling equipment) and Bulgaria (which sent artificial fertilisers and chemicals).[41]

Table 6 shows China's trade with leading partners in Eastern Europe from 1950–8, table 7 shows China's total value of imports and exports over the same period, as well as the years 1959, 1960 and 1986.

Equally important to China's foreign trade with the outside world were the shipping arrangements for exchange of goods between Eastern Europe and China, carried out principally through the ven-

Table 6   China's trade with socialist partners (in ten thousands US
Dollars)

	Total	Exports from China	Imports to China	Total	Exports from China	Imports to China
	The Soviet Union			Hungary		
1950	33 844	15 325	18 519	343	343	
1951	80 860	31 129	49 731	2802	2229	573
1952	106 421	41 204	6 547	5187	2681	2506
1953	125 823	48 061	77 762	6247	3046	3201
1954	129 124	58 663	70 461	6142	2893	3299
1955	178 985	67 021	11 964	6100	2883	3217
1956	152 377	76 168	76 209	6809	3010	3799
1957	136 470	74 697	61 773	5216	2638	2578
1958	153 857	89 887	63 970	8354	3294	5060
	Czechoslovakia			Poland		
1950	1 036	924	112	660	398	262
1951	7 062	4 836	2 190	5001	2877	2124
1952	9 774	4 895	4 879	4832	2611	2221
1953	10 965	5 488	5 477	5352	2864	2488
1954	12 209	5 453	6 756	6723	2780	3943
1955	12 851	6 378	6 473	7055	4115	2940
1956	12 938	6 448	6 490	7358	3162	4196
1957	15 590	6 948	8 642	8328	3653	4675
1958	19 005	9 305	9 700	9933	4263	5670
	East Germany					
1950	262	260	2			
1951	5 907	5 536	371			
1952	10 733	4 154	6 579			
1953	11 049	6 460	4 589			
1954	18 060	7 589	10 471			
1955	18 730	9 241	9 489			
1956	19 664	9 024	10 640			
1957	19 169	9 059	10 110			
1958	25 194	10 911	14 283			

Source: *Almanac of China's Economy*, 1982.[42]

ture of the Chinese–Polish Shipbrokers' Co. (CHIPOLBROK), but
also through visits by Soviet and Czechoslovak ships.[44] CHIPOL-
BROK was established by the Chinese and Polish governments on 15
June 1951, with each side holding 50 per cent of the company's stock.
The company acted as the general agent for Polish ocean-transport
interests in the Far East. Its head office was in Tianjin (until February
1962 when it was moved to Shanghai), and there were also representative's offices in Beijing and Guangzhou.[45]

Table 7   China's total value of imports and exports, 1950–86 (in 100 millions of US Dollars)

	Total	Exports	Imports
1950	11.35	5.52	5.83
1951	19.55	7.57	11.98
1952	19.41	8.23	11.18
1953	23.68	10.22	13.46
1954	24.33	11.46	12.87
1955	31.45	14.12	17.33
1956	32.08	16.45	15.63
1957	31.03	15.97	15.06
1958	38.71	19.81	18.90
1959	43.81	22.61	21.20
1960	38.09	18.56	19.53
1986	600.97	270.14	330.83

Source: *1987 Almanac of China's Foreign Economic Relations and Trade.*[43]

The company's first two ships, *s/s Pulaski* and *m/s Pokoj*, commenced service on the Poland–China route in March–April 1951, with Polish officers and Chinese crewmen, and flying Polish flags. Its original ocean-going fleet consisted of 10 vessels which averaged 18 years of age totaling 100 000 dead-weight tons. By 1957 another 6 vessels were added, increasing the tonnage to 166 392 dead-weight tons. They carried goods of Polish and Czech origin to Chinese ports, and there was a separate arrangement for the company's two tankers to carry oil from Constantza in Romania to China. From 1951 to 1957 the fleet carried a total of 3.02 million tons of goods, including 1.269 million tons for Chinese consignors and 1.378 million tons for Polish consignors. The undertaking was largely successful in breaking the shipping bottleneck caused by the blockade and Western shipping sanctions, in spite of the setback suffered by the company when two ships, *s/s Praca* and *s/s Gottewald*, were intercepted by Guomindang warships and detained in Taiwan in October 1953 and May 1954 respectively.[46] Throughout the 1950s the operations were kept top secret. The UK Consul to Gdansk, a Mr Littler, was understood to be keeping as close a watch on the China trade through Gdynia and Gdansk as the security arrangements of the polish authorities would permit, where possible, by attempting to obtain samples of the various commodities being handled there whilst he was engaged on 'routine consular business' in the harbour area.[47]

Mention may be made of two aspects of China's diversion of trade towards the Soviet bloc and away from the West. One aspect relates to the allegation of Soviet price discrimination: whether the Soviet Union took advantage of China's dependence on Soviet supplies by overpricing her exports to China.[48] The Soviet Union is known to have imposed upon China an unfavourable exchange rate of the ruble for Renminbi for Soviet-financed projects negotiated in 1950,[49] but that was exclusively in the area of non-trade payments. The Soviet Union returned the differential amount of payment to China after a negotiated settlement in July 1956. One argument is that while the actual published f.o.b. prices for Soviet exports to China showed them to be higher than quotations to the Western traders, it would be unfair to infer that the USSR was exploiting China as Soviet exports (being made mostly in European USSR) would have born very heavy costs during transportation to the border.[50]

One indirect indication of possible 'overpricing' was the exceptionally low price at which Chinese produce was resold to the West by East European countries, sometimes 30–40 per cent cheaper than that quoted by Chinese exporters, as was the case with Chinese bristles.[51] After comparing the expenses for two shipments of Chinese soya beans to Hong Kong after originally being consigned to Eastern Europe, the Foreign Office speculated that, whether the exchanges were in barter or monetary terms between China and the Soviet bloc, the 'satellite exports' to China might have been priced so high that China's trading partners could afford to lose over the resale of Chinese products whereas China was bound to lose commercially on these deals.[52]

This leads to the second, related question of whether China was more dependent on imports from the USSR than the USSR was on imports from China. Economically Moscow's bargaining position was much stronger than Beijing's in the trade between them. China's dependence on industrial supplies from the Soviet Union was all the more obvious since the Western embargo prevented China obtaining the capital goods it needed except from the USSR and its East European satellites, whereas the latter could elsewhere obtain most of the goods they imported from China as they were not strategic materials. In addition, in the bargaining relations between a fairly industrialised economy and a backward agricultural country, the former would generally have economic superiority.[53]

It may indeed be said that from a purely economic point of view China's diversion of trade towards the Soviet Union and its East European allies did represent a misallocation of resources at a greater opportunity cost. But in retrospect China did not seem to have any alternative, especially after the outbreak of the Korean war. The very fact that China was able, during this period of severe East–West tension, to get any trading partner to agree to exchange a fair abundance of industrial equipment and capital goods for China's raw materials, agricultural produce and gold reserves, so that China could get on with its economic recovery and ambitious industrial development programme, far exceeded expectations, and was far more important politically and strategically, whatever the economic cost might be. It is in this context that one can understand China's emphasis on imports as the starting side of its foreign trade planning process, its readiness in general to sacrifice exports in order to secure the required imports, meet its quantitative targets and overcome bottlenecks, and the priority given to stability and orderly development over profit motivation and competition.

Certainly China's early attempts at industrial development was by all accounts a success, not to mention the psychological effect of solidarity from like-minded governments on political fronts. The 304 industrial projects that the Soviet Union undertook to provide to China (with 154 basically completed by 1960) gave the Chinese government sufficient confidence to enable it to carry on with the socialisation of the private sector, and perhaps to forfeit any gains from British and other Western interests in China if and when circumstances compelled it so to do.[54] Since the effectiveness of the Western embargo very much hinged on its ability to create bottlenecks in those materials and goods in which China might have inelastic demand, and where China's terms of trade might be vulnerable, China's overall strategy in combating the economic warfare was to reduce economic links with the West to a minimum, shift the orientation of trade so as to make the economy less vulnerable, and to realign interests with friendly or neutral states for the bulk and weight of its international economic relations. For China the notion was no longer of a military power waging a people's war with this or that weapon against a foreign intruder, but of a dignified and injured nation reacting to an unjust political and economic world order. For the West, sanctions were 'the style most suited to an ideological age, in which nationalism may no longer appear naked, and military war has become a little dangerous'.[55]

REQUISITION EXCHANGES

Following the announcement by the US government on 16 December 1950 of a freeze on Chinese public and private assets in the US and the prohibition of American-registered ships from Chinese ports, China retaliated on 28 December by issuing an order putting US properties in China under government control and freezing American public and private bank accounts in China. Accordingly the Shanghai municipal government imposed military control on some 150 American-owned firms on 30 December, followed by similar actions in other cities and provinces.[56] The government issued a decree on 5 May 1951 to take over American firms through requisition, government custody, purchase or other forms of control according to different circumstances. By the end of 1952, 240 American firms had been disposed of in one way or another in various cities and areas, which accounted for 94.5 per cent of total American capital assets in China.

While there had been some early instances of government control of properties owned by British firms in some parts of country, China's formal sanctions against American companies did not affect the welfare of the British ones at large. However the situation drastically changed in the following April when China retaliated against the British government's decision to requisition the Chinese oil tanker *s/s Yung Hao* in Hong Kong on 7 April 1951, and then pass her on to the Royal Navy for use in the Korean War. Over the next year or so more requisitioning of British properties took place, specifically targeted in a tit-for-tat response to actions by the British authorities against Chinese interests.

The *Yung Hao* and Shell

The vessel *s/s Yung Hao* had been undergoing repairs in Hong Kong, and when these had been completed, the Chinese shipping company that owned her applied for permission for the tanker to leave. The Governor of Hong Kong Sir Alexander Grantham then asked Whitehall for urgent instructions. After extensive consideration at a number of meetings, the Cabinet decided that the tanker should be requisitioned and sailed out of Hong Kong at the earliest possible moment. The decision was quickly carried out, and more than 60 Chinese crewmen were expelled from Hong Kong.

The arguments in the Cabinet for the decision to requisition the *Yung Hao* included: (1) the ship's great value to China for supplying oil to troops fighting in Korea; (2) direct representation from the US government against the ship's release; (3) China's failure to take retaliatory action on previous occasions, such as when Britain had taken the more provocative step of refusing to supply oil to China; (4) the moral obligation under the UN 'aggressor' resolution of January, as well as the legal right to requisition the Chinese ship; and (5) the unsurmountable difficulty in justifying inaction to public opinion if the ship were allowed to pass into Chinese control. However the Cabinet decided that to ease the Governor's difficulties, the British representative should take this opportunity of raising with Beijing 'the general question of Chinese interference with British shipping and other British interests in the Far East'.[57]

The Chinese response was prompt and resolute, leaving no room for British imagination. MFA Vice-Minister Zhang Hanfu lodged a strong protest with Leo Lamb on 18 April, and on 30 April the Chinese government proceeded to requisition the entire properties of the Shell Company of China, Ltd (also called the Asiatic Petroleum Company), with the exception of its office buildings and sales departments in its head and branch offices. The government also decreed that its organisations would purchase the company's entire oil stock in China. In a statement which accompanied the order by Premier Zhou Enlai the government announced that the requisitioning was made in order to 'safeguard Chinese national security and the public interests'. It was noted in Hong Kong that the 'reasons for the requisitioning are similar to those given by the Hong Kong Government last month when the Chinese tanker *Yung Hao* was requisitioned in Hong Kong and taken over by the Royal Navy, and there is no doubt that the APC requisitioning is a reprisal'.[58]

On the same day, the decree was carried out by military control committees in Shanghai, Nanjing, Guangzhou, Fuzhou, Shantou, Hankou, Chongqing and Qingdao. In Shanghai the Foreign Affairs Bureau summoned James Nelson Bates, the company's general manager, to read out to him an official decree. Bates was said to be visibly shaken and dismayed. A military commissioner was appointed to supervise the change-over of the company. A general checking of the company's assets and inventory commenced on 2 May.[59] The actual transfer of Shell's requisitioned properties took place over a period of two years from late 1951 to 1953, while the company's day-to-day operation was run by the existing administration, subject to the approval of the military commissioner stationed in the firm. Most of the requisitioned properties were taken over by a government petroleum corporation which had offices in various parts of the country. Others were taken over by the military.[60] The company's bank deposits, Parity deposits and cash reserves, which were considerable, were not subject to requisition. On the other hand a related enterprise, Price's (China) Ltd, for which Shell acted as agents and managers, was requisitioned in October 1952 in spite of Shell's claim that they were entirely separate organisations with entirely separate capitals.[61]

At the time of the requisition the company had an oil stock of 10 749 tons in the Shanghai area, out of which 10 595.16 tons were purchased by the government. A controversial issue over the government purchase of Shell's oil stocks related to the prices, fixed by the government, at which the company was compelled to sell. This specifically concerned that part of the oil stock, 2 155.47 tons, on which customs duties had been paid earlier. The government calculated the average c.i.f. prices of petroleum products in US dollars at the exchange rate standing at the time of requisition, to which was then added an average sum of customs duties and other levies to become the purchasing price of the duty-paid stock. Official buyers would request each delivery by presentation of a formal letter from the military commissioner's office (called the Requisitioned-Purchase Notice) which spelt out the prices at which the company was to sell the required products.

The company complained to the government that some of the officially established prices did not make sufficient allowance for other charges under the heading of Maintenance and Operation, that is wages, administrative expenses, utility charges and various other local taxes, which in the aggregate amounted to a substantial part of the company's expenditure, and which were pro-rated against selling products and recovered in prices. The government in its part regarded the issue as non-negotiable, and under protest the company eventually issued deliveries of roughly 1423 tons of oil.[62] On the other hand, 8439.69 tons, comprising 79.7 per cent of the entire stock, was non-duty-paid and for which the government claimed it had established prices appreciably higher than the actual c.i.f. prices. The company did not challenge those prices either. On balance the company was allowed to make some profit on the requisitional sales of its entire stock.

Shell's history went back to 1897, and its Asiatic Petroleum Co.

was formed in 1913. For nearly half of a century the company, together with the Standard-Vacuum Oil Co., and the Texas Co. (China) Ltd, dominated the petroleum market in China. The American-owned Cathay Oil Co. Inc USA was smaller in scale. In addition, at the time of the liquidation of British-American oil companies in China, a number of trading firms dealt in oil under licence, including the British-owned Jardine Engineering Corp. Ltd, Frost Blend and Co. Ltd and nine American firms. Of Shell's 50 secondary branches in China (Shanghai being ranked as the primary branch) 36 had closed by the end of 1950. At the time of the requisitioning, the company's assets exceeded its liabilities fairly comfortably and 364 staff were employed in the Shanghai area alone. Admittedly most of the staff members were reticent about the change.[63]

The Chinese government never doubted that the requisitioned properties would not be restored to their original British owners and that compensation for them would be the subject of later diplomatic negotiations. The company's physical presence came to an end in 1966, when on 10 January T.P.G. Ruffett, Shell's Shanghai manager, signed an agreement with the China Enterprise Co. under which the company was to transfer all its properties and assets to China against the responsibility for the staff's employment and pensions. Nien Cheng, who is the widow of Shell's former general manager in Shanghai, Dr Kang-chi Cheng, was persecuted during the Cultural Revolution.[64]

Chinese Aircraft in Hong Kong

The decisions by Hong Kong and English Courts in 1952 to disallow the ownership of 71 Chinese aircraft and other related assets in Hong Kong by the People's Republic triggered off another series of public requisitions of British properties by the Chinese government.

As mentioned earlier, the events that led up to the Court decisions, particularly the detention of the aircraft by the Hong Kong authorities, had been one of the thorny issues hindering progress towards the establishment of diplomatic relations between China and Britain.[65] On the eve of the CCP nationwide victory in 1949, the two Chinese aviation companies involved – CNAC and CATC – moved the aircraft to Hong Kong under the orders of the Guomindang government, together with a good deal of equipment. Soon afterwards, in May, Shanghai – where CNAC's head office was located – was captured by the PLA and the

PRC was proclaimed on 1 October. On 9 November the majority of the employees of the two companies declared in Hong Kong that they no longer recognised the authority of the Guomindang, and instead submitted their allegiance to the newly founded Central People's Government in Beijing. They wanted to take back to China 71 aircraft and other equipment which Beijing had declared in several directives and public statements were state property belonging to the new government.[66]

The Guomindang authorities rejected the power of the Beijing government over the two corporations and retaliated by announcing that the registration certificates for all the aircraft and licenses for their pilots be suspended. In addition, two former Guomindang officials – concurrently chairmen of the Boards of Directors of CNAC and CATC respectively – signed an agreement with General Claire Lee Chennault and Whiting Willauer of the United States on 5 December 1949 (presumably in Taiwan) with regard to the two Americans' offer to purchase all the physical assets of the two companies, a major part of which were now located in Hong Kong. They also made paper arrangements in the United States whereby the titles to these assets were to be transferred under American law to Civil Air Transport Incorporated (CAT), which was hastily established on 19 December.[67]

None of these public actions and private manoeuvres on both sides resulted in the removal of the 71 aircraft grounded in Hong Kong, and the pro-PRC and pro-Guomindang employees of both companies applied court injunctions against each other. In fatuous fashion, CAT started court action against its patrons Chennault and Willauer, asking for an appointment of receivers of assets thus transferred to its name, which, while the 'defendants' whole-heartedly consented as expected, was opposed by the pro-PRC employees of the two corporations who were effectively holding the aeroplanes, and who subsequently appeared before the Court in Hong Kong as third parties sued for damages for wrongful detention.[68]

The Hong Kong Supreme Court heard the cases (entered separately for the two companies) on 23 February 1950 and refused the application for receivers, concurring with the third parties' objection of sovereign immunity on the part of the PRC, which the British government had recognised on 6 January 1950. On 13 May the Hong Kong Court of Appeal upheld the decisions and threw out the appeals.[69] It may be noted that the PRC was never formally associated with these court proceedings, nor has evidence come to light of formal diplomatic correspondence from the Chinese government specifically requesting the granting of sovereign immunity through intervention by the British authorities. However the question was raised during the first round of talks on diplomatic relations between Vice-Minister of Foreign Affairs Zhang Hanfu and J. Hutchison in Beijing, and the British government was asked to clarify its position on this matter.

It appears that the British government was considerably disturbed by the court judgments in Hong Kong. The political and psychological repercussions of a release to China of the aircraft against all principles and efforts of Western strategic export controls would be too serious to be neglected. In April, while the appeals were pending, the Cabinet met several times to discuss the matter. The United States government applied heavy pressure on Britain to deny the aircraft to the Chinese Communists. The British were warned that the US government would withdraw Marshall Aid and the Military Assistance Programme. After the initial judgments were made in Hong Kong, greater pressure came from the US government by means of the threat of being unable to defend UK policy or coordinate with the UK and France in Southeast Asia.[70] The crucial issue for decision, as Attorney General Hartley Shawcross (who in 1952 appeared before the Privy Council as counsel for the American CAT) put it,

> was not a question of law, but the political question whether the Government's action should be directed to placating the US Government or the Chinese People's Government. . . . It would be better for the UK Government to take the responsibility of changing the existing law by an Order-in-Council, made under the prerogative, enabling the Hong Kong courts (subject to appeal to the Judicial Committee of the Privy Council) to determine the question of legal ownership. It would then deprive the Chinese People's Government of the jurisdictional immunity.[71]

During the discussions, some ministers found it repugnant that British law should be altered to suit the convenience of American interests. However Shawcross, supported by Foreign Secretary Ernest Bevin, urged the government to agree to an Order-in-Council, which 'would not only provide for the detention of the aircraft, pending an adjudication as to the title to them, but would set up machinery for the trial of this issue'. When it was clear that other methods of finding a convenient legal subterfuge to hide the political intention proved ineffective, the Cabinet agreed and the Order-in-Council was issued on 11 May 1950.[72]

The government action enabled the Hong Kong authorities to continue the detention of the aircraft for another two years while court proceedings were be re-instituted. This decision was strongly criticised by the Chinese government as a manifestation of using judicial procedures for political purposes.[73] The final judgments were made by the Judicial Committee of the Privy Council with regard to CATC's 40 aircraft on 28 July 1952, and by the Hong Kong Supreme Court with regard to CNAC's 31 aircraft on 8 October. All these aircraft were awarded to the American Company CAT. The respondents were not represented in the proceedings.[74] Immediately after the Privy Council's decision of 28 July, massive forces of Hong Kong armed police raided the section of Kai Tak Airport where the aircraft were grounded, as well as several warehouses and factories where other equipment and assets were stored. The employees on guard were beaten up and arrested and all the aircraft and assets belonging to the two corporations were seized by the government.

Chinese Retaliatory Requisitions

The Chinese government reacted angrily to the outcome of these legal proceedings. Any chance of itself appearing before the courts to start new proceedings or to appeal was out of the question. On 2 August and 28 October 1952, Vice Foreign Minister Zhang Hanfu lodged strong protests with the British government, through Leo Lamb, against the Court decisions. Each of these protests was followed by a requisitioning of British-owned properties in China, to the accompaniment of considerable publicity in the press. On 15 August, two weeks after the Privy Council's judgment, Shanghai's Military Control Commission issued an order to requisition the British-owned Shanghai Dockyards and the Mollers Engineering and Shipbuilding Works Ltd, including all their assets, movable or immovable. Deputy director of the Foreign Affairs Bureau Yu Peiwen summoned D. MacCallum, assistant manager of the Shanghai Dockyards, and N. Penson, manager of Mollers, and the order was read to them. Military commissioners were immediately appointed to carry out the takeover.[75]

The Shanghai Dockyards Ltd. were the owners of four dry docks in Shanghai harbour. Their longest dock was 584 feet, the shortest 345

feet. The company also had steam and electric slipways accommo-
dating vessels up to 200 feet. Its London representatives were Matheson and Co. Ltd. Mollers' dockyard and factories stretched along
2150 feet of the Shanghai waterfront – they also owned two slipways.
The two companies, unlike the Shell Co. of China, Ltd, had been
losing money and, it was speculated, would probably eventually have
had to close down after a difficult settlement. In fact it was reported
that the Mollers' dockyard had been leased indirectly in February
1952 to the Chinese government and had set off the first five-year
lease against taxes. The requisitioning thus released to some extent
the company's obligations to their Chinese staff, to the surprise of the
management. All this seems to confirm the political retaliatory nature of
the requisition.[76]

Again on 20 November, in reaction to the decision of the Hong
Kong Supreme Court in October, the Shanghai authorities ordered
the requisitioning of three British-owned public utilities companies.
Moreover properties owned by Mackenzie and Co. in Shanghai,
Tianjin and Wuhan were requisitioned.[77] Of these interests, Mackenzie's appeared the better off. It had remained solvent without sterling
remittances to China, and was estimated to be of better value. In
particular the company had a press-packing plant in Hankou which
had been working profitably, and was said to have been the chief
factor in enabling the company to keep their heads above water since
1949. The company also had had some property in Chongqing which
was requisitioned some time later.[78]

The three British public utilities companies in Shanghai were the
Shanghai Waterworks Co. Ltd, the Shanghai Gas Co. Ltd and the
Shanghai Electric Construction Co. Ltd (the British Tramway). Their
entire assets (including all movable and immovable property) were
requisitioned 'in the Chinese public interests'.[79] Other public utilities
companies in Shanghai included the French Power, Water and Trams
Co. (Compagnie Française de Tramways et d'Éclairage Électriques
de Shanghai), the American-owned Shanghai Power Co. and Shanghai Telephone Co. The two American companies were under government control at the time, whereas the French company was
eventually put under official custody on 2 November 1953.[80]

In view of the important role played by the British public utilities
companies in the everyday life of the Shanghai population, their
takeover was a rather delicate process, requiring careful orchestra-
tion by the authorities in order not to cause any disruption to the
normal public services. The British Tramway carried 40 per cent of

the total passenger load in Shanghai and covered the major routes in town. It employed a work force of 3500. The Shanghai Gas Co. supplied gas to some 17 000 customers, including industrial units and family households. (A Chinese gas company, Wu Song, in contrast, had about 1000 clients.) The total number of its employees was 784 in 1952. The Shanghai Waterworks Co. had the capacity to produce more than half of the city's water supply, being the largest in the Far East. It had a work force of 3213, in addition to 17 foreign employees.

To ensure a smooth takeover, not only was it necessary to win popular sympathy, efforts were also made to ease the minds of foreign personnel working in these enterprises. In these respects the government was successful. Workers were told to draw a clear distinction between British personnel and the 'imperialist British government'; the requisitioning did not mean objection to establishing diplomatic relations with Britain. Strict orders were given to forbid any action by individuals or groups, political or otherwise, that would affect the personal properties of foreign personnel or respect for their national flag, or would hurt their personal feelings and self-esteem. Except for senior managers, foreign personnel were allowed to stay on if they so chose, while the level of their salaries and benefits remained unchanged. The entire complement of Chinese personnel was retained in employment. Eventually all foreign staff members – British, Italian and Russian – were retired on pension and most left China.

Within months of the requisition, a check of all the assets and liabilities of the companies was completed, and inventories and estimates were duly signed by both British and Chinese representatives.[81] Much of the equipment and facilities being used were found to be in need of maintenance and replacement. It was also noted that the Chinese authorities insisted on much curtailed inventories of the physical assets taken over, in contrast to the detailed lists of items required for closure purposes.[82]

The three British companies had been founded in the late 19th and early 20th centuries. They had thrived in Shanghai's international settlement and survived the vicissitudes of modern Chinese history.[83] Although they all had a long history, before 1949 they had developed at a relatively slow pace. In addition to the losses carried over from the Guomindang days, they incurred varying degrees of losses after 1949 and had to obtain loans from the People's Bank to carry on with their services.[84] Part of the losses could be attributed to inflation and fluctuations in the exchange rates, but there was also considerable criticism by the unions of the management for contributing to the companies' financial difficulties.[85] The labour's attitude towards the management was said to have been generally peaceful, and ever since liberation the companies had maintained a close working relationship with the municipal government. When in 1950 the Public Utilities Bureau and the Foreign Affairs Bureau heard that Mr A. Pollock, Manager of the British Tramways, had decided to go back to England they tried to persuade him to stay, saying that he was a good and able man who had operated the company successfully in the past, and that he was a friend of China. Pollock told them that he had not realised the Chinese appreciated his work, that his health did not allow him to remain, and that men of his race, once having made up their minds, did not go back on their decisions. He returned to Britain in May 1951 and, because of ill health, tendered his resignation as manager and secretary of the company in the July of that year.[86]

On 3 October 1952, Leo Lamb made a representation to the Chinese Ministry of Foreign Affairs on behalf of the British companies concerned.[87] Related to the British requisitioning of the *Yung Hao* tanker and the court cases, were the cases of five Chinese fishing trawlers over the period between June 1950 to January 1953, which had been either seized by the Guomindang elements (in three instances) allegedly under the armed protection of Hong Kong authorities, or awarded by the Hong Kong courts to the Guomindang against PRC claims.[88] On 24 February 1953, the Guangzhou authorities requisitioned the Pak Hin Hok property of Butterfield and Swire, as well as other properties such as warehouses and buildings, apparently in reprisal against those Hong Kong court decisions.[89]

The requisitions and the Korean war in general precipitated the deterioration of the economic ties which had been strenuously maintained between the Chinese economy and British commercial presence in China. There is no reason to believe however that this episode of requisitioning and counter-requisitioning was inevitable, and much of the antagonistic posturing on both sides may well be attributed to the atmosphere of mistrust and acrimony prevailing at the time. The Chinese nonetheless appear to have acted in response to the moves of the British government, which they saw as hopelessly bogged down by a policy of following the aggressive American government. The Chinese were not convinced by the British government's argument that the question of title to the aircraft was a matter solely to be decided by the courts. They had made it clear during and outside the negotiations – and the British were well aware of this position – that as the aircraft were Chinese state property, the matter should be resolved by the governments on the basis of a recognition of the political nature of the case, and not treated as an ordinary civil lawsuit in which the government of China would be reduced to a party before an English court.

Nor did the Chinese leadership doubt that the British requisitioning of the oil tanker and later the shipment of rubber on board *Nancy Moller* (see page 97) was a deliberate political decision. As a result the bilateral political relations reached the nadir, leaving no room for mutual understanding and accommodation, and very little communication until the truce in Korea in 1953.

4 Trade Restrictions and Embargoes

*In dealings with imperialists, the principle '**Seeking truth from the fact**' does not apply: neither they nor we can afford to tell what had happened.*

An official in Shanghai

Whitney [US Ambassador to UK] said [to BoT President Thorney-croft at their dinner] if Her Majesty's Government would only say that they did not now press for China to become a member of the United Nations, a deal could no doubt be done.

F.W. Gloves-Smith (BoT)

From early 1949 the British government began to restrict British exports to mainland China, and the level of the controls reached its peak during the Korean War. Driven by a logic of East–West contention, strategic commodity controls entailed further restrictions on civilian supplies, transit trade, financial transactions and shipping. The momentum thus built into the system gave rise to a strong official resistance to any reversal or even modification of the policy long after the embargo appeared to have lost its *raison d'être*.

To the extent the policy served as an effective security instrument, it paradoxically rendered Britain's effort to keep a positive profile in China largely ineffective. A key element in Britain's diplomatic recognition of the new People's Republic admittedly was to keep trade channels open with an independent China. The cultivation of China's good will, the alienation of her native communism from the mainstream of Soviet orthodoxy, the encouragement of Chinese appreciation of potential economic benefits from cooperating with Western powers, the preservation of British commercial interests and political influence in China, the prevention of communism succeeding in South-East Asia – all of these objectives depended to a considerable extent upon a de-politicised trading relationship with China and a generally friendly atmosphere in the Far East. The secret application of export restrictions and, after the Korean conflict broke out, the open interference with China's property rights, contributed not a little to the collapse of Britain's peace policy towards China. It also ran counter to the intention of maintaining Britain's role and status in the China market. British decision-makers were hard put to tackle these inconsistencies in export controls on China.

INITIAL RESTRICTIONS, 1949–MAY 1950

Eonomic sanctions against China were conceived by the British government in late 1948 as a means of exerting economic pressure on the CCP and for retaliation against possible CCP suppressive action against British economic interests in China.[1] On 4 March 1949, the Cabinet assessed the economic weaknesses of CCP authorities to see whether Britain could utilise these to her own advantage. It was then realised that Britain held no particularly strong cards, and that any action would therefore have to be taken from outside China. There was also the perceived strategic necessity to prevent goods of military value from reaching the Communist world, which would soon include China.[2]

Britain had by now already prohibited sales to the Soviet Union and other East European countries of not only war equipment, but also any other equipment which might significantly add to their war potential.[3] In this respect, Britain stressed the need to agree with the United States on a common list of articles to be withheld or restricted, since the Americans made such controls a condition for their aid. One aspect of the US system was to control through licensing the export of all commodities to Europe under a procedure known as the 'R' procedure, with its 1A and 1B Lists.[4] The 'R' procedure was eventually adopted by the United States towards China, and British export controls on China were subsequently founded on its basis.

In March 1949 an Anglo–French list of strategic items was formulated. Accordingly the British government extended its controls to cover all items which had been agreed with the French government. In order to avoid the appearance of discriminatory action, the controls applied to exports to a wide range of countries, with licences granted freely to destinations outside Eastern Europe and waved for OEEC countries, the US and the Commonwealth. Where export licensing was impracticable owing to the difficulty of definition, administrative control was exercised through the various production departments concerned.[5]

However the British government decided on political grounds in the spring of 1949 that Britain should keep a foot in the door in China and that British commercial interests should be supported as part of that policy. For one thing, a severe curtailment of exports would have the effect of depriving the established British merchants in China of the minimum business which they would need in order to carry on their operations, thereby forcing them to close down. There would be the added complication that the Chinese authorities might take measures against UK commercial and industrial interests in China. This did not differ substantially from the US calculations made during the first half of 1949, but as the Americans appeared increasingly inclined to see their business interests withdraw from China and to prepare for a tougher line, the British government was anxious to persuade the United States and other powers to impose no general sanctions on China 'for as long as foreign interests remain reasonably unmolested', and to work out a system of joint measures of economic pressure against China for future application. 'Action on these lines would not of course preclude the denial to China, by agreement with other Powers, of goods of strategic importance, where such denial would be effective.'[6] Work was then under way at inter-departmental level on the kind of economic sanctions Britain could apply to China, beginning with a denial of industrial goods, oil, ferro-alloy metals, tin and possibly rubber.[7]

Anglo–American Consultations

As early as February 1949, the US government asked the UK government to urgently study the question of export controls in the UK and Hong Kong. The Americans set out to seek British cooperation in extending the 'R' procedure to China, and in adopting measures to control trans-shipments through Hong Kong. In April Western envoys in China discussed a US proposal to adopt a uniform trade policy towards China with a view to exerting economic pressure at an early stage.[8]

In June American and British officials met in London to coordinate their export control policies on China. As a first priority, the Americans wanted to see a British control on strategic materials (mostly on the US 1A List). Britain was already in a position to ban their export to China without taking new powers which might involve undesirable publicity. Export licences were required for these for all destinations, and were largely subject to presumptive denial to Eastern European destinations. London then agreed to put a stop on direct export to China by adding China to the Board of Trade's Export Licensing

Department's confidential list of countries for which licences should be refused for security reasons. The British claimed that by this time all shipments of weapons to China from the UK, Hong Kong and Singapore had already been banned.

In addition the working arrangement with industry would be extended to China, by which the responsible production departments could exercise control over the export of certain strategic equipment which did not lend itself to export licensing.[9] The Americans also wanted the British to restrict certain other goods of particular importance to the Chinese economy, basing their selection on the US 1B List, including petroleum products, essential types of mining and power generating equipment, certain essential transportation equipment, and possibly steel working equipment. This was justified on the basis of their value as political bargaining counters with the Chinese government.[10]

The British government did not agree with an early imposition of such controls, especially in view of British vulnerability after the *Amethyst* incident. Nor did the British believe that ready and effective cooperation on a wide scale among allies would be forthcoming in the event of any proposed extension of this system of controls to China. They also rejected an American suggestion to extend the control at that time exercised in the UK over the export of List 1A items to cover transhipment in Hong Kong and Singapore.[11] It would be necessary to consider a huge area, including the Japanese ports, Fusan, Keelung, Haiphong, Macao and Manila. The geographical proximity of Hong Kong to mainland China made the colony particularly vulnerable to breaches of controls through smuggling. Above all British reluctance grew out of the fear of political repercussions.

Both Britain and the United States agreed about the urgent need to control petroleum supplies to China. To that end American oil companies (California–Texas and Standard Vacuum) and British firms (Shell and Anglo–Iranian) were requested not to meet the CCP government's huge demand by concluding any long-term contract with it. Instead of a formal ban, they agreed that the flow of oil traffic into China would be watched to ensure that China did not obtain more than was needed for civilian consumption.[12] While the British government was not yet prepared to introduce formal controls over 1B items owing to 'political and administrative difficulties', it agreed, together with the Hong Kong and Singapore governments, to check the flow of these items to China and exchange information with the

Americans. A list of 50 odd items for 'close watch' was to be finalised by both sides.[13]

The significance of the Anglo–American negotiations in the summer of 1949 on export control policy towards China lies in the fact that the principles, scope and procedures of the control system in the Far East were carefully laid out. At the same time they revealed serious disagreement between the two governments over the timing of the new controls. The US government decided late in 1949 to extend the 'R' procedure to mainland China and adjacent areas, with exports of 1A goods subject to presumptive denial except for special cases, and those of 1B and lower categories to be licensed on the basis of strict safeguards against excessive quantities and possible transhipments to the Soviet bloc and North Korea.[14]

After some more delays on the part of the Foreign Office and considerable urging by the Department of State, the delegates of the two countries to the Paris Group meeting in January 1950, approached the delegates of Belgium, France and the Netherlands with a view to coordinating controls on items on the US 1B List to China. This was followed by informal communications to Paris, Brussels and The Hague in March. Britain also urged other Commonwealth governments to pursue the same policy. All these efforts were eventually successful.[15]

Administrative Controls

The informal arrangements and administrative machinery were already in place in Britain to ensure that China did not receive those goods of strategic importance which were being denied to the Soviet bloc countries. While the government could not formally prohibit a firm from carrying out an order in the absence of law, there was little question that the controls, when within the scope of the government's reach, were largely effective. This was because most British trading firms and manufacturers felt obliged to seek government advice on the security aspect of an export to a Communist country whenever they were in doubt. For all practical purpose, the system was not dissimilar to formal government sanction as a matter of law. For instance ICI wrote to the Foreign Office asking how they should respond to an order from China for a consignment of certain chemicals to Tianjin. The matter was discussed at the inter-departmental Security Export Control Working Party, and the Foreign Office expressed to the firm 'His Majesty's Government's misgivings' and that it wished to 'dissuade' the firm from fulfilling the order. The same thing happened to an inquiry received from China by the Rail and Telegraph Accessories Export Group for 300 000 units of railway anchors.[16]

In cases where an order asked for a quantity of a commodity which, while of itself not prohibited, might be 'unduly large', government intervention often resulted in the failure of the firm's completion of the contract. This happened to Johnson and Phillips Ltd, who asked for permission to export electric cables and wires to China in 1950.[17] The government also requested British suppliers to provide a monthly statement showing against each of the specified destinations the value of an administratively controlled product they had directly exported in the previous calendar month, plus the value of any significant orders they had outstanding.

Understandably the government was reluctant to confirm in writing that it had been enforcing such export prohibitions. This caused a serious problem for British firms trading with Chinese government purchasing agencies, whose standard contracts stipulated that documentation was required in support of any *force majeure* claim. The British government's 'equivocations' upset the trading community. The British Chamber of commerce in Shanghai complained that even in those cases where written statements by the British government were finally produced, they were either too vaguely worded to be of any assistance, or arrived so late as to arouse considerable suspicion and embarrassment to the seller concerned.[18] U.K. exports to China were valued at £2.25 million in 1949 and £0.6 million in the first five months of 1950. The main items were iron and steel, copper and electrical and other machinery. The proportion of strategic items were negligible but that of US 1B List items probably very high.[19]

The Consultative Group – COCOM

The development of the multilateral export control system in the West was initiated by US efforts to secure parallel export controls by West European countries and Canada as a supplement to the US system. The French government then called a meeting in Paris of participating countries of the OEEC, at which they decided to negotiate a common set of control lists on the basis of the Anglo–French List, and to set up machinery which would allow for continuing consultations.

The OEEC countries held talks in Paris on 12 October and 14 November 1949, which resulted in the adoption of a common policy for the denial to the Soviet bloc countries of goods to be included in an agreed list. They eventually reached agreement on an International Munitions List (IML), and on International Lists I (IL I, covering more than 100 industrial items for embargo) and II (IL II, quantitatively controlled items). A further list of commodities was also worked out in 1950, the export of which would be watched and subjected to exchange of information among participating countries. This was known as International List III (IL III).

Thus Britain embargoed to Eastern Europe goods on IML and IL I, whereas the export of other goods such as merchant ships was severely restricted. In addition Britain put under quantitative control a range of items on IL II.[20] In May 1950 the United States began to urge the Paris Group to add the US 1B List items to the embargo category. This comprised 290 odd items which the US believed were being purchased by Soviet bloc countries for stockpiling. Progress in this aspect was slow within the Paris Group owing to opposition from its members, and the United States became increasingly impatient.[21]

In terms of institutional arrangement, delegations to the January 1950 session agreed to set up: (1) a Consultative Group (CG), composed of heads of participating delegations meeting once every quarter to consider major matters of policy; and (2) a permanent Coordinating Committee (COCOM), to be attended by representatives from interested participating countries as deputies. The Coordinating Committee would arrange for such meetings on an *ad hoc* basis to compile control lists, to determine the methods and extent of the restrictions, and to administer the organisation. CG-COCOM was proclaimed (secretly) on 20 January 1950.[22]

The establishment of CG-COCOM represented for the US the ultimate achievement of its 18 months of bilateral negotiations with West European countries for parallel action on export controls. One general objective for Britain in the Paris group was to see that controls exercised by other European countries were kept in line with its own.[23] Increasingly Britain found it necessary to co-ordinate with other countries, especially members of CG-COCOM, over export controls on both the Soviet bloc and China, although initially it was intended that the two sets of controls be kept separate.

THE KOREAN WAR EMBARGO 1950–56

When the Korean War started in June 1950, Britain placed a complete embargo on all shipments to North Korea. The government also proceeded to formally add China to the confidential list of countries to which export licences were in fact refused for items on IL I. Instructions were sent out to Hong Kong and Singapore to start to apply List I strategic export controls against China. The decision was promptly related to the American government. On 17 July COCOM agreed to impose an embargo on IL I and quantitative control for IL II exports to China, thereby bringing China controls in line with those applied to the Soviet Union and Eastern Europe.[24]

The British government also decided to take steps to interrupt the flow of oil to China from British sources. Since the US government had instructed US firms (mainly Caltex and Standard-Vacuum) to suspend all oil supplies to China, the only major supplier of oil had been the British firm Shell. Shell's total supply to China in the first six months of 1950 amounted only to some 26 000 tons, which was estimated to be about five per cent of China's total requirements, or less than 10 per cent of its civilian requirements. As the rate of supply was so low the British government had previously decided not to ban British oil supplies to China but to limit them to the current low rate of supply. In mid-July 1950, the government decided to stop all supplies of oil to China forthwith. Immediate measures involved stopping a tanker bound for Tianjin and the requisitioning by the British Services Departments, for their own strategic requirements, of all the oil stocks in Hong Kong. The UK also added oil products to List I, as extended to Hong Kong and Singapore, in order to relieve Shell of its contractual obligation to find supplies from other sources.[25]

The Korean List

After hostility broke out in Korea, the Minister of Defence reported that manufacturers and traders in Britain were receiving inquiries, from China in particular, for large quantities of items such as steel wire rope, copper wire, wireless sets of army type, heavy duty tyres, telephone equipment and steel rails, which it said might be used in support of North Korean forces in the war.[26] Consequently the inter-departmental Security Export Control Working Party recommended 45 items for proposed emergency controls on China and oriental Soviet Union (the so-called 'Korean List'), in addition to ILs I and II.[27] The idea was that, pending formal legislation in coordination with other countries, the departments which were in close touch with the traders in question should be allowed, as an interim measure, to use whatever powers or influence they possessed to refuse or discourage British exports to Asian destinations, either through the existing licensing system or by way of advising the reduction or refusal of abnormally large orders.

On 11 September Cabinet approved the Working Party's proposals for restrictions by administrative means on the export of goods on the 'Korean List', beyond the International Lists I and II. Cabinet also agreed as a matter of principle that emergency powers might be used for the purpose of requisitioning equipment and supplies which had been ordered from Britain by Communist governments but were required for defence purposes by Britain or other NATO countries.[28]

A turning point was reached during the tripartite talks in New York in September 1950, when the three Foreign Secretaries – Bevin, Schuman and Acheson – agreed that future extension of export controls should be designed not only to limit the short-term striking power of the Soviet bloc, but also to retard the development of its war potential in the longer term. To that end, the three governments agreed to considerable extensions to ILs I and II for immediate operation, and to persuade other member countries of the Consultative Group to go along with the new policy. Twenty-seven items of the original 45 on the UK 'Korean List' were subsequently agreed within COCOM for inclusion into the international embargo and quantitative control lists. By then, upon recommendation from Britain, the Paris Group had added petroleum products to IL I for total prohibition to all destinations in the Soviet bloc, including China.[29]

London then asked the governments of Hong Kong, Singapore, North Borneo, Brunei and Sarawak to institute the above controls; orders were promulgated in Hong Kong and Singapore to that end. All the colonial governments had been instructed to keep a close watch on trade in strategic materials. The British government made a pronouncement on the new policies in the House of Commons on 18 September. The control measures caused a hue and cry among the British trading community, typified by the remark that 'There is little doubt that a good deal of irresponsible and hysterical thinking is behind some of the actions of those who direct our export policy'.[30] The Foreign Office admitted that a considerable number of NATO members did not operate export controls comparable with those in force in the UK, especially with regard to non-strategic goods. It was stated that the government 'sympathise with the disappointment of the merchant community at seeing their reviving chances of trade apparently slipping away owing in part to United Kingdom export controls; but the present international situation and the increased defence requirements of this country make their continuance unavoidable'. Also, future export licensing policy 'depends on the actions of the Central People's Government'.[31]

China Entered the War

The direct Chinese intervention in support of North Korean forces in October triggered off on 3 December a complete US embargo on all exports to China. Shipments of commodities on various control lists would require licences not only for destinations in China but also when consigned to Hong Kong or Macao. All of China's US dollar assets in the United States would also henceforth be frozen.[32] In London, the Economic Policy Committee met on 21 December and requested the Minister of Defence to arrange for an urgent consideration by the Security Export Control Working Party of additional restrictions directed primarily against China.[33] It was subsequently revealed that, for the twelve months up to January 1951, all Chinese Sterling accounts had also been blocked, and that all payments from them had been subject to the permission of the UK Exchange Control.[34] Little evidence is available to reveal the circumstances of this secret government action, but it did in the end justify the early fears of the Chinese (see chapter 3, page 62.)

In early 1951, after the UN General Assembly had adopted a resolution on 1 February declaring China to be an 'aggressor' – with Britain voting in favour of the resolution – London concluded a further study on economic sanctions on China and their political and strategic implications.[35] In ensuing talks with Washington, the British rejected American suggestions to 'de-recognise' Beijing and impose a total embargo, a naval blockade and a host of other measures. For Britain the safest course would be to continue the present selective embargo but with an extended coverage of commodities and materials. Goods hitherto subject to quantitative control (IL II and part of the 'Korean List') could now be completely prohibited. This move was not as dangerous for Hong Kong as other measures, such as total embargo and naval blockade. Besides, it was initially thought, since this would be secured through the private negotiating processes of the Consultative Group (rather than be part of any wider UN arrangement), it would maintain COCOM's secrecy and avoid possible open confrontation with the Chinese.

As it turned out, the United States decided to take the case to the

United Nations. As a result of considerable pressure and a resolution by US Congress, Britain found it increasingly difficult to delay submission of a resolution by the UN Additional Measures Committee to the General Assembly recommending a strategic embargo on China.[36] The Cabinet gave authorisation on 7 May, 1951, and embargo resolution went through the General Assembly on 18 May.[37] In spite of its initial reluctance, the British government was not unhappy with this turn of events. A UN embargo would merely ratify existing British practice.[38] But it would also close to China sources of supply outside the Paris Group, which would help prevent leakage through re-export from countries other than the Soviet bloc which were not members of the Paris Group.[39]

The adoption of the UN embargo resolution changed the political context in which the Western economic warfare against China would be placed: henceforth it could be justified as part of an international police action and collective security, rather than a vindication of the West's policy of isolation and containment of communism in Asia. Above all its importance lay in its psychological effect on public opinion, which began to see the embargo policy as a concerted UN defence measure, a necessary complement to the common war efforts in Korea, and a useful way to shorten the war and save the lives of allied soldiers. The veneer of morality and legality was to prove most handy for the British government for several years to come when defending in public its stringent embargo policy towards China, even well after the immediate cause of that policy was removed.[40]

Once the political decision had been made at the United Nations, the entire machinery of British export control was set to full gear. On 19 June the President of the Board of Trade, Sir Hartley Shawcross, made a statement in the House of Commons, declaring that an Export of Goods (Control) Order had been prepared giving effect to the government's decision on export licence control on all goods to be sent from the UK and Hong Kong. The new Order came into operation on 25 June. A comprehensive list was published specifying those goods which were prohibited from export from the UK to, or transported as ships' stores in any vessel proceeding to, any port or destination in China or Hong Kong.[41] While the formal list was also communicated to the United Nations, other items which were quantitatively controlled in varying degrees in the UK and the colonies were not, so as to assume an appearance of uniformity and to maintain the secrecy of the Western export control operations. The British action delighted the US government; Department of State officials expressed the view that 'they had not expected so much so quickly'.[42]

Controls in Hong Kong

Whereas the US embargo covered all consignments to China, a special American licensing policy had, since December 1950, affected those to Hong Kong and Macao as well, be they of American origin or foreign goods in transit through America. The latter procedure in effect amounted to a complete embargo on Hong Kong. The Americans appeared to harbour a lot of resentment of the Hong Kong business community, seeing them as 'a bunch of pirates' who 'get rich by dint of skillful and continuous evasion of all regulations'. It was suggested that it might even be 'necessary to put Hong Kong out of business'. As a result, shipments of cotton, blackplate, tin plate, petroleum products and other essential raw materials were suspended.[43]

By now Hong Kong was already operating controls on the export to China of major strategic goods, as requested by the British government and implemented through the Exportation (Prohibition) (Specified Articles) Order, 1950 and two other Orders under the same title (No. 2 and No. 3, 1950).[44] A detailed record of trade in items on International List II and other strategic materials was reported regularly to London in order to check any 'abnormal' exports.

In addition, there was in existence an export control mechanism enforced under the Defence Regulations, 1940, which was mainly confined to essential supplies such as various types of foodstuffs, certain steel products, tinplate, black plate, raw cotton, cotton yarn, and cotton waste. The government had a great deal of discretion in such matters, and subsequently tightened control measures in response to American criticisms. A Mr Hansen from the US Senate visited Hong Kong and asserted that he had identified in the captured (communist) equipment in Korea some Hong Kong-made rubber shoes. The Governor of Hong Kong immediately stopped the export of rubber shoes to China.[45] In spite of this readiness to accommodate, the Hong Kong government had great difficulty in persuading Washington to relax its embargo on Hong Kong. Hong Kong's commercial community quickly felt the pinch, and a general mood of depression prevailed in the colony.[46]

After a good deal of debate within the British government, Cabinet approved a plan under which items on ILs I and II, and on the 'Korean List', were henceforth forbidden to be exported to China from Hong Kong regardless of their origin. Importation of such goods to Hong Kong from the UK were prohibited unless certified for local use, and a system of certification of essential supplies was put into place. Orders from Hong Kong for strategic or semi-strategic materials from UK and continental firms were referred back to Hong Kong for confirmation as to the end use of the goods in question.[47] All goods on the prohibited list were diverted upon arrival to specified warehouses in the colony in order to ensure their safe custody until being released to the final user. An immediate effect of this measure was that the monthly figures of exports by sea and rail to China – which amounted to 112 000 tons in December 1950 – declined to 40 000 tons in June 1951, and 17 000 tons in July 1951.[48]

Problems with the Americans persisted and contributed to a worsening of the economic situation in Hong Kong; especially hard hit were factories dependent on American cotton supply. Not until the spring of 1952 did the US government adjust its controls to permit certain non-strategic goods, such as cotton, to be exported to Hong Kong under a general license procedure.

Implementation of Controls

British authorities in day-to-day operations were constantly confronted with borderline cases of licence applications which might have political implications beyond the letter and spirit of the established control lists. A proposed transaction with China of UK refined sugar was eventually aborted for fear of running any risk of 'irritating United States' public opinion'.[49] On another occasion the Board of Trade expressed the view, in reply to an inquiry by Textile Machinery Makers Ltd, that although textile machinery was not embargoed, it should be regarded as having strategic importance and therefore should not be supplied to the Chinese.[50] The 'end-use' principle was applied to make sure that civilian products would not be used for strategic purposes. Thus the government refused to license the export to China of 10 000 heat and acid resisting bricks for the construction of a sulphuric acid plant in China, nor did it allow chart paper to be supplied on the grounds that its end-user was the Chinese Navy.[51]

Rubber was singled out for control. China's purchase of rubber in 1950 showed a considerable rise over those for 1949 – roughly 80 000 tons compared with 27 500 tons in 1949. In response to criticism in the House of Commons, in April 1951 the government decided to adopt a more restrictive policy. Exports of rubber to China were limited to 2500 tons per month. This was quickly superseded by a complete ban, announced by the President of the Board of Trade, Peter Thorneycroft, on 10 May 1951. Cabinet also decided to place an embargo on the export of rubber from Malaya to China, in spite of the information received from High Commissioners in Malaya and Singapore forecasting strong local opposition.[52]

Just at this time a Hong Kong-registered ship, *Nancy Moller* of the Moller Company, was carrying a cargo of 3775 tons of rubber from Singapore to Guangzhou via Hong Kong. The ship was chartered by the China Resources Corporation. Prime Minister Clement Attlee called an urgent Cabinet meeting, at which it was agreed that the ship should be intercepted and the cargo requisitioned. The operation was carried out on 18 May by the Royal Navy just outside the Chinese territorial waters. It was understood that the ship had left Singapore two days after the new controls had been announced in the House of Commons, but that the cargo had been cleared before the announcement was made so at the time there had been no legal necessity to detain the ship in Singapore.[53]

The export of pharmaceuticals to China drew considerable attention from American and British authorities. In February 1951 a ship of Norwegian registry, *m.v. Hoi Houw*, was believed to be carrying a large quantity of sulphur drugs, antibiotics and penicillin from Bombay to China. The Americans attributed this cargo a direct military significance since they were convinced that a typhus epidemic in the Chinese army in Korea had been partly responsible for the recent easing of Communist pressure in Korea. Having failed to get Hong Kong to take action to seize the ship, the Americans, it was understood, used the Guomindang government, whose destroyer the *Taiping* seized the *Hoi Houw* 70–75 miles east of Taiwan on 11 February and took her into Keelung, where the cargo was unloaded. The US joined Norway in lodging a protest with the Guomindang, but British intelligence understood it differently: 'There can be little doubt that the Americans were behind the seizure. . . . They were in the happy position of being able to get the Chinese Nationalists to do their work for them, and thus in theory being in no way connected with the incident. They even took their ingenuous bluff to the point where Mr Hunt (the Economic Intelligence Officer of the US Consulate-General in Hong Kong) asked [the] Staff Officer (Intelligence) [in] Hong Kong for information as to what was happening to the ship in Formosa, on the grounds that the US authorities there did not know anything about her!'[54]

Export of certain pharmaceuticals to China from the UK had been restricted since December 1950, at first by voluntary arrangement with manufacturers and, since 29 June 1951, by means of export licensing control. The Americans wanted to see a complete ban on China but the British only agreed to limit the exports to pre-Korean war level. The Americans maintained that despite China's vast man-power resources it was important that Chinese wounded should not be made fit to fight again. But the British argued that, given the shortage of medicine available to the Chinese, a ban on their export to China would mean that American and British wounded prisoners of war in the hands of the Chinese might be left to die first. Britain unilaterally controlled antibiotics, anti-malarials and sulfonomides, including streptomycin, which was widely used in the treatment of tuberculosis but valuable also in treating bubonic and pneumonic plague and for secondary infections caused by burns. The UK delega-tion informed COCOM of its government action and urged other members 'to watch the matter of drugs very carefully'.[55]

Exports outside the quota to Hong Kong were allowed only against 'essential supply certificates' for internal consumption. This system broke down in September 1952 because of foreign availability. The UK tried, but failed, to secure agreement in the Paris Group to add anti-malarials, antibiotics and sulfonamides to List II for quantitative restriction by all member governments. At the end of 1953, London decided to lift the quantitative controls on export of these drugs, with an understanding with the US that this should not act as a precedent for the relaxation of controls over items still being denied to China.[56]

The China Control Lists

Pressure from the US continued to mount after Congress passed the Kem Amendment in the summer of 1951 and the Mutual Defense Assistance Control Act (the Battle Act) in August. The Battle Act in particular provided for the mandatory termination of all US assist-ance to recipient countries which had knowingly shipped Category A goods to communist countries.[57] Britain went along with a US pro-posal in Paris to add more items to IL I for complete embargo, on the basis of a tripartite criteria adding technology and know-how, as well as items whose embargo would maintain or create a critical deficiency in the war potential of the communist countries. Items on IL II were subject to quantitative control because their strategic character was directly related to the quantitative extent to which they might be exported. Those items whose strategic importance had not yet been clearly established for the purpose of the first two lists would remain on the watch list (IL III). At the same time, a French proposal on a new rule of exceptions was accepted by the group (known as the 'doc. 782 procedures'). This had the effect of increasing the flexibility of the exceptions procedure from the previous requirement of unanimous approval to a system of information exchange and *post-facto* notification, without need for justification.[58]

The British, for their part, submitted a proposal on the principles and procedure for determining IL II items, including permission to export minimum quantities of them in return for the importation of essential supplies from the communist countries. This was called the 'doc. 471 procedure' for exceptions, which were made for exports subject to prior consultation with COCOM and *'quid pro quo'* justification.[59] In light of these, another round of tripartite talks were held in Paris to transfer the remainder of the new American list to the three International Lists. Thus, from August 1951 to June 1952, the Paris Group negotiated and succeeded in finalising the three International Lists, adding about 40 items to List I (originally 229 items were on IL I, plus 105 on IML). Also, as the result of some 80 meetings over nine months for List II review, 88 of the original 102 items remained on List II.[60]

While the Americans embargoed practically anything for China, the British list was longer than those of the German, Dutch, Belgian and French, among others. The British ban included quite a number of items which were on List II and quantitatively controlled by these countries, and some on List III. The rest however were not on any of the International Lists, but were regarded by the British government as of higher strategic significance than those on List III. In October the UK delegation urged COCOM members to adopt a common list of controls on trade with China, in line with the UK list. In response to Danish reservations on grounds of administrative difficulties, the UK delegate stated that his government held that 'the war in Korea was sufficient justification for accepting such extra difficulties as an extended embargo on supplies to China might involve'.[61]

With the Americans and the British taking the lead, COCOM had agreed by May 1952 to place under special controls for China all items on ILs I, II and III, thereby creating a gap between the Soviet bloc controls and China controls.[62] It had also agreed to recommend a special exceptions procedure for exports of List III goods, and that the regular exceptions procedure should apply to List II goods as though they were List I items. The Committee was unable to arrive at an agreement covering the non-International List items proposed by the UK. The difference was later known as the UK Supplementary List.[63]

The China Committee (CHINCOM)

In August 1952 the Consultative Group met to set up a new committee to handle export control matters in the Far East, which was given the name of 'China Committee'. The issue arose after the Japan Peace Treaty had been signed by a number of countries in San Francisco in September 1951, which was declared subsequently by Japan and the United States as entering into force in April 1952. The US feared that Japan might want to relax the severe controls on trade with the Soviet bloc, and in particular China, which she had hitherto been forced to adopt. Others thought it necessary to incorporate Japan into a framework of security export controls for fear of Japanese commercial competition in the China market.[64]

The US originally opposed the admittance of Japan as a full member into the Paris Group and wanted to see Japan continue with her existing restrictive controls on exports to China. The Japanese did not like the idea, nor did the British and French favour a separate organisation in the Far East.[65] The British, however, would not resist the setting up, within the Paris Group, of a sub-committee for the separate study of Far Eastern control problems 'if in practice such a course appeared to be desirable'.[66] The United States then sponsored a five-power meeting in Washington, involving the US, the UK, France, Canada and Japan, to negotiate a package deal. The meeting lasted from 28 July to 2 August, running parallel with singular American efforts to extract agreement from the Japanese negotiator Ryuii Takeuchi.[67] The Consultative Group endorsed the arrangement through a resolution on 19 September 1952 proclaiming the founding of the China Committee. The Committee was responsible for the development of detailed aspects of export control policy relating to China. The Group members agreed that the same five powers would become the founding members of CHINCOM for a trial period of six months, but that all fifteen members of the Group could participate at any time when necessary.[68]

By early 1953 the British had been able to get the Group to accept about two-thirds of the items on the UK Supplementary List, some with narrower definitions than those of the UK List.[69] The British persisted after the Korean armistice was signed in March, and as a result the China Committee succeeded in securing agreement to remove all discrepancies between the International China Embargo List and the UK China Embargo List. At the end of August 1953 the Committee accepted the inclusion of certain iron and steel products – chiefly through agreement between France, Germany and Japan – and in October the UK agreed to remove small passenger motorcars from the UK embargo list as a concession to Italy.[70]

The Korean armistice in 1953 did not affect the British embargo policy, with the government pledging to work 'as a loyal member of the United Nations' in carrying it out strictly while it remained in being, and that 'any change in this policy can be made only in co-operation with other Governments which maintain similar strategic controls'.[71] COCOM undertook a general review of the items on the International Lists from 27 April to 17 June 1954, culminating in a CG meeting at which a reduction was agreed on 21 July (the same day that the cease-fire in Indo-China was signed at Geneva) on all the lists as they affected trade with Eastern Europe. IL I (embargo) was reduced from about 260 items to about 170, IL II (quota) from about 90 to about 20, and IL III (watch) from about 100 to about 60. No change was made on either the Munitions or Atomic Energy Lists. Prior to this (in March) a tripartite conference had been held in London. On that occasion, and during the CG meeting in April–July, it was agreed in principle to continue those controls with respect to China and North Korea.[72]

In 1955 the Committee re-edited and consolidated the China Control Lists; it agreed to include in a single list all items which had been added to the Soviet bloc lists during and after COCOM's 1954 review. By June 1956 the UK China embargo could be summarised by the following six lists of goods, which also governed the issue of licences in respect to Eastern Europe (EE):

Munitions List	16 broad headings	banned to PRC and EE.
Atomic Energy List	35 items	banned to PRC and EE.
List I	176 items	banned to PRC and EE.

List II	25 items	banned to PRC, quantitative control to EE.
List III	64 items	banned to PRC, freely exportable to EE, subject to reports to COCOM.
The China List	207 items	banned to PRC, freely exportable to other destinations without any obligation to report.

Thus the China controls were much wider than the Soviet bloc controls and a large number of goods (some 296 items) could be sent to Eastern Europe but were prohibited for export to China, hence the 'China Differential'.[73] In addition there might be evidence to show the extent to which the British government subjected other exports to China to quantitative control as well as those under the CHINCOM obligation to report.

Transhipment and Shipping Controls

As the various embargo lists were being finalised, attention began to be increasingly focused on ways to make the system water-tight through transhipment and shipping controls. As early as 1949 control of shipping for the carriage of goods along the China coast was suggested, and there were cases, after the start of the Korean war, of British and other shipping to China which worried the British government.[74] The United States pressed the UK for transhipment and shipping controls since shipping was said to be 'the Achilles heel of China and that if the amount of shipping engaged in trade with China could be drastically reduced it would have a serious effect on the Chinese economy'.[75]

Technically, transhipment might take the form of direct transfer from one ship to another, or might involve unloading the cargo onto the quayside to await another boat or other vehicles to carry it by road or rail in bond. In either case the goods would be trans-loaded without going through local customs, a procedure which had previously been considered as not coming within the scope of export regulations obtaining in the place where they were transhipped. Despite the legal niceties, Britain introduced a set of transhipment control regulations in November 1951 to ensure that no ships sailing from a UK port could be carrying to China restricted goods loaded in a UK port. Furthermore Britain introduced an Import Certificates–Delivery Verification system (IC/DV) to make sure that goods consigned to innocent destinations would not be diverted to China.[76] COCOM found little difficulty in launching a similar programme collectively. In May 1952 all British colonies were instructed to issue IC/DV forms to member countries of the Paris Group when asked so to do. (As mentioned earlier, Hong Kong had a special system of import licensing in operation, which covered UK embargo items.)[77]

In December 1952, in a review of shipping controls, the British government decided that while port facilities such as bunkering, repairs and stores should not normally be withheld from ships of other countries on the ground that they were carrying strategic goods to China, it might be necessary on occasion to take exceptional measures against a flagrant case of the frustration of UK controls. The government then advised British oil companies to refuse bunkers to Soviet bloc ships on the excuse that shortage of supplies did not permit them to take on new customers. In practice however, this course of action proved to be untenable and ineffective.[78] On top of that was the irritating fact to the British control authorities that because the UK prohibited goods which other countries both in and outside the Paris Group did not restrict, British ships often carried for those countries goods which Britain did not allow to be exported to China.

In March 1953 Eden and Acheson discussed this issue in Washington. The British government decided: (1) to introduce a new system of licensing vessels registered in the UK and its colonies so that strategic materials from non-British sources could not be carried to China in British ships, and (2) to take additional steps to ensure that no ships of the Soviet bloc or other nationality carrying strategic cargoes to China would be bunkered in a British port.[79]

Voyage control was put into operation by an order (the Control of Trade by Sea [China and North Korea] Order, 1953) and a general licence (the Control of Trade by Sea General Licence, 1953), which became effective on 31 March. British ships of 500 gross tons or more (other than those registered in Commonwealth countries) needed to seek individual licences for voyages to China or North Korea, which would be granted only if non-strategic goods, as listed in the Licence, consigned to China or North Korea were carried. Neither oil nor coal bunkers should be supplied in British ports east of Suez to ships engaged in the carriage of strategic goods to those destinations. Since American and British oil companies provided most of the bunkering services in the West, it was hoped that the system of the embargo on China could thus be strengthened. Voyage licensing was introduced in Hong Kong also on 31 March.[80]

Oil companies were normally asked to accept a nomination for bunkering a vessel before she had sailed from her port of lading. Owing to the difficulty in establishing the innocence of a cargo when nomination was being sought, the British control authorities as a rule interpreted the new law in such a way that all ships of Soviet bloc registry, and most other ships sailing from Soviet bloc ports to China, or from non-Soviet bloc ports but proceeding to China, would be presumed 'guilty' and bunkers refused.[81]

Because the UK embargo list for China had a wider coverage than the International China Embargo List, and that the sole test was whether a foreign vessel was carrying strategic goods as determined by the British control authorities, it was inevitable that conflicts arose with other governments. Within the Paris Group, the point of contention was whether the British control authorities should recognise export licences issued by other COCOM countries according to their lists or as a result of an 'exception' granted by COCOM. A British official admitted, 'We could hardly contemplate suggesting to other countries that in granting Export Licences to China they should indicate whether or not each export would be authorised under UK rules'. Indeed friction was particularly serious with France and West Germany, who continued for some time to grant export licences for iron and steel goods as 'prior commitments' after these had been accepted for embargo to China. In October 1953 a French ship (*Falaise*) was on her way to China with a cargo of iron and steel goods taken on at Hamburg, duly licensed by the German authorities. When the *Falaise* reached Djibouti, Shell's agent declined to provide bunkers for the vessel. The Governor of Djibouti threatened to requisition Shell's bunkering station. The matter was in the end resolved by a compromise, which was to transfer oil from another ship to the *Falaise* in sufficient quantity to enable her to proceed to Saigon, where bunkering facilities might still be in control of the French authorities.[82]

In November 1954 Britain decided to amend its policy concerning voyage licensing and bunkering controls 'in a way which will bring it into line with the wishes expressed in the [China] Committee'. As from 1 December 1954, export licences issued by any member country of COCOM for listed goods consigned to China would be acceptable for the purpose of UK voyage licensing and bunkering controls, even if the goods in question were banned by Britain, with the assumption that 'the voyage licensing controls of Member countries will prevent the carriage of illicit exports from other sources.'[83]

The British government wanted in 1956 to introduce reductions in the China control list, and hoped that the voyage licensing control would either be automatically reduced *pari passu* or completely abolished together with the bunkering control. This proved to be abortive.[84] In assessing the operation of the measure, the British government concluded in 1954, 'Although by no means wholly effective as a means of preventing the carriage of strategic goods to China, bunkering and voyage licensing controls are known to have caused some inconvenience to Soviet bloc exporters to China'.[85] Four years later it was reported that Hong Kong's proximity to the Chinese mainland in effect reduced the shipping control to a mere token, because 'ships on the China run requiring bunkering facilities in Hong Kong can arrange, with little or no inconvenience, to discharge their cargoes in China and take bunkers on the return journey'.[86]

Within the British government there was no real dispute over the need to prevent goods of military value from reaching the 'communist world'. This had been made clear in two Parliamentary debates in September 1950.[87] After the outbreak of the Korean War, the government quickly reached consensus with the Americans on the formal imposition of a selected embargo on China. Despite her opposition to political sanctions suggested by the United States, Britain did her best to ensure that those economic sanctions which were believed feasible were effectively carried out. The existence of a 'hot war' situation in Korea was used to make the embargo a military necessity; the UN embargo resolution served as a basis of legal and moral justification for an economic warfare dictated by national objectives. As the focus of Britain's cold-war strategy was in Europe, where the special Anglo–American relationship was crucial, she could not afford to have it endangered by serious disagreement with the US in the Far East. As Attlee explained to Cabinet in August 1950, with regard to her economic sanctions against China, Britain had to accept positive sacrifices to align her policy with that of the US.[88]

There is no doubt that Britain's economic sanctions sharply reduced her trade with China. From 1950 to 1951 the volume of British and Hong Kong trade with China fell by 50 per cent, and reduced further in 1952. The intensification of a ban on exports reduced the cargo available and, together with the political uncertainty, induced the British ocean liner companies to be increasingly reconciled to a stoppage of trade with China.[89] It was also believed that the knowledge that UK shipping controls were tight tended to discourage continental shippers from enquiring about space in British ships even when the cargo would have been carried under UK voyage licence.[90] Britain's embargo policy added to the economic difficulties of Hong Kong, which tended to raise not a few critical and puzzled eyebrows within COCOM.[91]

To make such sacrifices was a political decision. But the sacrifices appeared to have been compensated for to some extent by the sheer amount of American aid. Britain was among those Marshall Plan countries which received the largest share of the aid during this period. As US Marshall Plan aid during 1949–51 was mostly given as outright grants, and surpassed the total turnover of East–West trade in Europe, Britain must have benefited a good deal from the dollar flow. In 1952, when US economic aid fell below the level of trade, the military aid started rising. It was suggested that, as late as 1954, the total US aid was still considerably above the value of European East–West trade, and that in 1955 the US economic aid alone equalled almost 20 per cent of the whole European East–West trade turnover, which might well equal the business profits of that trade.[92]

Whilst it may well be said that aid was not an ideal substitute for trade, Britain could not afford to go without it due to the need to make economic recovery. Thus section 117 (d) of the US Foreign Assistance Act of 1948 (the Mundt Amendment) and the Battle Act of 1951 acted as appreciable constraints on British foreign policy thinking on general East–West relations. This of course had its irritating effect. As one Foreign Office official put it at the time of the adoption of the Kem Amendment, Britain found itself constantly bumping against the ceiling of possible further concessions; no sooner had the Ministers agreed to an arrangement than Congressional pressure built up and they were asked to take yet another stage in the direction of the interruption of trade with the Sino–Soviet bloc.[93]

Paradoxically Britain took a leading role among the European members of COCOM in advocating and pressing for tighter embar-

goes on China. Not only was the UK China List longer and introduced earlier, but Britain also took the lead in imposing transhipment,
shipping and bunkering controls. The British control authorities in
their day-to-day operations tended to interpret International List
items more broadly, and would do everything to make sure that if
Britain did not allow an export to China, the same policy should be
adopted by entire membership of COCOM. This was the case with
various Chinese orders for British air compressors, external cylindri-
cal centreless grinding machines, lorries of 2.5 to five tons, X-ray
dosimeters, and iron and steel products.[94]

In general Britain was very active in various COCOM–CHINCOM
deliberations and took pride in playing a leadership role in the Paris
Group. This was bound to bring Britain into conflict with other
members. A British proposal for banning antibiotics was not accepted by a number of COCOM members. The British delegate to
COCOM blamed the French for being the chief obstacle to progress
towards adopting the entire UK Special China List, and took pains in
defending Hong Kong's export control record.[95] One might suggest
that Britain could have gone further but did not. This may well be
true. For political reasons the government could not bring itself to
accept the American suggestion to 'de-recognise' the Beijing government, or to join in any scheme involving naval blockades on the
China coast. It pondered for a long time, without taking action, over
the pros and cons of introducing financial or transaction controls.
Eventually Britain agreed to introduce transaction controls – controls
over offshore transactions with the British as intermediaries – in
return for other members of the Paris Group agreeing to a Transit
Authorisation Certificates scheme (TAC) in 1954.[96] In these respects
the British position fell short of American expectations. It is possible
that the UK tended to look at embargoes with suspicion. The British
propensity for secrecy and fear of publicity might have led to doubt
that embargoes – and certainly embargoes with clamour – were an
effective way of dealing with and securing concessions from an
opponent such as China, rather than due to any moral principles or
legal restraints.

The China embargo policy lost its military sense and political
cogency after the Korean armistice in 1953. The British government
was entrenched in its dogma, unable to initiate any relaxation for fear
of being out of step with the political tension between China and the
United States. The ultimate question in this connection might be: in
pursuing the export control policies towards China the way it did, did

Britain look at China fundamentally as a real enemy during the Korean War, and as a continuous threat after it? The psychology in this respect is undoubtedly one of the more difficult factors to establish, but if it did – as the Chinese at the receiving end of those policies tended to think – it was probably compelled by circumstances rather than by reason.

THE BEGINNING OF AN END TO THE EMBARGO 1956–7

In the summer of 1955 the British government put the Americans on notice of its desire to reduce the China controls to the level in force for the Soviet bloc. At the beginning of December 1955 Britain informed the US that it proposed making a unilateral reduction of the controls, on a gradual basis beginning in January 1956. At the request of the Americans Britain postponed action to allow the matter to be discussed during Prime Minister Harold Macmillan's visit to Washington at the end of January. Following the visit Macmillan informed the House of Commons on 13 February that 'The control of trade in strategic materials with China will now be reviewed'.[97]

One of the reasons for the delay of a review in 1955 was the Americans' hope that they could use the issue of the embargo in the Sino–American bilateral negotiations in Geneva.[98] The Americans held the counter for months; when they played it at a meeting on 23 November it was immediately spurned by the Chinese ambassador Mr Wang Bingnan, to the amusement of Macmillan who then pretended not to know anything about it.[99] Britain then urged an early Anglo–American talk. The Americans agreed to a summit in Washington in January 1956, fearing that a unilateral action by Britain would lead to a collapse of the entire cooperative structure and a high degree of ill-feeling between the two countries.[100]

The technical possibilities initially seemed to include the introduction of a 'minimum shipments' system, a pruning of the China list of some of its more harmless items or sub-items (the so-called 'peeling off'), and a revised policy of spare parts and trivial exceptions. The government also suggested that Britain should disinterest itself at COCOM in exceptions cases put forward by other members. Later the focus was shifted to the notion that all items in the 'China Differential' – that is those 207 items freely exportable to Eastern Europe – be deemed unimportant strategically. The proposed scheme thus took the form of a simultaneous decontrol by Britain of the entire complex of items, regardless of their individual listing. Britain proposed to the US a gradual, unobtrusive process of bringing the UK list for China into conformity with the agreed list for the Soviet bloc by removing items in groups of two or three at a time. The Foreign Office also submitted a list of priority items to be dropped from the China embargo list over two periods of six months each.[101]

France fully shared the UK's desire to secure a gradual reduction and, fearing that it might be left out in the cold by any Anglo–American deals, undertook a review of its own China control list. This upset the British, who had previously asserted that the French had been abusing COCOM exceptions procedures and acting irresponsibly with respect to bunkering controls.[102]

When the British got round to discussing the issue with the Americans, it touched on a raw nerve within the American government, with Pentagon officials 'talking wildly about the sacrifice of their boys in Korea having been in vain', and government officials and congressmen emerging from an internecine warfare 'gory with blood'.[103] Dulles stressed to the British the very real dangers to the Foreign Aid Bill from any concessions on the China control, and then offered a package deal which purported to trade the decontrol of certain items from the China list with new additions on the Soviet list.[104] The British objected, the talk threatened to break down, and President Dwight Eisenhower intervened, agreeing that the US would acquiesce in a liberal use of the exceptions procedure for some items on the CHINCOM list.[105] It looked as though the US government now preferred to wink an eye at 'exceptions' rather than accept responsibility for formally removing any items from the list. The British did not hesitate in taking the offer, and the US in return produced a liberalised list for exceptions exports. The private understanding was that there would be no specific change made to the present procedure for exceptions, but merely there would be no discussion of justification. The British were not satisfied with the American list but decided not to haggle about it for the time being. A statement was made in the House of Commons on 14 May 1956 that the discussions with the Americans were not yet concluded, but 'in the meantime more use will be made of the exceptions procedure to permit reasonable exports in appropriate cases to China of goods which are not on the Soviet Lists'.[106]

The effect of the move was to allow more freely the export of rubber, tin, sisal, motor vehicles, tractors, certain internal combustion engines, iron and steel products and some electrical equipment to China, which improved on the previous cases of exceptions. Further chemicals were also able to qualify for exceptional treatment. The French remained content with the procedure as it conformed with their previous practice, and they did not mind 'pausing for breath'. Meanwhile the Americans made a statement in CHINCOM denying any US–UK bilateral agreement on the problem and urging that 'great care and restraint would be observed in the application of the exceptions procedure'.[107] The Malayan and Singapore governments announced a greater degree of relaxation in their rubber trade with China, whereas Indonesia and Thailand formally called off their embargo of rubber and certain other non-strategic products.

Britain's total export trade with China increased in 1956 by £2.9 million in comparison with 1955, from £7.8 million to £10.7 million. Exceptions procedures were used for export of steel pipes, cranes, excavators and jibs, electric and electronic equipment, surveying instruments, cinema and motor vehicle equipment, and cutting and tool grinding machinery.

For the remainder of 1956 the US tried to forestall multilateral action on the China Differential by not consenting to a CG meeting. A US official report in September conceded that the government should agree to a CG meeting by the end of the year, and that the US would have to approve a sizable reduction in the differential if multilateral controls were to be maintained.[108] On 12 September the US requested all CG members to restrict the use of exceptions procedures until the next CG meeting at the end of the year. No COCOM country accepted this, whereas the UK agreed to refrain from accelerating their use until the end of 1956. After the events in Hungary and the Middle East, Washington was seen to have taken a 'much sharper line' on the whole subject of strategic controls. It retreated from its previous position, saying that a CG meeting would be held at a time when world conditions warranted a definitive settlement.[109]

On 21–3 March 1957, Macmillan and Foreign Secretary Selwyn Lloyd met with Eisenhower and Dulles in Bermuda. The British urged the Americans to urgently consider the matter of disposing of the China Differential quickly, citing Eisenhower's undertaking in February 1956. The Americans countered that while they were working on a proposal, they hoped that Britain would take a more positive attitude in respect of the continued denial of China's representation in the United Nations, so that the two countries could 'move forward on both fronts in a somewhat synchronised manner'.[110]

At a CHINCOM meeting on 12 April, the French delegate Noel-Mayer formally proposed abolishing the China Differential (the 'Consolidated China List'); to apply to China the COCOM procedure covering the export of IL III items (that is, de-control); to establish within six months quotas for China for items on IL II; and to suppress CHINCOM within one year so as to apply rules applicable to the Soviet bloc. The British suspected that the French wanted to steal a march on the Anglo–American bilateral talks, and had canvassed other governments for support.[111] The UK delegate nevertheless supported the French proposals, saying that the French arguments 'seem extremely cogent and their proposals very sound'. He also added that the British government had had to answer over 200 Parliamentary questions and to deal with a mounting flood of criticism, political and commercial, in Parliament and in the press on the subject of the China controls.[112] The US delegation made a counter-proposal which, after a few concessions, amounted to dropping 157 items from the China list, the rest of the Differential and those on IL III being subject to a stricter application of exceptions procedures. A few items would also be added to the Soviet embargo list and, to complete the bargain, the use of exceptions procedures should be tightened up in general. France, Japan and the UK declared the US proposal unacceptable.[113]

On the evening of 17 April American Ambassador to London John H. Whitney had BoT President Peter Thorneycroft to dinner, at which Whitney told his guest that the US government was willing to do a deal with Britain on the China controls if Britain could agree not to press for China's seat at the United Nations.[114] There is no evidence yet to show that the British agreed to this strictly *quid pro quo*, but the message must have been highly significant in view of subsequent developments.

At a CHINCOM meeting on 21 May the US proposed further concessions, which France, Japan and the UK rejected outright. The Foreign Office then instructed the British embassy in Washington to pass the message to the US government that since the US insisted on maintaining a substantial China Differential, including a formal embargo on those items which were only under quantitative control for Eastern Europe, the British government believed that the time had come for a clear-cut solution.[115] Cabinet met on the 24th and a decision was taken to make a statement in Parliament.

The UK delegate told CHINCOM on 27 May that the British government considered the abolition of the China Differential to be the only basis for an effective system of controls for China, and that Britain was prepared to negotiate agreed quotas in List II items and to accept minimal quotas for certain items destined for China. He also stated that Britain had no intention of leaving CHINCOM and would play a full part in its work in future. As it turned out the United States showed more resignation than anger when the British move was announced, most countries expressed regret that a unanimous solution had not been found, and Portugal and Denmark gave full support to Britain.[116] On the 29th Macmillan wrote a letter to Eisenhower. On 30 May Selwyn Lloyd made a statement in the House of Commons that the government had decided to bring the controls on trade with China to the level of those for Eastern Europe. He stated,

> Certain items now embargoed for China will either be transferred to the quantitative control list or to the watch list, or completely freed. The necessary detailed arrangements will need to be discussed in the China Committee.

He then added that licences would be granted on request for all items now embargoed for China but not subject to export licensing to the Soviet bloc. For items subject to quantitative controls for export to the Soviet bloc it would not be possible to grant licences (for China) until discussions were held in Paris about the size of quotas for China. The effect was that 207 items were freed from restrictions on export to China, and that these changes also applied to North Korea and Viet Nam. Someone during the House debate made the point that 'the Government ought to be congratulated on this belated if partial return to common sense'.[117]

While expressing disappointment at the British action, the US State Department stressed the agreement to maintain the present security controls for Eastern Europe as well as the declared British intention to control trade with China on the same basis as was applied to the Soviet bloc. Eisenhower conceded that he did not see as much advantage in maintaining the China Differential, and that trade in the long run could not be stopped.[118] The Chinese government gave a positive reaction, adding that 'China wants to develop trade relations with all countries, including America, on the principle of mutual benefit and a basis of firm supply'.[119] In the following months,

Belgium, Denmark, France, Japan, and The Netherlands followed the British example.

This was perhaps the only single occasion since the establishment of CG-COCOM on which a negotiated settlement was not found to the many problems inside the Paris Group. It was suggested that the British action was 'a unilateral act of insubordination'.[120] The British government justified its action by stating that the strategic controls were of no use unless they were effective and justified on strategic grounds, and that the additional controls for China were neither. Because of the lack of support from British exporters, the whole system of controls was being discredited and before long even the really important controls on trade with Eastern Europe would have been affected.[121]

Britain continued its role within CG-CHINCOM at discussions on the remaining issues on China controls, and its cooperation with the US remained unscathed in this area.[122] The US and some other countries continued their embargo policies in varying degrees but, as Britain stated at the time of the 30 May decision, once the problem of the China Differential was out of the way once and for all, a serious source of friction between the members of CG-CHINCOM would thus be removed.

The conflict of interests between Britain and the US over the China embargo drove their bilateral relationship to a crisis point in 1956–7, and it involved the leaders of the two governments at the highest level in a search for a definitive settlement which would balance their national objectives with the unity of the alliance. If indeed Britain can be said to have exercised its right to dissent in the summer of 1957, just as the US had done the previous year over the Suez crisis, then the two allies can also be seen to have drawn level with each other over their foreign policy differences in an otherwise peripherial area. It may also be suggested that Britain had imposed on itself, consciously or inadvertently, a moral obligation vis-à-vis the US over its long-term policy towards the PRC, in such a way that on none of the key issues relating to China – China's seat at the United Nations, strategic export controls within CG-COCOM, and normalisation of diplomatic relations – was Britain able, over the next decade and half, to bring itself to move a single step ahead of the US even if it had so wanted.

5 The Departure

All the good things of this world are no further good than as they are of use.

Daniel Defoe

The next dreadful thing to a battle lost is a battle won.

Duke of Wellington

In the previous chapters we have examined the political and economic environment in which private British businesses were compelled to operate. This chapter will examine the process of British commercial withdrawal from China as a direct consequence of pressures from all directions and loss of confidence. The Chinese government seemed to have finally made up its mind by mid-1952. Without a push from the political front, a clear-cut solution to the closures would not have been possible. While it is evident that British firms began to close down and leave China from the very early days of the People's Republic, if not earlier, this chapter will focus on those who shared similar problems but whose decisions to leave were compelled in the end by the deterioration of Sino–British relations after the outbreak of the Korean conflict.

COMMERCIAL CLOSURES 1949–52

It may be recalled that when the PRC was proclaimed in 1949, British commercial interests appeared to concentrate largely on three sectors of the Chinese economy, that is raw materials, the manufacturing industry, and trade and services. These included coal mining, textiles, foodstuff, tobacco processing, ship repairs, chemical manufactures, petroleum supply, export and import, banking and insurance, shipping and port facilities, and public utilities. Except for export and import, British interests were either in the hands of transnational corporations, in which case operation in China was but an extension of an international network for one line of business or another, or controlled by leading merchant 'hongs' of old China hands, whose operations cut across a whole range of economic activities in China.

In the field of export and import, British-owned firms were numerous and varied in financial strength and background. These can be further divided into trading agencies operated by individuals with domiciles inside China, and trading firms controlled by head offices in Hong Kong and Britain. In terms of capital formation, businesses by individuals tended to be in a much weaker position and historically had a high mortality rate owing to uncertain market conditions, keen competition from Chinese firms, and the speculative nature of their business. We now know that prior to the outbreak of the Korean war, owing to a nationwide recession and the Chinese Government's trade reorganisation, many of these small trading firms, together with an even larger number of Chinese ones, were never given permits to recommence and had to cease operation right away. Many of them appear to have closed down without much delay, although lack of evidence does not permit any detailed studies of this group.

The second group in contrast consisted of big merchant houses, which had over the years accumulated a fairly large stock of capital (paid-up capital and surplus). Part of the capital they reinvested in various businesses and real estate in China; the rest was remitted to their head offices outside the country, creating a considerable net outflow of capital. Some firms, such as the Sassoons, were able to sell the bulk of their landed property during the last days of the Guomindang rule, and thus escaped with large amounts of capital before the CCP takeover.[1] The process by which this latter group of firms tried to wind up their business in China after 1949 lasted much longer, and it coincided with their attempt to seek other ways of retaining their business connections with China under changed circumstances.

Early Cases Related to Ownership

The legal and corporate structures of various British businesses in China were varied and complex, and this may have had a direct bearing upon the ways in which their capital and management was subsequently transferred. Some firms were registered as British-owned, notably in Hong Kong, but were really Chinese compradore capital in disguise. Some others were managed predominantly or totally by the British but in fact had only a very small percentage of British capital. Hutchison observed in 1950 that some British firms were largely Chinese owned; some had already to a great extent freed themselves of debenture and similar liabilities (that is investments had already been repaid and profits had been remitted home); and some had been capitalised largely from the proceeds of their local activities, presumably to avoid taxation at home. His conclusion was that even if these British firms had to incur a loss on their existing assets in China, it would not necessarily mean equivalent net loss on their investment.[2]

The CCP devoted a good deal of resources and energy to a meticulous investigation into the ownership of private businesses; a positive determination that a foreign firm was really owned by the Guomindang authorities would immediately lead to its categorisation as 'big bourgeois bureaucratic capital' and subject to official confiscation, whereas private interests would be protected by law.[3] An example of such disguised ownership is the case of a British car manufacturing plant, the Auto Palace Co. The company was registered as a British Company in Hong Kong, but in 1946 some original shareholders liquidated their shares by transferring them to the name of the Yangtze Finance Co. Ltd. The majority of shares were then transferred to some eight Chinese shareholders, presumably acting on behalf of the Kung family, one of the four large Chinese monopolistic money groups under the Guomindang. These shares were then transferred to the personal name of its manager F.X. Gutierrez and again in March 1949 to the name of A.B. Rothwell, one of the original British shareholders. After extensive investigations, the Chinese government was satisfied that the company was in effect owned by the Kung family. The Auto Palace Co. was taken over by the government and amalgamated with the National Automobile and Supplies Corporation to form a new Chinese company known as the China Automobile and Supplies Corporation. Gutierrez resigned from his post, but he was later instrumental in helping to sort out Auto Palace's financial accounts abroad, notably in connection with General Motors, New York, and the Austin Motor Export Corporation, London.[4]

A more complicated issue was mixed ownership, such as in joint ventures, which was common in the field of mining. The Fushun colliery and the Kailan mines, the two largest coal mining enterprises in pre-1939 China, were under Japanese and British control respectively. Prior to World War II there were some eighteen cases involving British interests acquiring rights of mining in China, including incorporation or takeover of Chinese-owned mines, such as Kaiping (1901), Mentougou (1911), and Jiaozuo (1915). Under the Ching and Guomindang authorities, areas were allocated to foreign investors for mining as concessions, usually for a period of 60 years. The CCP government denounced these concessions, and declared its intention to restore them to Chinese control as soon as possible.

A case in point was the Kailan Mining Administration (KMA), which had been under British–Chinese joint administration as a result of an amalgamation in 1934 between the British-owned Chinese Engineering and Mining Co. (CEM) and the Chinese-owned Lanchow Mining Co. This merger completed the process started at the turn of the century in which British interests first acquired control over the formally 'government-supervised' private Chinese joint-stock mining enterprise – the Kaiping Company – and then dominance over its sister company – the Lanchow Company – the latter having been created by Chinese authorities to compete with Kaiping, which had fallen into British hands. Subsequently the 1934 merger built on an agreement of association of 1912 which had given birth to the KMA. The Lanchow collieries were about ten times larger than the Kaiping mines, and produced 70 per cent of the total KMA coal output. Under the 1912 agreement, if the total net profit of the new administration was less than £300 000, the British-controlled Kaiping company would receive 60 per cent and Lanchow 40 per cent. Profits in excess of £300 000 would be divided equally between the two companies. In management the British enjoyed the greater control.[5] Prior to the CCP takeover the British-owned Chinese Engineering and Mining Co. Ltd had held a half share interest in the KMA, which had its head office in Tianjin. The CCP authorities for their part were determined that the mines would be restored to Chinese control, claiming that the British company CEM had acquired all the property and assets of the old Kaiping without one single pound of fresh capital having been subscribed thereto.[6]

The Mining Permit issued to the KMA by the Chinese government on 1 December 1930 was due to expire on 30 November 1950. It included a provision that if the Chinese authorities wished to terminate the mining rights, they should purchase the British share of the assets at a fair valuation. One complication arose from the fact that in 1936 the British were reluctant to submit the Mining Permit to the East Hopei Government because the permit was apparently irregular in form, and because it was feared that the provincial government might contend that it was vitiated by the manner of its issue.[7] Realising that the lease of the British concession of Kaiping was due to expire in 1950 and that there was little hope of an extension, the British Company instructed its manager in China to write to the

Ministry of Fuel of the CPG on 17 April 1950, offering 'to hand over forthwith to the Central People's Government all this company's share of interests in the Kailan Mining Administration provided only that the Government will agree to discharge all liabilities of the Administration that cannot be covered by its own funds'.[8]

By this time production at the collieries of the KMA was under the supervision of the government. A chief military representative, Xu Daben, was appointed in July 1949 to supervise production, sales and transportation, and the rationing of government-supplied commodities among staff and labour. In addition to direct contact with Xu, KMA's British chief manager Pryor had personal talks with CCP leaders Liu Shaoqi and Yao Yilin about KMA's affairs, and also with Wu Chengming and Ji Chaoding of the Foreign Investments Bureau of the State Financial and Economic Commission.[9] In 1950 Pryor left China for a visit to Japan and never went back; he never received a government reply to the company's request for a transfer of British-held assets in KMA.[10]

Prior to this the local Chinese authorities had at one point requested the British manager to obtain financial help from the UK amounting to £500 000, but the issue was never pursued. The Chinese knew that the British management had made certain remittances to London out of the proceeds of sales of KMA coal to Japan (one remittance in early 1950 alone was some £180 000) and claimed that because of the unnotified departure of the British manager the accounts for the Administration's revolving fund in London had never been sorted out in a final settlement. The Financial and Economic Commission of the Central Government held a special session on the future of Kailan mines. The Chinese board of trustees of the KMA later submitted an application to the Ministry of Fuel to put the KMA under government custody; they also requested government financial support.[11]

Two other Sino–British joint ventures – the coal mines in Henan Province controlled by the Pekin Syndicate within the Chung Fu Joint Mining Administration, and the Mentougou Colliery near Beijing – seemed to have lapsed in a similar way with the departure of their British managers, leaving behind them a number of unanswered questions about British legitimacy and rights. No evidence, however, is yet available for any accurate portrayal of these business ventures during the final days of their operations in China.[12]

British Thinking: From 'Staying Put' to 'Guild'

For many British firms in China, the British government's policy in 1949 of keeping a foot in the door had some appeal. They hoped that once Britain recognised the PRC, formal diplomatic relations would be established and new prospects would be created for improved commercial activities in China. In spite of grave difficulties they were not yet prepared to abandon their assets, but were determined to stay put so as to maintain their presence in the country. They felt disappointed with the impasse in Sino–British negotiations and with the continued adverse circumstances they had to face. They wanted the British government to act decidedly with regard to the Guomindang blockade and to make direct representations to the Chinese authorities for a remedy for their difficulties. Already, word of warning came from the British Chamber of Commerce in Shanghai to the China Association in London that unless the situation improved materially in the near future, 'a great number of British firms, large and small, will have no option but to close their business and quit'.[13] Some individual businessmen approached British officials with the suggestion that, to break the present deadlock and stagnation of trade, the British should offer some kind of trade inducements to China, including definite offers of business and capital investment. These were not acceptable to the British government. Others urged that the British government should despatch an ambassador to discuss the future of British business in China with top-level Chinese officials. This also appeared impossible to realise as long as no progress was made towards the establishment of official diplomatic relations.[14] Hutchison however did despatch a note to Chinese Vice Foreign Minister Zhang Hanfu on 24 May 1950, conveying British government concern over conditions for foreign business in China. The Chinese government did not give any formal reply, but trade conditions showed an improvement afterwards, coinciding with the massive government purchases upon the outbreak of the Korean conflict.[15]

While enlisting government support, the British business community began to think hard about the best way to strengthen their collective bargaining position. They knew that the conditions under which British traders had operated in China during the last century had changed completely. With the treaties of privilege and extraterritoriality gone, the British would have to live and trade in China under Chinese law, subject to Chinese habits and customs, with only such protection as British officials were able to give them, and subject to inevitable political changes. It was then thought that British interests should be organised so as to present a united front on all political and commercial problems in negotiations with the government; to provide an agency for the competent conduct of inter-state trade and inter-governmental barter deals; and to secure the highest degree of efficiency among member firms by utilising fully their human and physical resources and eliminating competition.[16]

It was therefore proposed that a Joint Stock Company be formed. It would acquire a controlling interest in the business of its members by exchange of its own stock for their shares. By virtue of its financial control it would also control the management of such business. A Board of Governors would then group the various businesses of member firms under a number of specialised branches, viz: Banking, Shipping, Airways and Wharves, Industries and Factory Management, Insurance and Real Estate, Trading, Shops and Stores, Utilities, and so on. This proposal became known as the 'Shanghai Scheme', and was considered side by side with an earlier scheme – the so-called 'Schlee Scheme' – for forming a non-profit agency representing all British trading firms in their commercial dealings with Chinese Government-controlled trading organisations.[17]

Neither the 'Shanghai Scheme' nor the 'Schlee Scheme' however came to fruition, owing largely to a lack of consensus among manufacturers, large cartels, merchant houses and banks on the desirability of such a vast organisation. Nor perhaps were they yet prepared to change their traditional policy and business practice. In August 1950, after conflict broke out in Korea, the same idea was again revived in the form of a plan known as the 'British Guild Scheme'. Its proponents argued that to prevent the Chinese from dealing with British private ventures piecemeal as they saw fit, the British should get themselves organised on the basis of the principles of a British Guild so that 'an attack upon it would be transparently a Chinese government move to oust the whole of British business and could not be cloaked by guerrilla attacks on the fringes'.[18] This suggestion was put forward just when the Chinese government had introduced a number of readjustments to ease the difficulties of private industries; import and export trade was also beginning to look up. As a result of renewed business and hopes, nothing concrete came out of the discussions about possible steps to strengthen the British community along these lines.

The international situation began to change dramatically with China's military involvement in the Korean war in October. A meeting was held in the General Chamber of Commerce in Hong Kong in November between Sir Esler Dening of the Foreign Office and British business representatives for the purpose of taking stock of the new situation and discussing future policies. The British government's position was that while it 'does regard the maintenance of our trading interests in China as a valuable contribution to our policy of keeping a foot on the door', this did not mean that the British government would be willing to subsidise those interests which 'must in the final analysis make up their own minds whether they would go or stay'. The meeting also applied a *coup de grâce* to the idea of a 'Guild system', as the participants appeared united in the opinion that it could not be made to work.[19]

The 'Peking Démarche'

By May 1951 it looked as though the trend of international affairs was becoming increasingly damaging to the business of British interests in China. Early that year Britain joined in the UN resolution condemning China as an 'aggressor', which was followed in May by the UN embargo resolution against China. As British consulate officials saw it, Britain had now been singled out by the Chinese government as an enemy and the number one accomplice of America. It was feared that 'in all these circumstances it appears impossible to avoid the conclusion that many, if not most, British concerns here must expect their activities to come to an end before very long, not necessarily with a bang but merely with a series of whimpers'.[20]

Throughout the period many firms found themselves pouring large remittances into China in order to keep their firms afloat. There was a great deal of debate within the business community in China and between the business men and British officials in China, Hong Kong and London as to the desirability of stopping remittances into China, so as to bring pressure to bear on the Chinese for a more lenient application of rules to foreign firms. In the end firms decided against making a joint approach to the Chinese authorities to announce the cessation of remittances.[21] Subsequently a number of firms continued to send money into China in order to pave the way for negotiating their eventual pullout with the Chinese authorities.

Unable to compel the local authorities to change their policies, the British Chamber of Commerce in Shanghai appealed to the British government to make a concerted protest with other Western governments to the Central People's Government on the deteriorating conditions. The British diplomatic officials in Beijing were not very enthusiastic about the idea, fearing that the Chinese were more likely to contemplate measures of apprisal rather than relief under the adverse political climate. The China Association then took up the issue with Whitehall in June 1951.[22]

The Foreign Office finally agreed to authorise British Chargé d'Affaires in Beijing, L.H. Lamb, to discuss with representatives of other governments in Beijing the possible method of approach to the Chinese government, and also the terms of representation. There followed in London an exchange of diplomatic correspondence between the Foreign Office and the Scandinavian, Swiss, French, Italian, US and Belgian governments, while in Beijing Lamb sounded out the Indian and Pakistani envoys, and indirectly even the Soviet ambassador, for support for a joint protest. After a basic draft note was worked out among the various countries it was decided that, in order to stress the appearance of independent action, it was best that the Swiss minister on behalf of some governments proceeded with his representation, followed later by Lamb with the UK's representation, which Lamb duly performed on 1 September 1951. This became known as the 'Peking démarche'.[23]

The joint protest focused on a set of alleged problems which included: (1) difficulties and delays experienced by Western businessmen when making application to local authorities for an exit or entry permit; (2) the practice by Chinese authorities of holding individuals responsible for transactions or liabilities of commercial or other organisations to which they belonged, and of penalising them on account of their representative capacity; (3) the crippling handicap of not being able to go into voluntary liquidation and to reduce staff at will; (4) the burden of taxes and surtaxes; their assets had in several instances been seriously reduced by the requisitioning of properties without compensation; and (5) arrests of foreign nationals and detention without trial.[24]

By this time Sino–British talks on the establishment of diplomatic relations had been suspended. Nor was there any possibility of face-to-face communication between Chinese and British officials in Beijing on a regular basis. Some requisitions had already started or were being contemplated by both sides. Similar difficulties with regard to travel documents were experienced by Chinese nationals, overseas Chinese in Southeast Asia and Chinese students in

America, as well as political detentions and deportations in Hong Kong and elsewhere.[25] The Western embargo also became increasingly stringent and restrictive. The Chinese government seemed to be stepping up their attack in the public media, while at the same time both China and Britain were quietly retaliating against each other.[26]

The 'Peking démarche' elicited no official Chinese reply and resulted in little improvement in general business conditions for British firms. Early in 1952 the Chinese government launched a large-scale campaign against official corruption and economic crimes, known as 'Three Antis' and 'Five Antis'. This made the foreign business community very nervous, although the campaign was largely directed against Chinese organisations and individuals. In March, representatives of the China Association met with British government officials on a number of occasions, and informed the British government that many firms were making decisions to pull out of China. A Cabinet paper stated, 'Closure of these firms will be a serious blow to our world trading interests'.[27]

At the insistence of the China Association, Cabinet agreed to authorise Lamb to deliver another similar note to the Chinese authorities on 12 April 1952, with a warning that there was a distinct possibility that British business interests would not be able to carry on if the situation continued.[28] The possibility of a massive withdrawal of British firms from China seemed to be imminent; the subject was discussed extensively between the firms' representatives in London and government officials. As a result, the Foreign Office instructed Lamb to deliver another note on 19 May formally informing the Chinese government that a whole list of British firms with commercial assets in China 'feel that the proper course is for them to arrange for the transfer as going concerns, custody or closure, of their businesses'. The note asked the Chinese authorities to facilitate the measures to be taken by individual companies in the lead up to their withdrawal. Subsequently Foreign Secretary Anthony Eden made a formal statement in the House of Commons on 20 May about the intention of the firms to dispose of their businesses in China. The Chinese Association also issued a press release to the same effect.[29]

The Chinese government reply came on 7 July in an official note, with a statement by Vice-Minister for Foreign Affairs Zhang Hanfu. This statement did not mention Lamb's notes of 1 September 1951 (the 'Peking démarche') and 12 April 1952; it purported to respond to his note of 18 April in connection with the Moscow International Economic Conference (which will be discussed later), his note of

19 May and Eden's statement in Parliament on 20 May. It admitted that British companies and manufacturing firms in China had met with serious difficulties but cited the depressed state of the trade between the two countries, their 'bad management', and the British government policy of trade control and embargo as the main causes of the firms' predicament. It then suggested that those which wished to wind up their business voluntarily should apply to the local authorities to have their cases dealt with, each according to its own merits and the regulations.[30]

At a superficial level, these exchanges of official communications appeared very much like a dialogue of the deaf. The Chinese reply did not answer any of the charges raised by the British. Nor did any of the British notes make mention of the discriminatory trade policy against China, let alone defend it. However the British did not find the Chinese response prohibitively negative, especially with regard to passages on due protection of British business interests and promotion of Sino–British trade that 'give an impression of reasonable consideration of general desiderata' in the British note of 19 May.[31] Official statements of intent nonetheless, could hardly automatically resolve the dilemma faced by the British firms, but they did not lead to a rush of closures either. Indeed several firms changed their minds and wanted to carry on, and others wanted to delay their final withdrawal. It seemed apparent that there was no complete unanimity about what they should do, no matter how much it was sought. In the end, as in the case of the Guild Scheme, British firms all went their own way.

Two events in particular contributed to this outcome. One was the negotiated transfer of properties by the British–American Tobacco Co. Ltd (BAT) into Chinese ownership on the basis of what was later known as the 'Yee Tsoong formula'; the other was the Moscow International Economic Conference early in 1952 that led to the conclusion of huge trade contracts between China and British businessmen. These are discussed below.

The Yee Tsoong Settlement

On 2 April 1952, H.V. Tiencken, Chairman of the Board of Directors of Yee Tsoong Tobacco Company Ltd (YTT), signed an agreement with the Shanghai Tobacco Corporation, a Chinese government-owned company. Meng Ya-ren signed the agreement on behalf of the Chinese side. Witnesses to the agreement were representatives

1. G. E. Mitchell, Butterfield & Swire's General Manager, 1935–41, in a Peking cart, Manchuria, 1927–8. He worked for the China Association in London in the 1950s.

2. (*above*) A welcome photo for Mr Curry of Butterfield & Swire, with B&S Tanggu (Tangku) shore and floating staff, 5 August 1949, Tanggu, China.

3. (*below*) Humphrey Trevelyan (later Lord, *right*) and Dudlay Cleland (Hong Kong and Shanghai Banking Corporation) at Cleland's residence in Beijing, *c.* 1954.

23. (*above*) Sir John and Lady Keswick watch a skilled ivory carver at work in the Chinese Pavilion at the 1976 Ideal Home Exhibition. Sir John was then Vice-President of SBTC.

24. (*below*) British and Chinese traders at a reception at the Savoy Hotel, London, for the 30th anniversary of the founding of The 48 group, 1984. (*left to right*) S. G. Sloan; Lord Bessborough; Chinese Commercial Counsellor; Shi Weison from the Chinese Embassy; Roland Berger; Lord Beswick; John Keswick *et al*.

25. Photograph of the meeting which culminated in the signing of the Business Agreement 'ice-breaker' mission 1953. (*left to right*) 3rd from left Cao Zhong shu (CNIEC); 4th from left Lu Xuzhang (CNIEC); 6th from left Ji Chaoding; 7th from left Roland Berger (48 Group); extreme right H. H. Spencer.

4. Photomontage displayed at Leipsig and Poznan Fairs in the 1950s showing: a page of the Business Arrangement, 1953; Lord Boyd-Orr, Berger and Chinese business people; the meeting hall of the Moscow International Economic Conference.

5. The meeting hall of the Geneva Conference, 1954, attended by the Chinese, British, Soviet, US and other delegations.

Chinese Delegate Qiao Guanhua (later Chinese Foreign Minister)

Chinese Premier Zhou Enlai

UK Foreign Secretary Sir Anthony Eden

Humphrey Trevelyan

6. A close-up of the Geneva Conference, 1954.

7. Mao Zedong, Chairman of the Central People's Government of the People's Republic of China, receives Mr Attlee and the other members of the British Labour Delegation in Beijing. Photograph shows Mao, wearing grey summer tunic, with fan in hand, with the delegation. (*left to right*) Mr Wilfrid Burke, Labour Party Chairman; Mao Zedong; Dr Edith Summerskill, MP; Mr Clement Attlee, MP; and Mr Sam Watson, the Durham miners' leader.

8. Sir Anthony Eden, Britain's Foreign Minister (*left*), shares a joke with Zhou Enlai, Premier and Foreign Minister of China, at an informal meeting during the Geneva Conference in 1954. In centre, Dr Pu Shouchang acting as interpreter.

9. (*above*) Huan Xiang, first Chinese *chargé d'affaires* in London with Lord Boyd-Orr, 1950s; in the background Dan Stobart, a British trader.

10. (*below*) Blott mission arrives in Beijing, 1955. J. A. Blott, vice-chairman of the 48 group (*3rd right*); Cao Zhongshu, deputy director of CNIEC (*2nd right*); R. Berger (*3rd left*).

11. (*above*) The Chinese delegation in Britain, 1957; Chinese visitors with Massey Ferguson.

12. (*below*) Dr Ji Chaoding (CCPIT), Pan Yonghua (Bank of China) and Lord Boyd-Orr (BCPIT) during the 1957 Chinese mission to Britain.

13. (*left*) Xie Shoutian, first Chinese commercial counsellor to the UK, with S. G. Sloan, late Chairman of The 48 group at a 48 group reception, late 1950s.

14. (*below*) The Chinese mission to Britain led by Dr Ji Chaoding (*far left*); Sir Alfred Owen (*2nd left*); S. G. Sloan (*1st right*); a Chinese trader and others.

15. (*above*) Professor Joan Robinson (BCPIT), a Chinese businessman and Li Shude (Chinese commercial official in London) at a 48 group reception in the early 1960s.

16. (*below*) (*from right to left*) Zhou Enlai (Chinese Premier), Chen Yi (Chinese Foreign Minister) and interpreter Qi at a British Industrial Exhibition in Beijing, early 1960s.

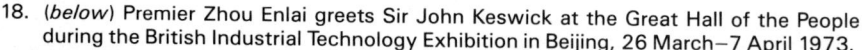

17. (*above*) Lu Xuzhang, Vice-Minister of Chinese Foreign Trade, in London, March 1963, greeted by Mr F. Erroll, President of the Board of Trade.

18. (*below*) Premier Zhou Enlai greets Sir John Keswick at the Great Hall of the People during the British Industrial Technology Exhibition in Beijing, 26 March–7 April 1973.

19. (*above*) Zhou Enlai visits British Industrial Technology Exhibition, March 1973. Sir John Keswick on his right. Between them is Vice-Premier Li Xiannian.

20. (*below*) Premier Zhou Enlai visits Peter Walker, Secretary of State for Trade and Industry, and Michael Heseltine, Minister for Aerospace and Shipping, March 1973, at the time of the British Industrial Technology Exhibition, Beijing.

21. (*above*) Lord Nelson of Stafford, President SBTC, and Mr Feng Kuo-chu, Vice-Chairman of Shanghai Municipal Revolutionary Committee, at the opening of the British Maritime Tools and Scientific Instruments Exhibition, Shanghai 1975.

22. (*left*) Prime Minister Edwar Heath meets Premier Zho Enlai, June 1974.

of the Shanghai Federation of Industry and Commerce, and of the
Shanghai Committee of the China Food Products Industry Labour
Union. This agreement purported to assign all properties of YTT,
Capital Lithographers Ltd, Tobacco Development Co. Ltd, Tobacco
Products Corporation (China), Hung An Land Investment Co. Ltd,
Wing Tai Vo Tobacco Corporation Ltd, Chi Tung Tobacco Company
Ltd, A. Lopato and Sons Ltd, and Provident Trustees Ltd at various
places in the Eastern, Central South, South-West, and North-Eastern
areas of China to the Shanghai Tobacco Corporation. The agreement
listed maladministration, depletion of funds and heavy liabilities as
reasons for this transfer, which made it impossible for the firm to
carry on operations. The agreement was based on the specific instruc-
tion given by BAT's Head Office to Tiencken earlier that year to
offer to the Chinese a voluntary assignment of all YTT's physical
assets, and in return for the Chinese to accept and take over all
YTT's liabilities and obligations both outstanding and current, including liability to workers and staff in respect of termination of
employment.[32]

The 1952 agreement was the culmination of a series of closures,
leases and transfers of BAT interests across the country which had
been occurring since before the 1949 revolution, and it brought to an
end the operations in China of this multinational corporation, which
had assumed the characteristics of an empire for over half a
century.[33] Yee Tsoong was never able to recover from its post-war
decline, and its financial situation plummeted rapidly after the CCP
takeover in 1949. In 1937 BAT (China) operated 11 sizable cigarette
factories, 6 leaf-curing plants, 6 printing plants, one packing material
plant and one machine shop, which together employed more than
25 000 workers. The period of 1945–9 was one of contraction and
continued outflow of funds; between October 1945 and September
1949 the average annual production was only 210 000 cases, less than
20 per cent of the pre-war level. 1946–8 were recorded in Yee
Tsoong's statistics as years of losses for the first time ever, but its
enterprises still managed to remit abroad £4.59 million and US$12.1
million between 1946–9.[34]

After 1949 Yee Tsoong realised that it was faced with the most
unfavourable combination of conditions: heavy dependence on the
government-controlled supply of tobacco leaves, reduced output
under a nationwide quota system, increasing competition from
government-run enterprises, poor sales owing to the high elasticity of
its product at times of economic depression and low consumption, its

large workforce, expensive overheads in terms of taxation and rents, and low realisation of funds.[35] On 28 December 1949, Capital Lithographers Ltd leased its premises and equipment in Hankou (the Ta Chi Men Factory) to the Yee Min Company. On 13 January 1950, BAT's Kung Hsin Tobacco Co. Ltd (Shanghai) went into liquidation. On 3 June of the same year, BAT's Lopato Co. (Harbin) leased its assets to the Harbin Tobacco and Liquors Company.[36]

The crucial point lay with unfulfilled capacity and redundant labour. In April 1950 the company tried to negotiate with its Shanghai labour for temporary suspension of manufacture in its Shanghai and Pootung factories, but the union refused for fear of layoff.[37] As a result, surplus employees remained on the payrolls in their thousands at the Shanghai, Tianjin and Qingdao branches, and the company was hopelessly in arrears with payment of wages and taxes. In May that year the company approached the government with the request that it either lease or purchase the company's enterprise as a going concern, a request which was renewed at the end of 1950.[38] Wu Chengming of the Foreign Investments Bureau of the CPG Financial and Economic Commission then discussed the company's difficulties with its management, but explained why the government did not want to take it over at this stage. Wu stated that the government's policy was to allow private foreign enterprises to operate without hindrance and that a takeover might well give the impression that the government was opposed to the operation of foreign industries. Wu agreed that production quotas could be increased for the company. Subsequently agreement was reached with labour at Shanghai, Tianjin and Qingdao for a scaling down of wages and salaries. Production improved briefly as a result. Government departments tried to help with loans for raw materials and with the marketing of finished products. Later on the company even contracted to manufacture spare parts for automobiles in its machine shop, to the great dismay of British export control officials.[39]

The company's difficulties first appeared most intractable in the Northeast. Following the leasing of the Lopato's factory in Harbin, the Shenyang Municipal Labour Bureau gave permission to the Chi Tung Manufacturing Co. Ltd in Shenyang to discharge its entire workforce on 6 October 1950, and in November BAT officials were able to confirm that all property in Shenyang had been taken into trust, in return for exemption from taxation and the conditional retention of certain premises.[40]

In May 1951 the Northeastern authorities for the first time indicated that the Tobacco and Wine Monopoly Bureau was prepared to take over YTT's properties and premises in Harbin, Shenyang and Yingkou if Yee Tsoong would surrender everything and forgo any right to receive compensation. Two months later there were indications that the Qingdao authorities would accept the proposition to take over all liabilities and obligations in return for voluntary assignment of all YTT assets in that area. YTT officials in Qingdao confirmed that their failure so far to make effective the previous production arrangements with banks, government supplying and selling agencies seemed to have compelled the government to move in this new direction.[41] The company directors also seemed to prefer this development, having taken the position that, 'No funds will be remitted to Tsingtao from anywhere', and that in any case 'any payoff must be regulated to [the] amount . . . realised from the disposal of assets . . . [which] would include the assets in Shantung only.'[42] This policy was soon made applicable to all BAT properties in China.

Earlier that year, both the Capital Lithographers and the Tobacco Development Co. Ltd (Shanghai) had applied to the city's Bureau of Industry and Commerce for permission to close down on grounds of their inability to continue with their operations.[43] Yee Tsoong's cigarette factories in Shanghai employed some 7500 workers and staff, in addition to those employed in Tianjin and Shandong Province. It dawned on the company that a combination of circumstances – including the government's carefully maintained balance between its objection to massive layoffs of workers, its encouragement of workers' voluntary scaling down of wages in return for the management's agreement to keep production going, and the low level of production quotas – would soon compel them to give away their properties as the only way of extricating themselves from their liabilities in China. The company seized the initiative and submitted a petition to press for an exchange of liabilities for assets in August 1951.[44]

There is no evidence yet to indicate the background of increased properties and materials that Yee Tsoong were said to have obtained from Japanese interests and Chinese 'bureaucratic capital' (presumably of Chinese collaborators) after the war. According to the Chinese claim, they amounted to some 85 per cent of the assets transferred to the Shanghai Tobacco Corporation under the 1952 agreement. Liabilities in the form of severance pay amounted to more than 20 per cent of the total assets transferred. This added to the 85 per cent above (which by logic should have been restored to the Chinese government after the war) gave a figure in which the liabilities exceeded the assets by more than 5 per cent.[45]

Thus closed a chapter in the history of one important aspect of British investment in China – the tobacco industry. During the last days of BAT's operations in China it faced heavy financial burdens, which eventually led to the Company's decision to cut losses against any fresh remittances. Hence this all-for-all exchange. In the entire process a crucial element seems to have been the attitude of the workers. As a manufacturing concern with large stocks of materials and assets on hand, Yee Tsoong negotiated with a labour force of several thousands for the terms of their pay-off, which must have been very different from small firms negotiating with an office staff of thirty or forty clerks. All the same, as in many cases prior to and after Yee Tsoong, since the government tended to refrain from any action until agreement between labour and management was reached, it was thought that matters could be held up almost indefinitely if labour refused to discuss the terms. Thus it appears that unless and until the government intervened in favour of a speedy settlement, the workers would enjoy almost unlimited bargaining strength.[46]

One cannot state categorically that the 'Yee Tsoong formula' was applicable in all subsequent cases of British withdrawals; in many cases other factors worked at the periphery to make a simple surrender of assets against liabilities an impracticable proposition. Insofar as a large workforce was involved in any liquidation negotiations, it appears that the position of the workers, combined with the willingness or reluctance of the authorities to intervene at an early stage, was invariably an essential factor in the outcome of the settlement. To the remaining firms, the Yee Tsoong settlement could be nothing but an ill omen for things to come, which made them all the more anxious about the urgency of their banding together to resist a total collapse of the British commercial empire from within through individual firms' abandonment of their assets in China.

THE INTERNATIONAL ECONOMIC CONFERENCE IN MOSCOW

From 3 to 12 April 1952, an International Economic Conference was held in Moscow. China's participation highlighted Beijing's desire to trade with the West through new channels. This significantly influenced the thinking of the established British firms in China and convinced them that successful negotiations for their closure would need to include arrangements which would ensure their continued trade opportunities with China after they withdrew.[47]

The conference was sponsored by an official Soviet organisation, the World Peace Council, with governmental and non-governmental delegations representing many countries. The 26-member delegation from China included such prominent bank and trade officials as Nan Hanchen, Lei Zhenmin, and Dr Ji Chaoding. The British delegation had 29 members, led by Lord John Boyd-Orr, and including MPs Henry Charles Usborne and Harold Davies, Peter Wile, Alexander K. Cairncross (now Sir Alec), Joan V. Robinson, Jack Perry, and others.[48] The conference gave China a major platform from which to condemn the 'policy of embargo, blockade and discriminations' pursued by Western governments. At the same time the Chinese delegation declared, 'We are prepared to conduct trade negotiations with any delegate at this conference; we are ready to conclude agreements based on the interests of both parties'.[49]

It is clear that the Chinese delegation, many of its members being specialists in various fields, went to Moscow with concrete plans to contract sales and purchases with Western businessmen. China's call for negotiating trade deals at the conference received support from British delegates, who made the specific suggestion that delegates organise themselves into commodity groups so that buyers and sellers could meet and do business together. Chinese and British members then got together and concluded a barter trade agreement for 1952, with a value of £10 million each way. The goods which the Chinese were required by contract to buy from the British included textile goods, wool, cotton yarn, synthetic silk, chemicals, metals and pharmaceuticals. In return they were to supply large quantities of traditional Chinese exports such as soyabeans, hog bristle, tung oil, frozen eggs, oil seeds, and cattle products. The Chinese conceded that in order to accommodate the supply difficulty of British traders resulting from the embargoes, the contract would state that 35 per cent of the British goods would be in textiles.[50]

To the established firms and 'old China hands', the news that Chinese trade officials were negotiating deals with businessmen with little previous experience in the China market was alarming indeed. They were all the more resentful as they felt that they themselves were compelled to operate under difficult conditions. Nor were they prepared to yield their position easily. The British government on its part was very sympathetic towards the old firms' position. While skeptical about the Chinese sincerity to do business with the West, the Foreign Office nevertheless decided that the signals coming from Moscow should not be ignored, and consequently instructed L.H. Lamb to deliver a carefully worded note on 18 April to the Central People's Government. Alluding to the reports that China was prepared to substantially increase her trade with Britain, the note stated:

> Her Majesty's Government have noted this decision with interest and hope to receive from the CPG an early intimation of the nature of its proposals and of the channels through which it intends to pursue the suggestions outlined in Moscow. In this connection Her Majesty's Government point out that there are numerous established British merchants in Shanghai and Hong Kong who are well qualified to negotiate any such arrangements with the CPG or its representatives.[51]

In an official reply dated 5 July 1952, Chinese Vice Foreign Minister Zhang Hanfu confirmed that following the agreement in Moscow in May, Chinese and British representatives had signed in Berlin on 9 June a pro-forma contract to the amount of £6 500 000 for the first instalment of goods. The statement suggested that this exemplified what China wanted to see develop between China and Britain, 'a normal trade relationship on an equal and mutually beneficial basis'.[52]

It was apparent that Beijing did not follow the British government's advice to involve the old British firms in Shanghai and Hong Kong in the Moscow–Berlin deals. There existed a huge gap between the old familiar way of colonial-style business undertakings that the firms stood for and the new pattern of trade relationship that the new Chinese government aspired to. British firms soon realised that unless they extricated themselves from the present hindrance and awkwardness the China market, into which they had invested so much human capital and for which they had developed so much expertise, would be in one way or the other lost forever.

WINDING UP OF BRITISH INTERESTS 1952–7

Having decided to cease their unprofitable operations in China, the British firms wondered in what way they should go about their withdrawal in order to realise maximum gains from the bargain and still retain a foothold in the China market. From the ensuing debate among the merchants and British officials in China and Whitehall, two ideas emerged, which were largely derived from the experiences of Yee Tsoong and what had happened at the time of the Moscow International Economic Conference. One idea advocated collective bargaining – not by virtue of a 'Guild Scheme' but through preliminary negotiations in Beijing – on principles applicable on an all-China basis. The other called for a linkage between their withdrawal and the setting up of a trade mission.

These ideas were first developed by the British Chamber of Commerce in Shanghai in April 1952. Previously closure negotiations with local authorities had been unsatisfactory to the firms concerned not only because officials were unable or unwilling to give decisions speedily, but also because several local Government Bureaux would necessarily be involved, each one of which would be likely to pull in a different direction and impose its own conditions.[53] Thus the Commerce and Industry Bureau would want to ascertain that a given business had reached rock bottom and that there were no movable stocks or assets left which could be realised in order to fulfill its obligations. The Labour Bureau on its part would see to it that all demands from workers were dealt with by management. The firm would then face the Tax Bureau for the purpose of paying off its staff, outstanding taxes and other claims. The biggest headache was the organised labour, who would fight for their 'pay-off' irrespective of whether or not a firm qualified as a 'going concern'. Also it had not been possible for large firms with offices scattered nationwide to settle their problems on an all-China basis.[54]

In view of the past experiences, British managers in China proposed that preliminary negotiations be conducted with the Central People's Government on certain basic principles governing closure procedures. Specifically, they wanted to see:

1. A government agreement to purchase or lease the assets of the withdrawing firms, with payment made in foreign currency or exports, paying local currency only to cover local liabilities.
2. An agreed clear-cut procedure for assessing the labour liability and, where applicable, for the pay-off of labour; and agreement on the principle of and the period of notice for the termination of employment without question after due notice.
3. Agreement on the procedure for the settlement of other outstanding

obligations and claims, applicable to withdrawing firms and going concerns.
4. The possibilities of a settlement involving a surrender of pooled local assets against pooled local liabilities among withdrawing firms.

The British Chamber of Commerce in Shanghai wanted to see these ideas reflected in the note to be delivered by Lamb to the Chinese government on 19 May 1952, but they were evidently overruled by British government officials and the head offices of the firms in London and Hong Kong. Lamb in particular regarded the proposal for negotiations in Beijing as 'impracticable and unrealistic'.[55] This greatly upset the Shanghai managers, on whose behalf the China Association in June once again urged that the possibility be considered of initiating discussions between a party of British businessmen from Shanghai and the authorities in Beijing so as to first establish a general framework of guidelines.[56]

The firms in Shanghai were fairly optimistic about the prospects of overall withdrawal arrangements, partly because of their long-held belief that China would need their expert service in her foreign trade, which they were in an indisputable position to provide. There was also some suggestion that the Chinese authorities might have agreed to the proposal had the British side broached the idea in the first place. After the unorthodox Sino–British trade agreement was initiated in Moscow, and in view of official Chinese statements about the importance of continuing Sino–British trade, it was particularly felt that in any subsequent communication from British officials in Beijing to the Chinese government, a suggestion regarding a commercial mission should also be considered.[57] It was argued that if it was correct to assume that the Chinese 'intended to retain at least some of us [British firms] as a trading contact with the Sterling Area until they can replace us with something more suitable to their own trading methods . . . then the offer to replace the old organization with some form of Commercial Mission . . . might well meet with a favourable reception'. In this connection, some form of British government sponsorship would be required.

Although the British government did not take up the proposal of preliminary discussion in Beijing, it espoused the idea of a trade mission, which fitted in with the policy of securing some kind of foothold for Britain in China. Hence a paragraph in the note of 19 May 1952 commending the idea of a permanent trade mission to the

Chinese government. The Chinese government's initial response was fairly encouraging. There was some indication that the Chinese Foreign Ministry thought the idea of a representative trading group 'to be quite a good one'.[58] Apparently encouraged by the prospect of a successful encounter with the Chinese on this score, a small party of British business representatives, composed of managers of Jardines, ICI and the International Export Corporation, held a meeting with a senior Chinese foreign trade official in Shanghai in September, during which the latter unofficially discussed with them the idea of a trade mission. Whereas this official, Mr Lu Xuzhang from CNIEC's Shanghai branch, was cautiously sounding out the British position, the managers insisted firmly that there would be 'no Trade Group before withdrawal'. They probably also left the Chinese official with an impression that the Trade Group would be narrowly represented, with only two further candidates – the two Arnhold Companies, Swire and Maclaine and GEC – being added to the original three.[59]

This latest British position, which resulted from a misreading of Chinese intentions, was supported by British officials in Beijing. Thus Lamb wrote that as a matter both of principle and of expediency 'the satisfactory closure of firms must be insisted upon a prelude to the foundation of the Trade Group', which, he argued, 'could be a useful bargaining counter'.[60] But already news had come from Shanghai that the Chinese had abruptly postponed a scheduled meeting between British business representatives and officials of the local Department of Commerce. The British reported with alarm, 'The Chinese have been taken aback by the British insistence that the closure of firms must be coupled with discussions on the Trade Group'. Foreign Office officials subsequently confirmed that the attempt at a 'linkage' had suffered a setback. It was then urged that, 'on the whole it would be better that no reference should be made to the Trade Group proposals', as there had been evidence that 'the Chinese were willing to talk about the Trade Group, but lost interest when we made it clear that such discussion could only be in connection with the closing down of the firms'.[61]

There is no evidence to suggest that the Chinese government was initially averse to either the idea of establishing general principles governing the closure of British firms or to the proposal of a trade mission in China. This was in spite of the fact that it would have been highly unlikely that the Chinese government would have found many of the British demands contained in the memorandum of BCC at Shanghai acceptable in their original form. The British on their part hesitated about the feasibility of preliminary discussions, and then appeared unnecessarily aggressive with regard to the trade mission. Thus, proceeding from an instinctive desire to ward off further application of the Yee Tsoong formula, the British firms in the end gained little from this intensive process of calculation and manoeuvre, which lasted throughout 1952.

Final Closures

As a result of the British decision not to pursue the idea of preliminary negotiations in Beijing, a number of firms filed separate applications for closure with local Chinese authorities. These proposals were then referred to Beijing for instructions, and the firms were told by local officials that the applications would be dealt with on a general, and not individual, basis.[62]

The government must, by early July 1952, have formally taken a decision that the time had come for most of the British commercial interests to leave China. Lamb suggested that, judging from Zhang Hanfu's statement, the Chinese central government might have sent instructions to the local authorities to discuss terms of withdrawal with the individual firms and perhaps also not to be unduly obstructive. This would mean the firms 'now have more assured grounds for holding out for more equitable terms and for not disposing of their assets too cheaply'.[63] In late July 1952, British consular officials in Tianjin reported that the Foreign Affairs Bureau had asked several British firms to complete before 25 July a questionnaire with regard to their business operations for the past two years, and, in the case of factory owners, also for 1946–50. All this suggested a connection with proposals for the withdrawal of British business.[64]

Industrial Concerns

Among the first British firms to follow the 'Yee Tsoong formula' was the China Soap Co., a subsidiary of the Lever Brothers and Unilevers Ltd. The firm, in difficulty over taxation and wages (for 668 employees in 1950), first proposed a lease to the authorities early in 1952, which they understood was referred to Beijing. After a few months the firm's head office in Hong Kong instructed their Chinese manager in Shanghai that if he still could not arrange to lease the property in China, he was to offer to hand it over to the Chinese government in return for release from all liabilities. This upset the British Foreign Office, who tried to get the China Association to persuade the Levers not to give up their property, but to press for lease, for fear it would prejudice 'the negotiating position of other British firms who want to press hard and long for sale or lease'. Roger Heyworth of Unilevers in reply insisted that the offer was on the same lines as the BAT agreement and under the circumstances they felt they were not creating a precedent.[65]

Around the same time, Liddell Brothers and Co. Ltd reached agreement with the Harbin authorities to sell its plywood factory at the price of HK$750 000 in local currency, which the firm said would be used for paying off its staff in Harbin and Shanghai. The Harbin authorities later chose to issue an Order for Compulsory Purchase in the name of its mayor Yao Bin. For the sale of its plant in Tianjin, the Liddells received export cargo in partial payment from the government. Payment to the Liddell Brothers had in fact not been completed by the time of the Sino–British talks in Geneva in 1954 owing to continuous problems, on which Humphrey Trevelyan made a representation to the Chinese on behalf of the firm.[66] Other cases in Tianjin along the lines of all-for-all arrangement included International Export Co. (Tianjin) Ltd, the Court Hotel, and possibly also Mackenzie and Co. Ltd.[67]

In November 1952 the Jardines agreed with Tianjin to surrender all the company's local assets against the remission of liabilities, and a final agreement was signed some six months later. The assets included houses, godowns and other properties in Tianjin and Tanggu, as well as all movable assets; the liabilities included claims in court by government corporations for compensation for outstanding contracts, and pre-war claims from the staff. The firm also needed to pay off the staff and workers prior to the final agreement. The Jardines later alleged that the firm's assets in Tianjin exceeded liabilities by a large margin. 'We had to sign on their terms, otherwise permission for closure would have been withheld; in fact we had to sign under a form of duress'.[68] In order to facilitate the closure, the Jardines arranged for a supply of valves from Switzerland as part of an unfulfilled contract for the import of a boiler to a Chinese concern. The British government had previously refused an export licence for the shipment of valves from the UK, and the Foreign Office immediately condemned the deal, saying that it was 'shameless of Jardine to try to obtain the missing parts from Switzerland'.[69]

Land and House Properties
A greater part (more than 65 per cent) of the British assets being

disposed of was in landed property and real estate. The PRC government had all along regarded the restoration to Chinese control of foreign-held land as an issue of high political significance. It first took steps to reduce the land holdings by public foreign entities, including the requisitioning of military barracks and other acreages occupied by foreign diplomatic or consular missions. It then introduced laws under which private land was subject to state requisition if deemed necessary, with appropriate compensation. British real estate included, on the one hand, factory premises, office buildings, godowns, wharves, storage structures attached to industrial enterprises and, on the other hand, apartment buildings and other kinds of real estate for renting purposes.[70]

Over 95 per cent of British-occupied land and house properties transferred to Chinese hands (in terms of value) came from private British business concerns.[71] In the case of British industrial concerns, transfers of their land and housing possessions were usually arranged under an overall liquidation agreement with Chinese government organisations. An example was the disposal arrangement by Butterfield and Swire with regard to their Holt's Wharf in Shanghai. B and S had been the agent for the Blue Funnel Line in Shanghai and other Chinese ports. On 15 December 1954 Holt's Wharf and B and S's other port facilities closed down; the Blue Funnel Agencies in China were then handed over to the China Ocean Shipping Agencies, a People's Government concern.[72]

With regard to British housing properties to let, these were allowed by Chinese law. Since there were comparatively small overheads involved, companies which managed them were able to maintain these properties with modest proceeds for some years. In most cases however, owners eventually cooperated with the authorities to dispose of their holdings through sales, leases and trusteeship.

In late 1949 the government promulgated a set of measures governing the disposal of ownerless land, or landed properties held in the name of absentee owners of foreign nationality. The government initially allowed a period of three years for registration by the original owners, at the end of which time any unregistered land would be taken over as public owned. Trustees who intended to establish ownership would have to find and appoint by power of attorney a local agent to attend a re-registration of the title and pay the necessary land taxes. In 1951 the government initiated the second re-registration process. Within a time limit of three months, application for registration would need to be made by the claimants, or if they were absent, by their legitimate agent.[73]

In 1952 local authorities began to take over control of ownerless or unregistered land and houses. The forfeited landed properties, together with various properties requisitioned by the government with compensation, may have constituted 50 per cent of private British housing property which passed to Chinese control in 1952.[74] It seems that British owners failed to re-establish title through registration either because of their absence, or because the rates for land and house property taxes were too high, for the sort of premises which foreigners usually owned, to make the idea of their coming back to claim them a sufficiently attractive one. Besides, relevant regulations provided for accumulative fines for failure to pay on due dates. Some British owners thus preferred to let their ownership interest lapse tacitly by taking no action about registration.[75] A related category of housing property were private British clubs in various cities, which were at first leased to Chinese government agencies. Some of them were later taken over by the government.[76]

Trading Firms

It seems that the majority of British firms still carrying on in 1952 were in the import and–or export business. Some of them had extensive business activities and properties. Unlike industrial concerns, these firms handled trade transactions for commissions, which usually involved lower overheads and labour costs. Some of them had decided that there was insufficient business to warrant their continued presence in China and were in the process of winding up, whereas others were not keen to withdraw at all costs, such as along the lines of the Yee Tsoong settlement. Their expertise in the trade business and extensive overseas connections – many of them were sole agents for British manufacturers in the Far East – in effect enabled them to do some business on behalf of China's foreign trade organisations. By 1954 however, British government officials had become increasingly inclined to see British commercial interests pulled out without further delay.[77]

Among these was the International Export Co. Ltd, which specialised in the export of foodstuff and native products. IEC also had major properties in Nanjing, Shanghai and Hankou, which it wanted to sell to Chinese government organisations in order to settle its liabilities. Another case was Imperial Chemical Industries (China)

Ltd, which shipped to China materials such as dyestuff, chemical fertilisers and pesticides, and distributed them to Chinese customers through various regional offices. The company also exported peppermint, eggs and vegetable oil from China. Having gradually trimmed its operations, ICI still managed to do a considerable volume of trade in 1954.[78] Swire and Maclaine Ltd did not do so well in commission trading and was on its way out. B and S's liners called on Chinese ports regularly. In August 1954, J. March of the Swire Group visited China from Hong Kong and held talks with Chinese trade officials in Shanghai. March's visit was aimed at improving business opportunities both for the firm's shipping and for its trading subsidiary, Swire and Maclaine Ltd in Shanghai.

The Jardines' activities covered the export and import of a wide range of commodities. This was in addition to shipping, real estate business and management of textile mills and machine plants, spreading over Shanghai, Tianjin, Qingdao, Hankou, Guangzhou, Fuzhou and Shantou. The firm had disposed of its assets in Tianjin and Qingdao by 1953, and was in the process of closing down its offices in Shanghai, Hankou and Fuzhou in 1954. Other specialised firms included Harvey Main and Co. Ltd (import of instruments as well as metals and chemical products), Inniss and Riddle (China) Ltd (import of machinery, electric equipment and metal materials), Postro Trading Co. Ltd (import of chemicals and export of silk, feathers and other native products), China Engineers Ltd (import of industrial machinery, components and spare parts, wool tops and chemicals, and export of animal products and silk), Bank Line (China) Ltd (shipping service and some commodity trading), and Shell Co. of China Ltd (import of petroleum products).[79]

Trading firms withdrew gradually. In Shanghai 99 British firms re-registered in June 1949. Their number decreased over the years, to 34 in June 1951, 30 by 1952, 21 by 1953, 15 by 1954, and eight by the end of 1955. (The total number of foreign trading firms in Shanghai followed the same trend of decrease, from 376 at the end of 1949, to 214 by 1950, 108 by 1951, 75 by 1952, 25 by 1953–4, and 15 by 1955–6, with another four in the process of liquidation.) Some firms were able to sell their property and settle their liabilities in China. During the Geneva conference in May–June 1954, Trevelyan discussed various aspects of British interests in China with the Chinese delegation, and obtained Chinese assurances that they would facilitate a speedy settlement of some outstanding matters with regard to tax, payoff and court actions and would help find appropriate government agencies to purchase British properties.[80] Parallel with this development, their import–export trade in China was increasingly replaced by their correspondent transactions with China, executed offshore from either Hong Kong or Britain itself. After 1956 the withdrawal of British trading houses from China was quickly completed. Some firms, such as China Engineers Ltd and ICI, were persuaded by the Chinese authorities to maintain their presence in China for a few more years, but most of the British community did not survive the 1956 socialist transformation.

Banks
The three principal British banks operating in China were the Hongkong and Shanghai Banking Corporation, the Chartered Bank of Australia, India and China, and the Mercantile Bank of India, all of which had by July 1952 filed applications to close down their offices in various cities. Earlier they had pinned their hopes on some group action or negotiation with some close representatives of the authorities, such as the London office of the Bank of China who, it was believed, 'are in better favour with Peking than their other branches'.[81]

Like the Yee Tsoong Tobacco Co., the British banks finally agreed to set off all their liabilities in China against the surrender of their assets in China (with one possible exception of a few office buildings and residences in connection with their post-closure representation in China).[82] After the banks announced their decision to close down, the financial control departments of local governments sent teams of inspectors to go through their books with a fine toothcomb, examining vouchers, letters referred to in the accounts, and other details. They also asked the banks many questions.[83] The banks first managed to close down their offices in various cities on an assets against liability basis and voluntary discharge of employees, and transferred outstanding matters to their principal offices in Shanghai. The Chinese government also approved a sale agreement between the Hongkong Bank and the Indian embassy in Beijing, under which the bank would sell its Beijing premises to the Indian embassy; the proceeds from the sale were used towards the bank's liabilities in China.[84]

The Hongkong Bank first closed its offices in Qingdao, Tianjin, Beijing, Hankou and Guangzhou, and then entered into negotiations with the Ta Hua Trading Corporation in early 1954 for the purpose of disposing of its properties as well as liabilities in Shanghai. An agreement was finally signed with Ta Hua in June 1955, including an

arrangement of a new, smaller office for the bank on Yuen Ming
Yuen Road. One disappointment to the British was that Ta Hua
refused to let the Bank have the bronze lions standing at the entrance
of the old HSBC building, 'As bronze is a prohibited export, we can
do nothing unless they acquiesce'.[85]

The final winding up of these banks was considerably delayed by
the stumbling blocks of pre-war deposits and frozen US dollar accounts with the banks. From the very outset, the banks were determined to resist all claims to the pre-war deposits by Chinese public
and private clients on the grounds that '100 per cent cover was taken
over by the Japanese and the deposits could and should have been
withdrawn in full'.[86] Their position was directly opposed to an order
by the Central People's Government to banks to pay pre-liberation
deposits, with detailed provisions on the exchange rates and calculations.[87] In the end settlement was achieved on the basis of an understanding (in the case of the Hongkong Bank, along the lines of an
agreement reached in Guangzhou) to the effect that pre-war liabilities to Chinese depositors would be transferred to the Chinese
government within the overall arrangement of liquidation, whereas
the pre-war Sterling and other currency deposits belonging to people
outside China would be retained abroad.[88]

The problem of frozen US dollar accounts in the United States
proved to be more intractable. These were principally deposited by
Chinese trade and financial organisations with the British banks,
which were subsequently frozen by the US government in December
1950 under Foreign Assets Control Regulations.[89] The total dollar
assets held in the US in the blocked accounts of these three British
banks amounted to approximately US$9.3 million, of which approxi-
mately US$4 million consisted of balances of branches of these banks
in mainland China.[90] The banks argued that it was not in their power
to obtain a release of the dollars, but the Chinese government
refused to permit their closure until these accounts were settled. The
issue was discussed between Chinese and British representatives in
Geneva in 1954, without any prospect of finding a solution.[91]

The key then seemed to lie in getting the US government to agree
to a *modus vivendi*, which the Foreign Office tried to obtain in 1953
and on subsequent occasions without any success.[92] In 1956 the US
government agreed to issue a licence to the Mercantile Bank of India
to pay from free funds the amount of the blocked dollar accounts
(which would remain frozen in principle) in non-US currency to the
Chinese government on the basis of a precedent created for two

American banks. This enabled the bank to settle its foreign currency liabilities with the Bank of China.[93] Neither the Hongkong Bank nor the Chartered Bank wanted to follow the Mercantile's example for fear that their much bigger accounts might be subject to confiscation by the US Treasury should there be a deterioration in Sino–US relations.[94] For the two banks however, the problem seemed to have receded to the background by 1955 since both of them had accepted, somewhat reluctantly, the proposal from the Bank of China that they keep their presence in China and act as its correspondent banks.[95]

The general deterioration of business conditions in China, the overall losses, and difficulties in running and managing their offices contributed to the three British banks' decision to wind up. After the outbreak of the Korean war, they came to believe that the ensuing barter trade arrangements would limit the banks' discretion and involve them in large foreign currency risks, which the British banks were rarely prepared to accept.[96] Partly because of that they had decided by early 1951 to cut their business operations to a strict care and maintenance level in anticipation of an eventual withdrawal, even though that would mean heavier losses from their large over-heads which would otherwise have been compensated for by income derived from small business.[97]

There seems hardly any doubt that throughout the process the central authorities in Beijing were firmly in control. Various applications for closure, together with suggested plans from local governments on specific procedures of negotiations, were submitted to Beijing for final approval. Actual closures were spaced out to avoid massive unemployment and abrupt economic dislocation, in addition to the care taken to ensure that disputes were settled strictly within the rule of law. Supplementary measures were also taken to preserve a number of British firms which were willing to operate within the requirements of the new government.[98] On the other hand there were complaints from firms about delays and insufficient responsiveness by the authorities for quick settlements.

At the local level, British firms were advised by the Foreign Affairs Bureau to show sincerity in negotiations with the workers on the basis of fairness and reason. It was pointed out to them that the People's Government gave due consideration to the interests of capital and that labour's demands were put forward only as a basis for discussion. The British complained that since labour unions were well aware that until a settlement was reached the foreign merchant would have to continue to pay wages and would not receive an exit permit, they rarely agreed to modify their demands.[99] While it was expected that government officials at the local level sympathised with workers, it seems also true that they exerted a certain restraining influence on the militancy of the workers. The Foreign Affairs Bureau in Guangzhou, for instance, was reported to have returned the workers' demands for severance pay to their unions for reconsideration because it deemed them excessive.[100] Nevertheless there were common charges in 1952 that firms were being faced with 'increasing exorbitant demands for wages or severance pay from their trade unions'.[101]

The assurance given by the Chinese government in Zhang Hanfu's statement of 5 July 1952, to the effect that the Chinese authorities in respective localities would expeditiously and reasonably settle any question arising out of the winding up of British firms, upgraded the issue of foreign private commercial operations in China to the level of state relations. It thus gave the British government a legal standing with which the British chargé d'affaires in Beijing was able to pursue the matter with the Chinese government regarding any problems and disabilities experienced by British nationals and entities in China. To the extent that the British held the Chinese government ultimately accountable for these otherwise private matters, it exercised an implicit form of restraint on the Chinese against taking more forcible administrative measures. British officials in Beijing, upon instructions from the Foreign Office, kept on bringing the difficulties and requests of the firms to the attention of the Chinese Foreign Ministry in numerous communications. Short of direct negotiation, this was perhaps the only effective way under the circumstances for the British government to compel the Chinese central authorities to exert a modifying pressure to bear on the provinces and to speed up the process of the closures.[102]

From the Chinese point of view, the 'Yee Tsoong formula' perhaps appeared the most cost-effective way, both economically and politically, of ending the presence of British commercial interest in China. In reality this proved possible only in cases where the British concerns in question shared similar vulnerabilities with the Yee Tsoong interests. It emerged that most were industrial enterprises, which relied on Chinese supply of materials and allocation of market shares, and were burdened by large administrative overheads (principally in the form of property tax) and labour costs. Having thrived on special privileges and extra-territorial rights in the past, they now had to cut their losses and withdraw from a revolutionary China. Other forms of settlement besides all-for-all deals were long-term leases, sales and trusteeships, in which cases liability was cleared from the original British owners. By the end of 1952 a total of 236 British businesses had liquidated their assets in one way or another; this amounted to 63 per cent of British capital in China. A few British firms managed to carry on until the late 1950s, such as the woollen mill of Messrs. Patons and Baldwins Ltd, which was purchased by the Chinese government in June 1959.[103]

6 A New Pattern of Trade

Sino–British relations should be kept running like a narrow winter stream, cold at the official level and uninterrupted in people-to-people contact.

Mao Zedong

Controversy should always be so managed as to remember that the only true end of it is peace.

Alexander Pope

As old firms beat their retreat from China, new British business interests were stepping in. The traditional mode of trade had had to go, but it did not mean the end of Sino–British economic relations. On the contrary, it ushered in a new pattern of trade, built on a respect for China's independence and a sense of mutual advantage. Chinese state trading dominated the scene, while the 'old China hands' competed with a group of newcomers on the British side. But the Chinese also learned from experience that in forging new links with their British partners, they could not very well ignore the position and attitude of the British government.

Indeed political interactions continued to set the tune for trade and other forms of exchanges between the two countries. The Korean armistice and the Geneva conference of 1954 gradually brought about a relaxed atmosphere in East–West relations. This in turn warmed the official ties between Beijing and London, and precipitated a scaling down of Britain's trade embargoes on China. Both governments were realistic enough to realise the limitations on a comprehensive rapprochement in the Far East. But they saw value in keeping up contacts at a personal level and in fields outside the arena of political contention, however precarious that process might be amidst huge political differences.

PRC–UK POLITICAL RELATIONS AFTER THE KOREAN WAR

The death of Stalin on 5 March 1953 initiated a new phase in Sino–Soviet relations. Progress towards an end to the Korean war, which had been very difficult since the opening of cease-fire talks at Kaesong on 10 July 1951, was expedited at Panmunjom by diplomatic initiatives from Beijing in 1953. On 27 July an Armistice Agreement was finally concluded to mark the end of the three-year long hostilities in Korea. Despite tremendous sacrifices, China viewed her military involvement a justifiable one for her national interests against aggressive American intentions.[1] The Chinese leadership must have felt very relieved when a general relaxation of tension followed the armistice, with Mao Zedong's exultation that a new phase of China's comprehensive diplomacy had come.[2]

Although the war had stopped, the Korean issue remained unresolved. The Chinese blamed the Americans for their refusal to discuss the possibility of withdrawing all foreign troops from Korea, which reinforced their belief that this formed part of a larger American scheme to surround China with a ring of hostile regimes. They also believed that the American plan was not popular, and that the international environment after the Korean war, which was conducive to détente, was favourable for China.[3] Thus, when all the blocks were finally removed to the convening of a conference in Geneva on the Korean question, the CCP Central Committee instructed the members of the Chinese delegation that they should at the conference 'increase diplomatic and bilateral activities . . . and seek some agreed solutions so as to pave the way for the settlement of international disputes through consultation among the big powers'.[4]

Following such a policy, and with a view to increasing the diplomatic isolation of the Americans, the Chinese government began moving towards a partial détente with the British even before Geneva. This was based on the calculation that the capitalist world was not a monolithic one, and that in particular, as Britain's view about the Korean war and the situation in the Far East was different from that of the United States, this difference should be explored to China's advantage.[5] Given their fundamental differences and some bilateral problems of immediate concern, the shift in Beijing's official attitude towards Britain was bound to be gradual and subtle. This was all the more so since the British government in public statements repeatedly stressed the common objective of the Anglo–American alliance.

Early in 1954 the Chinese began their pre-preliminary diplomatic minuet. On 24 March Zhang Hanfu attended a supper party at the house of British Mission chief Humphrey Trevelyan for the Coronation film 'A Queen is Crowned', and he in return entertained the

Trevelyans and other British officials at dinner at the Ministry of Foreign Affairs on 2 April. A vice-minister for foreign trade (possibly Lei Zhenmin) and some senior MFA officials were present. As Trevelyan later commented, this was the first such function given for non-recognised missions.[6]

China played an active part at the Geneva conference on Korea and Indochina held in April–July 1954. Her image of reasonableness and moderation was striking when contrasted with the hostile position of the US, who during a greater part of the conference was under-represented by Forster Dulles's deputy, Under Secretary of State Walter Bedell Smith. Trevelyan later recalled, 'The Americans appeared to want people to think that they were not there, like a guest at a party which he thinks is not quite up to his social standing'. They were 'not on speaking terms with the Chinese and were seen to be carefully avoiding contact'.[7] Trevelyan accompanied Foreign Secretary Anthony Eden to his meetings with Zhou Enlai, and – for the first time able to do what he had not been able to do in Beijing – held regular meetings with Director of MFA West European and African Affairs Department Huan Xiang, and with Vice-Minister for Foreign Trade Lei Zhenmin. As a result of the talks many of the troubles of the British community in China were resolved. Substantial progress was made in trade matters, which will be discussed later on.

At a luncheon given by Soviet Foreign Minister Molotov on 30 April, Eden complained to Zhou that the Chinese government had not been helpful in regard to their relations with Britain, having no corresponding representative in London to Trevelyan in Beijing. Zhou replied that Britain did not recognise the Chinese position in the United Nations and that he did not think this helpful. In reply Eden was reported as saying that that was a question quite apart from the subject under consideration at Geneva and that he did not wish to discuss it. This was the first time both sides had touched upon the subject of upgrading diplomatic representation in each other's capitals.[8] Concurrently a Parliamentary delegation led by Harold Wilson and William Robson-Brown went to Geneva for meetings with the Chinese delegation. They gave the message that the British government would consider positively the possibility of a Chinese commercial representative's office in London. This reassured the Chinese of their grounds, and after careful consideration they decided to reach out. Huan Xiang met with Trevelyan and informed him of the Chinese government's decision to upgrade Sino–British diplomatic relations to the level of Chargés d'Affaires by sending a corresponding representative to London. The Chinese logic seemed to be that since a commercial representative's office would be semi-official in diplomatic status, the British would not feel too upset or embarrassed by a Chinese counter-request that a Chargé d'Affaires be sent to London. Once that was accepted a proposal for a commercial counsellor, to be incorporated into such a London office, could hardly be turned down.

The British side seemed caught slightly unprepared. The Foreign Office thought it an offer that the British could not very well refuse, but given the American mood at this time, the announcement of Britain's acceptance of a Chinese Chargé d'Affaires in London, on top of an invitation to a Chinese trade mission to Britain and the news of a Labour Party delegation visit to China, might well produce very unfavourable reactions.[9] The concern about possible strong American reaction was dissipated by General Bedell Smith himself when Eden told him about the Chinese approach and asked for his opinion. According to Eden, Smith said that surely there was no other course the British government could follow but to accept. 'I asked him whether it would not upset American opinion but he was inclined to brush this off, added somebody must keep a contact with those people [the Chinese and the Soviets].' Much reassured, London decided that Britain should go ahead.[10] On 16 June 1954 Eden held a meeting with Zhou Enlai, and informed him that the British government was prepared to receive a Chinese Chargé d'Affaires on an equivalent basis to that of Trevelyan in Beijing. Zhou was pleased. The news was announced on the following day, and was warmly received both in Parliament and among the British public.[11]

Outside the conference Trevelyan acted as a go-between during the early stage of preparation for ambassadorial talks between China and the US, and his role was much appreciated by the Chinese. Thanks to Trevelyan's good offices, talks were initiated between China and the US which led to the repatriation of American nationals from China. Trevelyan returned from Geneva to a situation in China very different from the earlier years of the People's Republic. Now treated as a recognised mission, the British could do business in the same way as others, both in Beijing and in Shanghai, keeping regular contact with the Chinese authorities. F.F. Garner replaced A. Vaitch as British Consul-General to Shanghai in September 1954, and Trevelyan was replaced by Con D.W. O'Neill in 1955 as British Chargé d'Affaires to Beijing. In October 1954, Huan Xiang arrived in London as the first Chargé d'Affaires *ad interim* to Britain. This event formalised a partial normalisation of diplomatic relations between China and Britain.[12]

The partial normalisation was no doubt a political move, initiated by China as part of a strategy to drive a wedge between the United States and its closest ally, Britain. The Chinese used the occasion of an international conference to negotiate directly with British counterparts on bilateral issues, and cautiously paved the way by holding talks on bilateral trade between specialists from both countries. Once again China displayed its sensitivity towards the issue of recognition, which was used to set limits on intentions and consequences.

THE NEWCOMERS

The International Economic Conference in Moscow in 1952 (discussed in Chapter five) was an event of particular significance to Sino–British trade relations because it brought to the fore a new group of British businessmen. Many of them looked on the Chinese revolution with sympathy and were averse to the Cold War in East–West relations. In Moscow a decision was made to form a 30-member multinational Committee for the Promotion of International Trade.[13] Nan Hanchen and Dr Ji Chaoding, President and Vice-President of the People's Bank of China, were among the members of this new body. Those from the British side included Joan Vidlet Robinson, a Fellow and Lecturer in Economics at Cambridge University, and Jack Perry, director of a British company of dress products, home trade and export.

Jack Perry had met Dr Ji in autumn 1951 when the latter was travelling in Europe. With the encouragement of those supporting British participation to the Moscow conference, notably F.J. Erroll (later Lord Erroll of Hale) and Joan Robinson, Perry took part in the preparatory work as a member of the International Initiating Committee and was elected as vice-chairman of the conference.[14] He and his colleagues were instrumental in bringing about the conclusion in Moscow of an unorthodox agreement between Chinese and British delegates on a trade programme in 1952 of £10 million from each side.

By this time the Chinese government trade organisation, CNIEC, which had been set up to handle trade matters with the West and other non-communist countries, had opened an office in East Berlin. Its members were conducting business negotiations with individual businessmen from West European countries.[15] It was in East Berlin that the Chinese took the first initiative in fulfilling the targets of the trade programme, and placed an order with London Export Corporation (LEC, set up by Perry) for £300 000 worth of wool tops, a line of business which the firm admitted they had never done before.[16]

It appeared that the newcomers had wanted the established firms to join them in their ventures. In January 1952 Bernard Buckman, a textile merchant and distributor, had lunch with G.E. Mitchell from the China Association and first raised the possibility of reviving the China trade through an exchange of business visits with the Chinese. Mitchell rejected the idea as one which 'would get no response whatsoever, either from British business or diplomatic circles'.[17] The China Association's position was approved by the Foreign Office, who advised them to 'tread warily, stressing the fact of basic Anglo–American solidarity as well as the fact that it is entirely up to China to behave in such a way, as to make better trade relations a practical possibility'.[18] In early February Bernard Buckman told the China Association that he had recommended to the British organisers of the Moscow conference that Tony Keswick and G.E. Mitchell, among others, should be invited to join in the British delegation, but the offer was turned down. Mitchell recalled his reply thus:

> We felt that there would be no object in our accepting the offer as we have no status or authority for discussion of broad issues of international trade, and that for our own individual problems ample facilities already existed for discussion of business in China.[19]

In the middle of February Tony Keswick and G.E. Mitchell turned down an invitation to lunch to meet Jack Perry who, as they understood, was organising the British end of the Moscow conference.[20]

Following the Moscow conference, the Chinese government established on 4 May 1952 a China Committee (later Council) for the Promotion of International Trade (CCPIT), which consisted of 17 members with Nan Hanchen as President and Dr Ji Chaoding as Secretary-General. According to Wu Chengming, CCPIT was evolved from the former Foreign Investments Bureau under the Financial and Economic Commission of the Central People's Government as the latter's functions gradually faded away.[21] A similar unofficial body was organised in Britain in July – the British Council for the Promotion of International Trade (BCPIT). Lord Boyd-Orr became Chairman, Joan Robinson Vice-Chairman, and 21 other delegates to Moscow (with some later additions) members of the Council. Roland Berger, a former United Nations official, was appointed as its Director. Lord Boyd-Orr in the early years had been the first Director-General of the United Nations Food and Agriculture Organisation, and it was possible that their common background with the UN had got Boyd-Orr and Roland Berger together. Lord Boyd-Orr visited China in 1956 and was received by Zhou Enlai.

BCPIT fell into official disfavour by promoting trade with the so-called 'Eastern Area' countries, including China. The fact that the Moscow Economic Conference was sponsored by the World Peace Council was enough for the British government to condemn it. Anthony Eden declared in the House of Commons on 6 November 1953, that BCPIT was a 'Communist front organisation'. This position was reaffirmed in February 1954 and was supported by other established commercial bodies. It was suggested that the various country councils (committees) for the promotion of international trade were 'being used by the Russians as political front organisations through which trade with the Communist world was to be channelled.'[22]

Admittedly British firms in Hong Kong had different views from the China Association in London in the wake of the Moscow conference and follow-up deals in East Berlin. H.J. Collar, Chairman of the British Chamber of Commerce in Hong Kong, stated that he for one would go over to Berlin to see the Chinese trading agency there as he thought that the Chinese had done a rather shrewd stroke of business for themselves in setting up this agency. In the case of his own firm, ICI, it meant that the Chinese were able to secure lower prices in East Berlin, because of competition from other continental suppliers, than if they concluded contracts in Hong Kong or China.[23]

There was also a debate within the British government about whether they should allow CNIEC to open an office in London as some firms suggested that they should. Neither the government nor the established businesses liked the idea of conducting trade through East Berlin, nor could they very well compel the Chinese to confine their business venues to within China or Hong Kong. The matter was deferred, giving way to a fear of American sensitivity and a suspicion about Chinese sincerity. The Foreign Office suggested caution at first sight: 'It was one of the few cards we had in our hand and I thought we should not play it prematurely'.[24] It resurfaced in 1954 during the Geneva trade talks, and was supported by the Board of Trade but firmly opposed by the China Association lest it hurt the business of those firms in China and Hong Kong. The consideration was eventually overtaken by events in Geneva, where the Chinese government agreed to establish a Chargé d'Affaires' office in London, and which would include a commercial non-trading section.[25]

Meanwhile it became increasingly apparent that the 'newcomers' were serious about new business opportunities with China. LEC pushed hard in talks with Bradford wool top makers who initially refused to accept Chinese terms of payment, under which China's letters of credit would be confirmed by the Bank of China's office in London rather than by a foreign bank. The breakthrough came when Mr (later Sir) Kenneth Parkinson of B. Parkinson and Co. decided to sign a contract with LEC on Chinese terms. Scores of other companies followed suit. In addition to the initial wool top purchase, which had been successfully completed, LEC reported that other offers had been placed with British suppliers by the Chinese, including cotton and worsted piece goods.[26] These were the times when such unorthodox trade deals and unconventional practices were derided in Britain as 'midsummer madness'. The Moscow trade programme of £10 million each way fell considerably short of target. One of the first things LEC learnt to do in its new import business was to persuade the British importers to accept the Chinese requirement for payment by letters of credit prior to shipment, which was met with some success.

Considerable agitation flared in early 1953 over the news of a possible economic conference in Beijing and the desirability of British participation through the medium of BCPIT. Established firms within the Federation of British Industries (FBI) and the China Association turned to the government for a clear lead. After much debate about possible political pitfalls, Cabinet decided to advise the firms that the government would prefer them not to send representatives to the conference. It was also suggested that the Foreign Office should inform friendly governments of the action Britain was taking and hoped that they would follow a similar line.[27] The Chinese subsequently decided to arrange with BCPIT for British businessmen to visit Beijing for direct trade deals, which they thought was a more effective way than a conference to convince the West of business opportunities with China. The China Association decided to follow government advice and discourage people from joining the proposed group.[28]

BCPIT eventually succeeded in organising what was later known as the 'ice-breaker' mission to China, led by Joan Robinson. The group gathered in Hong Kong and went to Beijing via Guangzhou. On 6 July, 16 members of the mission signed with CNIEC a Business Arrangement of £30 million – £15 million from each side – as well as contracts for individual firms implementing the first half of this programme.[29] The Business Arrangement was to run from July 1953 to 30 June 1954. Some 12 contracts were signed for British exports to China totalling £710 000 in value, and 10 contracts for Chinese exports to Britain for £5.1 million. This was in addition to some 67 preliminary contracts with a worth of £6.78 million, pending confirmation by the British within three months. LEC moreover agreed to act as correspondents for CNIEC in the United Kingdom, and to act both as their selling and their purchasing agents.[30]

There were some signs of a conflict of interests between representatives of manufacturing concerns on the spot and merchant companies acting on behalf of their numerous clients at home, in regard to how to distribute business orders. In general the 'ice-breaker' mission seemed to have succeeded in securing large orders from Chinese trading partners, particularly because the timing of their visit to China corresponded with the formulation of a new Five Year Plan, which was yet to be published.

In the event, as many of the export items from Britain in the Business Arrangement were embargo goods, British suppliers were hard put in trying to obtain export licences from their government. Board of Trade President Peter Thorneycroft made it clear that there would be no licences for most of the vehicles ordered from Austin, as well as other Chinese orders for cables, electrical equipment, machine tools and most of the instruments. 'Our strategic controls would not, of course, be affected in any way by any arrangements that had been made in Peking.'[31] As a result, the firms concerned kept on putting off confirmation of their tentative contracts for want of export licences. But a number of transactions did get through, including the sale of compressors, tinplate, small motors and Austin A40 cars, many of which were being traded for the first time since the embargo had been imposed. For that reason, the 'ice-breaker' mission probably contributed in no small measure to the liberalisation of Britain's trade with the People's Republic.[32]

On the basis of the 'ice-breaker' mission was formed a China Trade Committee within BCPIT, with Roland Berger as chairman.[33] The mission subsequently came into a good deal of criticism, and its members were under heavy pressure to leave the group. Five firms from the original mission later resigned, one of the reasons being that they felt that their association with the members of BCPIT reduced their chance of obtaining export licences from the British government. J.B. Scott, a director of Crompton Parkinson and Co. Ltd, wrote to Lu Xuzhang, General Manager of CNIEC in Beijing, that it was impossible for Crompton Parkinson and Co. Ltd to work through BCPIT or associated organisations since the latter were *persona non grata* with the British government.[34] S. Gordon Sloan, sales director of Messrs Rubery Owen, who had obtained a large order from China for cart wheels and axles during the 'ice-breaker' mission, recalled the stern warning given him by Anthony Eden when he was summoned to the Foreign Office after the trip. It was clear to the enthusiasts for the China trade that unless they had the blessing of the British government it would be extremely difficult to make this a successful undertaking. The best course of action would be to steer clear of political implications and to focus on the commercial benefits of such trade for Britain and on the tradition of Anglo–Chinese friendship.[35]

The China Trade Committee's subsequent efforts to invite the Chinese to Britain to negotiate the balance of the contracts under the Business Arrangement proved abortive owing to their inability to obtain visas for their Chinese visitors. Through their contacts with the CNIEC office in East Berlin, the Chinese there agreed early in 1954 to receive a group of interested businessmen – about 30 of them – in March. The Foreign Office made a public statement on 13 March to the effect that the government did not wish to see British businessmen go to East Berlin under the auspices of BCPIT.

In spite of this discouragement from the authorities, representatives of 48 firms eventually made the trip to East Berlin in April. They included 18 large manufacturers, 13 medium-sized and six smaller firms, ten merchant companies and one shipping company. In order to coordinate the somewhat factionalised interests of manufacturing concerns and merchant companies, and to better represent their position in negotiations with the Chinese, the group met in a Kempinski Hotel in Kurfürstendamm, Berlin, and decided to form a Liaison Committee, with S. Gordon Sloan appointed as Chairman and Roland Berger as its consultant. The move was a sensible one and was welcomed by the Chinese. A business package of £3.6 million was concluded on 30 April, with some contracts on a tentative basis in anticipation of a relaxed export control by the government.

The Liaison Committee continued to meet after the Berlin trip to discuss ways and means of continuing trade with China on behalf of the firms it represented. This was the beginning of The '48 Group of British Traders with China' under the chairmanship of S.G. Sloan, which was to carry on and expand in the next 30 years. Berger worked full-time on the job, and the association used the BCPIT secretariat due to its own limited staff. In spite of its association with BCPIT, The '48' Group in general maintained its non-political, commercial character by eschewing political comments and focusing instead on the themes of trade and friendship with China. The association stated that it did not expect a monopoly in the trade with China, nor did it have any wish to appear to be competing with other bodies now in the field under the leadership of FBI. As the contracts under the Business Arrangement duly expired at the end of June 1954, the Liaison Committee set as a priority item on its agenda the exploration of the possibility of a further visit by the group to Beijing.[36]

From the inception of this unofficial trade association, a central task was to remove the obstacles to the China trade by mobilising public opinion against embargoes and bringing pressure to bear on the government for a greater number of contracts to get through. In early 1955 the '48' Group organised its first delegation of British businessmen to China; which will be discussed later in this chapter.

GENEVA TRADE TALKS

Faced with the new development in Sino–British trade, firms who had declined to associate themselves with BCPIT became anxious over lost business with China. Some argued that it was illogical for the government to try to eliminate BCPIT by political pressure whilst giving them the credit of conducting a successful mission to Beijing and bringing about a relaxation of licensing regulations on goods such as motor cars and compressors.[37] The Foreign Office was anxious to find a way to get the old China firms involved in the new reorientation of Sino–British trade. The BoT agreed that the government would give the old firms support if it could associate any possible relaxation in future with some group or mission other than BCPIT or its associates. An official intimated, 'We cannot hope to reinstate the Hong Kong channel of trade straight away: we may never succeed in that. We therefore must proceed gradually and if we can assist a pale pink organisation to get itself established in place of a red one we are at least moving in the right direction; and at the next stage, we may be able to go to a still better colour'.[38]

At the end of 1953 the Federation of British Industries, London Chamber of Commerce and China Association consulted to explore ways of increased trade with China within the permitted limits imposed by the strategic embargo. FBI Overseas Director Peter Tennant (later Sir Peter) knew H.J. Collar and John Keswick of the China Association personally, and they were the driving force behind the new endeavour. In March 1954 the three organisations decided that they would sponsor a responsible group in order to establish direct contacts with Chinese trade organisations and even to organise business trips to China. With the approval of the British government, on 29 March 1954 the three organisations addressed a letter signed by their presidents to the Chinese Minister for Foreign Trade Ye Jizhuang. They raised their objection to the arrangements with BCPIT 'whereby all enquiries from China are channelled through one small and unrepresented organisation in London'. They also declared that the three bodies would set up a joint organisation to approach the Chinese on trade matters, having between them 'a membership of several tens of thousands of firms, including practically all British manufacturing companies of substance'.[39]

The Chinese government appeared to be keenly interested in seeing trade grow, which it welcomed as part of the political thaw. The letter, having been pruned by the Foreign Office, was eventually delivered on 24 April with its original postdate to the MFA, attached to a diplomatic note, so as to be forwarded to Ye Jizhuang.[40] Trevelyan also informed the MFA that he would soon be going to Geneva to accompany Anthony Eden at the conference on Indo–China.

The Chinese quickly followed this up by sending Vice-Minister for Foreign Trade Lei Zhenmin to Geneva as a member of the Chinese delegation. On 27 April Trevelyan met Lei in Geneva and discussed the letter with him. At a dinner party for Lei on 30 April, Trevelyan told Lei that the three organisations were still awaiting a reply from the Chinese government. Commenting wryly about the ongoing negotiations in East Berlin between CNIEC and some 50 British business firms (that is the '48' Group, who were to conclude their deals with CNIEC on that very day), Trevelyan remarked that should the Chinese opt for the three organisations there would be 500 British firms at China's doorsteps, not 50. Lei said that he would like to talk with a representative of the three groups in Geneva if it could be arranged.[41]

Trevelyan suggested the name of Peter Tennant from FBI, whom he knew well through their earlier work together in Germany for the British Foreign Service. The Foreign Office made considerable effort in avoiding publicity about Tennant's unexpected trip to Geneva. For fear that 'in the present state of opinion in America this might cause all sorts of undesirable repercussions', the Foreign Office suggested that Tennant should say to the press that he was going to see Gilbert Holliday, the UK Commercial Counsellor in Berne (where FBI had an office), and was simply passing through Geneva. Berne, Beijing and Washington were all warned about this fiction.[42]

Two series of meetings took place in Geneva on 6–7 May, and on 26–28 May. The Chinese were represented by Lei, Shi Zhi-ang and interpreter Zhou, and the British by Trevelyan, Tennant and Joe Ford. Sir Peter Tennant later recalled the ambience of those meetings, which were held inside a suite occupied by the Chinese delegation in Hotel Beau Rivage in Geneva. The room 'was equipped with sufficient stage props specially brought from China. . . . The homely atmosphere of respectability and indiscriminate mid-Victorian taste is one that seems indissolubly linked with modern communism, a faithful tribute to the English lodging house days of Marx, Engels and Lenin. In spite of the standard lamp it did not appear that the room was wired for sound and our hosts were discreet enough to unplug the only telephone in the room from its wall socket. The conversation took place in an atmosphere of general courtesy and grinning affability, punctuated with rounds of luke-warm China tea and Chinese cigarettes'.[43] The following issues were discussed.

(1) The British agreed with the Chinese suggestion that lists of goods should be exchanged on a regular basis. When the British provided their first lists, the Chinese stated that though they contained much of their needs, they were narrow in scope. In the end Trevelyan had to break diplomatic convention by stating that the issue of embargoes was not up for discussion at this juncture because this was beyond their competence.[44] The British seemed nonetheless aware of possible political leverage if they could play the card of embargoes to their advantage.

(2) The Chinese raised the possibility of an inter-governmental trade agreement in view of their need to plan ahead for their production requirements and their fear of interruptions of trade in the absence of a government agreement. In spite of the careful and patient efforts by the Chinese negotiators, who knew how sensitive the issue was, they failed to bring their British counterparts any

closer to agreeing to work on an agreement, or even some general statement of intent by both sides. The British authorities suspected that this Chinese proposal was 'primarily designed for political effect'.[45]

(3) Both sides agreed to an exchange of business visits. Peter Tennant in particular grasped the opportunity to drive home the point that the organisations he represented could be very useful to Chinese visitors when they came to Britain. The plan for a Chinese trade mission to Britain was announced by FBI President Sir Norman Kipping at a press conference in London on 3 June, and was confirmed by the Chinese delegation in Geneva in a press release on the 7 June.[46]

One achievement of the talks for the Chinese was that they seemed to have dispelled doubts in the minds of the British about their eagerness to trade. Tennant noted that the Chinese Vice-Minister 'warmly responded' to Tennant's expression of hope that the Chinese would visit Britain. Later Lei told Trevelyan that 'he would like a visit by the Chinese delegation to be in May or June, because the contracts concluded last year by British commercial representatives had expired', evidently in a reference to the Business Arrangement with the 'ice-breaker' mission. Also the British seemed to have a good impression of the Chinese they dealt with. After the first Chinese trade mission left Britain later in the year, Trevelyan was to write that 'they were clearly interested in trade for its own sake, not only for its propaganda value. This represents a great change from 1953'.[47]

SBTC, THE '48' GROUP AND BUSINESS VISITS 1954–5

Peter Tennant took back to Britain what had been agreed upon by the two sides for a Chinese trade mission to Britain, as well as Harold (later Baron) Caccia's promise to issue visas on behalf of the Foreign Office.[48] This led to a discussion as to what body should receive the Chinese visitors on their arrival, and also arrange their programme. It was decided that direct sponsorship by some leading business organisations in the country would give it enhanced standing in the eyes of the Chinese. In the event, five bodies decided on 11 June 1954 to form themselves into a Sino–British Trade Committee. Sir Harry Pilkington was elected its first chairman.[49]

These five bodies were the Association of British Chambers of Commerce, The China Association, the FBI, the London Chamber of Commerce, and the National Union of Manufacturers. Together they had a very wide coverage of British trade and industry through their membership and affiliated trade associations, and thus represented a powerful force entering onto the scene of Sino–British trade.[50] It was agreed that the Presidents of each association should in turn occupy the chair of the new body, and that each should in turn provide secretarial services, with the five organisations sharing the modest expenses. In 1957 SBTC reconstituted itself into a Council. Through years of development it became a quasi-official body in the 1980s – the Area Advisory Group on China to the British Overseas Trade Board (BOTB), with an annual subvention from the British government.

In their press release the Chinese delegation in Geneva announced the intention of their trade mission to contact BCPIT and other business groups while they were in Britain.[51] This upset the sponsoring organisations of SBTC who feared that BCPIT would either make propaganda or reap their own commercial profits out of the visit, as well as make SBTC look ridiculous. It was suggested that BCPIT was 'not merely a political, but also a commercial racket, whose trading practices are most undesirable'. It looked as though the entire arrangement would be jeopardised because of the bad feelings thus generated. The FBI and its associates threatened to withdraw their sponsorship if the Chinese did not give a satisfactory assurance not to see BCPIT people, and insisted that if they failed to do so the government should withhold visas from the Chinese, or at least impose administrative delay.[52]

The Foreign Office quickly came to the rescue by instructing Trevelyan to tell the Chinese delegation in Geneva about SBTC's objection to BCPIT stealing a march on them in the visit. Both Huan Xiang and Lei Zhenmin in their meetings with Trevelyan gave reassurance that the visit would be arranged exclusively by the five organisations. On the other hand the Chinese group would not wish to be prevented from seeing firms and individuals other than those recommended by the five bodies. The British government decided that to withdraw now would be unwise. 'To withdraw now would play right into the hands of the B.C.P.I.T. We could not justify withdrawal by the Chinese wish to visit firms which invite them, but which are not on the associations' list'. Trevelyan then told the Chinese delegation in Geneva of the British decision to proceed with the visit, and that the British government had no intention of restricting the activities of the Chinese mission in Britain.[53]

The trade mission consisted of 11 members, led by Cao Zhongshu, Deputy Director of CNIEC, and arrived on 28 June. They were given specific instructions by the authorities in Beijing to explain China's good faith and desire to normalise trade with Britain, and to be even-handed towards various British trade groups. The mission held discussions with about 25 trade associations, visited some 19 works, attended two well-arranged exhibitions, and held business talks with 56 firms. The official functions lasted from 29 June to 9 July.[54]

The visit brought the Chinese into direct contact with British manufacturers and drove home to them the advantages of broadening their avenues of contact. The Chambers of Commerce at various localities gave the Chinese visitors VIP treatment, especially in Manchester where they were met personally by its Chamber's president at the station. Their hearts were warmed at seeing 'WELCOME!' and their national flag on display at some plants and hotels where they were guests. The Chinese visitors left it in no doubt that they were anxious to see the embargo lifted or modified. The fact that they were shown only part of some manufacturing factories in Sheffield and elsewhere disquieted them. Nor did they fail to notice a lack of orders, which caused some of the plants they visited to operate below capacity, including two alloy steel works in Sheffield, the GEC, ICI and Austin Motors facilities.

They said that they preferred to finance their buying on letters of guarantee terms and their selling on letters of credit because, as they believed to be the case, if they were owners of goods on the high seas they would run the risk of capture from the US-inspired blockade by the Taiwan authorities and other possible interceptions. They wished also to avoid the risk of credits opened abroad being frozen. On the other hand, they recognised the need to make exceptions to the present system under which final inspection of goods and arbitration were to be conducted in China. They equally realised that although dealings with manufacturers were more direct they could not overlook the possibilities of the service offered by merchants to both the sellers and the buyers. They reassured their British hosts that Chinese trade organisations would choose their trade partners on the basis of commercial considerations and would not reject business on the pretext of any political reason or beliefs.[55]

The Chinese visitors refused to be deterred from seeing other people after the official programme was over. Unofficial visits included a dinner party arranged by William Robson-Brown (Conservative MP for Esher), a visit to the South Wales Steel Works, a lunch with the '48' Group, a dinner by BCPIT, and a supper buffet by LEC – all crowded into three days. Finally, on 13 July, the mission gave a farewell cocktail party which was attended by some 400 guests. They left London for Geneva on the 14 July, 'having gone through an ordeal which must have taxed their stamina as much as the famous thousand-mile march to Yenan'.[56]

At the end of July SBTC accepted a Chinese invitation to send a return British trade mission to China. Since it would be impossible to include all the 62 applicants in one trip, SBTC suggested splitting their delegation into two groups. They also wanted the Chinese to put emphasis on light industry for the first group, and on heavy industrial products for the next trip in 1955, in the hope that the second visit would be so timed as to coincide with government measures to ease the China trade controls.[57] The visit took place in November–December 1954, the first of its kind organised by SBTC. Led by W.G. Pullen, General Manager of the Chartered Bank, and accompanied by H.J. Collar, the delegation was 37 strong and included members from both Britain and Hong Kong, representing 27 industrial establishments, two banks and one shipping concern.[58] Together, they signed about £4 million worth of business with CNIEC, to the great delight of the established firms.[59] The results of the visit confirmed the impression that China's major object was trade rather than politics. The Chinese hosts were also able to reciprocate British hospitality with the efficiency of their arrangements for both travel and business discussions.[60]

The trade mission finished formal negotiations in Beijing and then went in small groups to Wuhan, Shanghai and Guangzhou for varying numbers of days before crossing the border to Hong Kong. Some of them picked up small business deals on their way out, others were able to revisit their old acquaintances and settle business problems. It was a complete contrast to what many of the Old China Hands had experienced just a few years before.

In 1955 two more business trips to China were organised in the first half of the year, one by the '48' Group, the other by SBTC. The Chinese government apparently wanted to strike a balance between the two organisations by giving an equal amount of business to both. Some firms participated in group visits sponsored by both organisations for the sake of business flexibility.

The '48' Group arranged their first trade mission to China through the Chinese commercial counsellor's office in London and CNIEC's office in Berlin. The visit began on 5 February 1955 and was led by J.A. Blott and S. Gordon Sloan, with 24 individuals representing 19 firms. Approximately half of them were buyers of Chinese produce, the rest were selling firms and firms wishing to explore business opportunities for the future. By the time the mission left for home on 22 February, the business which the members concluded with the Chinese amounted to about £4 million in all, with a rough balance in trade in either direction. The Chinese agreed to export a total value of £1.75 million, in return for £2.25 million worth of British exports.[61] It was reported that the largest amount of business was done by LEC (about £900 000), followed by Biddle and Sawyer (about £500 000). On the whole, the trip was regarded as a success under Berger's expert guidance. One of the purposes of the mission was to reassure the Chinese trade organisations that the '48' Group would remain in being, specialising in trade with China on the principle of equality and mutual advantage. Both sides in their talks agreed to maintain close contact in the period ahead through exchange of enquiries and business visits.

The Chinese refused to enter into provisional contracts in respect of strategic goods as suggested by competing British businessmen. However they issued to one or two firms letters of intent against the time when restrictions might be relaxed. Enquiries were particularly directed towards high-grade steels. The Chinese hosts showed thoughtful consideration in respect of the mission's activities in China and were very helpful in arranging visits to Shanghai, Tianjin and other cities when requested. They added new commodities to their export lists and negotiated contract terms with rapidity and sensibility. After the visit to China, and arising directly from the mission's negotiations, a further volume of business amounting to £132 000 in British exports was concluded through correspondence.[62]

The '48' Group's mission was followed hot on the heels by the second SBTC group, which was in Beijing from 30 March to 15 April. Fifteen members of the delegation also visited Shanghai for some 10 days. The total amount of business done was much less than the first group, about £1.25 million, mainly Chinese exports. In spite of the disappointing amount of business concluded, its members agreed that the visit was 'well worth while'.[63] It was suspected that the small amount of business done was due to Chinese commitments to the Soviet bloc and possibly also to trade with Japan, and that it was likely that the Chinese were holding back their exports lest the members of the British mission, who were mostly in heavy industrial fields, did not have a lot to offer in return owing to the trade embargo. A basic scarcity of Chinese produce for export appeared to have forced the Chinese leadership to divert their limited amount of foreign exchange away from buying raw materials such as cotton and wool from abroad.[64]

Notwithstanding CNIEC's expressed preference for this method of doing business, neither SBTC nor the '48' Group was able to fix a date for further group visits to China or Berlin during the rest of 1955. The Chinese expressed the hope that the visits would soon be resumed after some restrictions had been removed. Another, perhaps related, reason was suggested that Chinese trade organisations had already undertaken heavy commitments over the next months for the reception of business parties and trade delegations from other parts of the world.[65]

Throughout the rest of 1955 and in 1956, expectations were raised among British businesses over the imminent possibility of the British government getting ready to remove certain controls over exports to China. This led British firms to postpone further visits to China. Through the Chinese commercial counsellor in London the '48' Group did succeed in organising a businessmen's trip to the Leipzig Fair early in 1956, which resulted in the conclusion with CNIEC of some export deals from Britain with a value of £780 000.[66]

Thanks to the direct contacts that had been made during the visits in both countries, and more importantly as a result of agreement on some basic principles and trading procedures, both sides were able to improve the channels for inquiries and placing orders through correspondence. The Chinese for instance wrote to ask for advice on the marketing in Britain of Chinese green and black soya beans, machines for the manufacture of needles, and plywood. They also made inquiries about goods produced in Britain which could be considered marginal in terms of strategic significance. In the spring of 1956 representatives of the China National Native Produce Corporation were added to the office of the Chinese commercial counsellor in London, who also undertook to negotiate on behalf of other corporations concerned with the export trade. The new system was understandably still fragile and not nearly fully satisfactory, but a basic structure was laid down for the new type of trade to operate between the two countries, and over the years certain improvements were made in those problematic areas of trade as experience accumulated.

BILATERAL TRADE: ISSUES AND PROBLEMS

Conditions for trade between China and Britain improved after the Geneva talks in 1954, thanks to the vision and efforts of people in both countries. Lei Zhenmin met with visiting British politicians in Geneva to discuss ways of developing better trade relations, and Zhou Enlai and Anthony Eden gave their support to the initiative. In respect of the reception given to trade delegations from Britain, there is evidence to suggest that the Chinese hosts endeavoured to avoid any possible discrimination affecting the standing of either SBTC or the '48' Group.

In addition the Chinese became increasingly relaxed with regard to contract terms. This included an informal switch from letters of guarantee terms (payment conditional on the arrival and inspection of goods) to confirmed irrevocable letters of credit (bank promise to pay prior to actual delivery) with respect to British exports; and from payment against telegraphic advice of shipments of Chinese exports to Britain before the documents of title had been received, to payment against presentation of the original shipping documents (air-mailed to the buyer directly after the goods had been loaded on board ships).[67] While they had maintained the provision for the final inspection of Chinese goods in China, by the time the Blott party was in China, CNIEC waived their earlier insistence upon inspection of British products in UK factories by 'experts' chosen by them.[68] A number of key issues which affected trade during this period may be identified as follows:

Government Policies

That the British government discriminated politically in favour of SBTC and its associates against BCPIT and the '48' Group, there was little doubt. Anthony Eden made another statement in Parliament on 8 November 1954, in which he reiterated the advice given by the government to British firms not to associate themselves directly or indirectly with the activities of BCPIT. A Foreign Office official referred to these communist-sponsored channels of trade 'which we want to see perish, and might even kill'. A controversial figure was Roland Berger, whose association with BCPIT (besides his employment by the '48' Group as consultant) continued to set the '48' Group against the displeasure of the government. LEC was also deemed by the government as suspect.[69]

As a result, while the British Chargé d'Affaires was specifically instructed by the Foreign Office not to give the Blott party a reception nor to attend any reception given to the '48' Group by the Chinese hosts in early 1955, the British officials in Beijing acted as an intermediary to facilitate SBTC's missions with the Chinese government.[70] Berger's public statements opposing embargoes were not of much help in endearing himself with the establishment.[71]

This political division sharpened the differences between trade associations, which in turn threatened individual firms' business opportunities. As much as some of the members of both SBTC and the '48' Group desired to see it happen, the two trade associations failed to reconcile their views about a better form of cooperation or even a merger largely because of the latter's BCPIT connection. As early as 1954 SBTC considered the possibility of including on their Committee 'a representative of the Sloan Group' and asking Sloan himself for co-option to the Committee.[72]

On the part of the Chinese authorities, while they were careful to avoid giving impressions of favouring one group of British firms over another, for some time they did place considerably large orders with a few firms such as LEC.[73] There were indications that the Chinese authorities were concerned about unfavourable opinions among their British friends and partners with respect to this state of affairs, and wished to correct the imbalance in favour of a few firms while giving them full credit for their contributions to Sino–British trade.[74]

Always looming large in the background were the ideological animosity and political mistrust of the cold war, which dictated foreign policy choices for China and Britain. Other than Britain's stance on China's representation at the United Nations, China's sensitivity to Britain's handling of certain crisis issues, such as the military tension in the Taiwan Straits, the riots in Kowloon and the Suez crisis in 1956, dampened Beijing's mood and threatened to negate the modest gains which had been made in trade exchanges between the two countries.[75]

Britain on its part was forced to fall in line with the rest of the Western world in enforcing the multinational embargoes, and in so doing found itself straitjacketed over any bold steps to expand trade with China. This was apparent in the government's dilemma between an instinctive reaction against British businessmen engaging in any form of negotiations with China for the future sale of strategic goods, and its desire to see provisional contracts concluded in anticipation of the imminent relaxation of the embargo. On this matter optimism was initially fuelled by the British government after the US government, on 12 November 1954, expressed its readiness to discuss with Britain whether the China and Soviet lists should be equated. The Americans later retreated from this position and the matter was deferred. The Chinese made reference to the failure of Austin Motors, Crompton Parkinson and China Engineers to supply against provisional contracts, which had obvious adverse effects on plans. Disappointed, the Chinese refused to sign provisional contracts with the British, although they did not mind entering into initial discussions on embargoed goods, which required lengthy considerations on technical grounds prior to contractual talks.[76]

Foreign Competition

An important factor affecting Sino–British trade was competition from other countries for such trade. There is no doubt that the embargo caused structural damage to Sino–British and Hong Kong trade, one of its effects being the Chinese inability to obtain spare parts for British machinery already installed in China. There were reportedly some 2000 power plants in China made by Babcock and Wilcox alone, whereas their spare parts were not allowed to go to China. In some instances this forced the Chinese to learn how to make their own spares, specifically regarding certain turbine generators, automobiles and machinery. In the longer run however China switched its attention to other countries for capital goods. While the Soviet Union and other East European countries remained China's main industrial suppliers, its trade became increasingly diversified after the Korean armistice, especially with other West European countries.

During the Geneva conference in 1954 the Chinese delegation held talks with West German and Belgian business representatives on the exchange of visits. Later that year China began to import a limited amount of goods (not permitted by Britain) from other West European countries, among which were complete electric power plants from Switzerland and Sweden.[77] Chinese sources reveal that some of the goods were manufactured in Britain and West Germany and transhipped through Austria and Sweden. Chinese officials also went to Japan, Italy, France, West Germany and Austria for trade talks in 1955 and 1956, which resulted in agreements for the supply of tractors from France and West Germany, galvanised steel and other steel products from Japan and other countries.[78]

There were other problems which gave foreign suppliers a competitive edge. While there was probably a natural tendency for some Chinese to identify all difficulties of current British supply with the embargo itself, it was recognised that in effect a shortage of some industrial supplies existed in British industry, such as heavier grades of steel. Also British prices compared with those on the Continent of many iron and steel and non-ferrous metals were said to be 'substantially higher'[79] In the face of increasing competition from European suppliers of industrial equipment and machinery, it was feared that Britain might fall back in the race.

Standardisation of Trade Practices

Many problems in Sino–British trade arose from disparities in each other's trade procedures. Their causes could be traced partly to the anomalies of the international environment, and partly to the features of China's state trading. The problems were discussed extensively among British businessmen and Chinese trade officials during their visits but some of them were to remain unsolved for many years to come.

For instance the Chinese told British visitors that, under the Chinese Regulations on Trade and Patents of 1950, revitalisation of previous British trade marks through re-registration was a matter for the two governments, possibly to be covered in a commercial treaty. However in the absence of full diplomatic relations this appeared to be out of the question. Both sides agreed in principle for future exchanges of technicians and the desirability of individual visits, which the British believed would give them added advantage in influencing the way China placed orders with British suppliers. But these were either difficult to arrange or subject to government control on each side. The British government held that 'there may be serious security objections to our training young Chinese technicians at this stage', especially in factories also manufacturing defence equipment and embargoed goods. It was also argued that given China's security consciousness 'it seems very unlikely that they would allow British technicians into China for training Chinese in the use of "strategic" equipment'. The Chinese cited the limitations on the export to China of capital equipment and a virtual absence of deals for installing complete British plants as one reason for the deferral of actual implementation of such exchange programmes.[80] In October 1957 a modest step was finally taken when the first group of Chinese technicians visited Britain.

In respect of actual contract terms and execution, no progress was made over the years concerning the question of *force majeur* clauses bearing on interception of goods on the high seas. Nor for that matter was there much to be said about uniform letter of credit terms being brought into line with international practice. The British deemed the terms of payment not satisfactory, in particular regarding certain categories of goods such as Chinese native produce, for which the Chinese organisations concerned would insist on payment by TT before the documents of title had been received rather than payment against presentation of documents. Also, while China insisted on the final inspection of goods for Britain, British traders pointed to the lack of facilities for rapid and independent inspection in China.[81]

It was assumed that once inspection procedures were placed on a mutually advantageous footing the need for recourse to arbitration would be much less likely to arise. As things stood at the time, many disputes arose over allegations of shortcomings on the part of either Chinese or British traders in quality, selection, weight outturns, in addition to late shipments and even failures to obtain freight, which could not be resolved speedily through normal legal channels. Cases which were brought to the attention of Chinese trade organisations included the discovery of salmonella in hen albumen, the delayed shipments of feathers, quality problems concerning meat, hog casings and bristles, losses in weight outturns in gallnuts, failures in shipping soyabeans and sunflower seeds, the lack of a standard description of textiles, the incompetence of officials of the China National Native Produce Corporation – which earned it a bad name among British traders – and British shipment problems related to tinplate and other products.

An added complexity was that British traders would not agree to arbitration being held in China on grounds of the absence of any known arbitration law and facilities in China, nor did China agree to use the rules of the International Chamber of Commerce. The Chinese government promulgated a set of provisional rules governing the procedures of CCPIT Foreign Trade Arbitration Committee in 1956, and another one on maritime affairs in 1959, but the problems persisted. British critique of the provisional rules of procedure for CCPIT's Chinese Foreign Trade Arbitration Committee was that there were various references in the rules to decisions which would have to be made under Chinese law, whereas in fact no definite Chinese law was known to have been published. The main point was that the rules were clearly intended to cover arbitration in China only. If the principle that arbitration should be held in the country of the defendant was accepted, to which the Chinese said they would agree, then difficulties were bound to arise since it was extremely unlikely that the rules of the Chinese Foreign Trade Arbitration Committee could be applied to arbitration in the UK. In their reply to ICC enquiries CCPIT admitted that there was no domestic Chinese law relating to enforcement of arbitral awards – such enforcements would therefore be entirely subject to arrangements agreed with other countries as part of trade agreements.[82]

Marketing

British traders pointed to a number of factors which militated against increasing the sales of Chinese produce in the West: (1) lack of statistical information about crops and supplies; (2) the difficulty in obtaining standard samples; (3) changes in long established classifications; (4) sporadic offers of produce rather than a regular flow of offers to keep buyers interested, and unsatisfactory Chinese replies to firm bids from the UK.[83]

Some typical Chinese cable clichés which the Chinese themselves later criticised include: FUTURE BUSINESS HOPEFUL DO YOUR UTMOST THIS WILL LEAD TO FUTURE BUSINESS; PRICE TOO HIGH REQUEST LOWEST; COMPETITION STRONGEST BUSINESS DEPENDS ENTIRELY ROCKBOTTOM CABLE UTMOST REDUCTION; OFFER LOWEST; OFFER ROCKBOTTOM. As China expanded her trade with an increasing number of countries, her internal supply lines for goods to be exported became more strained. At one point CNIEC officials admitted that it was possible to vary the pattern of internal consumption in accordance with the need for exports. This genuinely surprised the British. To go with it was a Chinese tendency to overprice their exports, presumably for want of up-to-date information on world market movements.

A point which was very much debated in the discussions on China produce was the serious disadvantage to the Chinese of allowing their produce to be sold through Eastern Europe at a discount. Representatives of firms which were traditional buyers of China produce told the Chinese that if a merchant in the UK knew (as he was bound to in many cases since so much China produce was carried in British ships) that a consignment of China produce was en route to an East European country which was not itself a consumer of these goods, the natural tendency was for the UK merchant to hold off buying direct from China until the East European country had had to unload the goods and the price had fallen.[84] The Chinese admitted that by selling China produce to the East European countries they were able in return to buy machinery which the West denied them under the embargo, even if this meant that they had to trade at a loss in both directions.

The possibility of China bringing to an end such resales by East European countries was discussed, and CNIEC eventually agreed to give preemptive rights to British importers for certain products. Union International Co., for instance, obtained preemptive rights over the Chinese export surplus of eggs in 1955 and 1956. The total volume in the two years would be about 30 000 tons, worth £5–6 million. Under the terms of the arrangement the Chinese would sell only small quantities of eggs to other countries and those entirely for internal consumption. UI would have to exercise their option to buy by a certain date each year. After that date the Chinese would be free to sell where they liked. Other suggestions included an arrangement whereby China would sell her bristles in the London Auction Market or through the medium of companies such as Rouda and Fongas Ltd.

MODIFICATIONS OF THE CHINA EMBARGO

While the British government ought to be given credit for taking the decision to remove the China Differential in 1957, concerted political pressure from the business community and the general public in Britain and elsewhere provided the driving force which ultimately compelled the government to come to grips with reality.

A major argument was that Britain was not likely to make any proposals which would appeal to China so long as the goods she could supply were restricted to the existing narrow range.[85] It was also stated that the embargo was not effective, either because other Western countries continued to supply goods to China as a result of their national rules differing from those in Britain, or because goods manufactured in Western Europe eventually found their way into China through Eastern Europe. The Chinese trade organisations for instance found that a product which was on the embargo list in

Britain was not embargoed but only on the shipping prohibited list in the Netherlands, and that therefore it was possible for a Dutch exporter to obtain an export licence for it and put it onto a British ship, to be carried via a British port to China. It was also reported that Czechoslovakia and the Soviet Union supplied their trucks and tractors to China and then obtained their supplies from West European countries. 'Leyland trucks were found in China although Leyland avowed they had not supplied them.'[86] More and more people in the British government recognised that the additional items prohibited for China but allowed for export to Eastern Europe were not justified on strategic grounds. Indeed, as one official document stated, US Secretary of State J.F. Dulles himself said at a press conference in May 1956, 'If they had been strategic they would have been on the Soviet list'.[87]

In the summer of 1956 the British government declared that it would make a greater use of COCOM's 'exceptions procedures' with regard to those goods considered to be marginal in strategic significance. The Chinese trade organisations welcomed the move, and British traders felt that they should urge the government to go further. There was increasing hope that export licences would be considered for goods not on the Soviet list, which promised to open up prospects of a substantial increase in the trade between China and Britain. On the grounds of trial assignments, export licences for agricultural tractors were issued in April 1956 to three British firms in three consignments of 20 each, with a total value of £115 640. Such tractors were on the China 'Special List', and official cooperation of CHINCOM became essential for such transactions to go through.[88]

The sense of insecurity continued to haunt trading partners on both sides of transactions. In some cases the Chinese hedged their bets by providing 'stiff penalty clauses' lest unexpected changes delayed or prevented actual deliveries. Tractor firms reported that their contracts provided that 0.5 per cent of the value of the shipment would be payable as a penalty by the exporter for each week's delay beyond the contracted date of delivery up to 10 weeks, and that thereafter the purchaser was at liberty to cancel the contract.[89] There was criticism of the length of time required for applications to get through, and it was understood that this was partly due to the continued need to refer to COCOM. Each British firm would need to find out how the procedures applied so far as its own commodities were concerned for the China market, and the Chinese said that they did not wish to create embarrassment by making inquiries which would receive a negative answer. Thus uncertainty was aggravated simply because neither the government, nor the two sides to the transaction, knew exactly what to expect of the application.[90]

If the Chinese were cautiously optimistic at first, they soon began to express displeasure at the haphazard manner in which trade would have to be conducted. They did not place many orders during the latter part of 1956, much to the dismay of the '48' Group and firms such as LEC. The Chinese could not help viewing the procedures in a larger political context. They objected to themselves having to be at the mercy of British licensing authorities, who could conceivably turn the tap on and off as they wished. Nor were they prepared to appear to concede to the legality of the restrictions by corroborating that the goods they ordered were for civilian end-use. The China Resources Corporation, a Chinese-owned trading firm based in Hong Kong, was known not to have agreed to issue such corroboration documents.[91]

Early in 1957 British trade associations made strong representations to the government urging that the Prime Minister should raise with Eisenhower during their talks in Bermuda the question of bringing the embargo on exports to China at least into line with the strategic list which applied to the Soviet Union. They also urged the government to take unilateral action if agreement could not be reached at COCOM–CHINCOM.[92]

As Trevelyan later wrote, in the end the British Government summoned up their courage, ignored American pressure and came off the China Differential. Foreign Secretary Selwyn Lloyd made a statement in Parliament on 30 May 1957 to that effect.[93] Con O'Neill, the British Chargé in Beijing, reported that the Chinese officials at MFA felt a good deal of satisfaction at the British step and spoke warmly about it. It was hoped that such satisfaction, even if it was for a wrong reason, 'may have, temporarily, its trading advantages'.[94] In effect the Chinese viewed the British step from both political and economic angles. In a document issued on 15 August 1957, the Ministry of Foreign Trade held the view that Britain appeared to pursue a more independent political line after the Suez Canal crisis, but that it was also pressured at home for greater overseas markets for its exports. Judging from the American attitude to the economic restraints which led to such British actions in the past, the Chinese felt that it was entirely likely that the Americans had acquiesced in the British move this time. They also knew exactly how many items were thus freed from the embargo and how many more were still banned for export to China.

There was no doubt that the Chinese viewed the partial relaxation as an important step towards further widening the scope of normalised trade with West European countries and Japan. The campaign was by no means over for a complete abolition of the trade restrictions, with Britain as its focal point. In China's overall trade relationship with the capitalist world, the emphasis would continue to be placed on Japan. The economic factors could hardly be overlooked. Freed from the limitations of the China Differential, British exporters would face the greater challenge of competing with Japan, Switzerland, Sweden and other countries for a share in the China trade. Thus O'Neill wrote, 'It may well be that following the relaxation of the controls we shall obtain more of this share than before provided that our prices and delivery dates justify the Chinese in giving us the preference'.[95]

The British were determined to keep up the momentum and to take advantage of the new development. In June 1957 SBTC reached agreement with the Chinese commercial counsellor in London on an exchange programme of trade missions in the second half of the year. Lists of British businessmen applying for the China mission were being prepared throughout the rest of the year. After extensive preparations F.J. Erroll, Parliamentary Under-Secretary to BoT, visited China in October for three weeks and was received by Zhou Enlai. His mission covered many cities in Northeastern and Central China, with the focus on further trade possibilities in both directions between China and Britain.[96]

Meanwhile, the Sino–British Trade Committee reconstituted itself into a top-level Council to receive a Chinese economic and technical mission led by Dr Ji Chaoding.[97] The main body of the mission arrived in Britain on 22 October and was received by Sir David Eccles, President of BoT, the following day. The Chinese guests visited various academic, technical, research and professional institutions, including the nuclear power station at Calder Hall, the British Standards Institution, the Patent Office, and the UK Atomic Energy Authority. They also contacted nearly 200 firms during their visits to factories and production centres within the five-week schedule. A textile machinery advance party, authorised to enter into direct commercial negotiations on behalf of the China National Technical Import Corporation, concluded contracts worth more than £700 000 for the supply of textile machinery, including a complete woollen textile mill.

Most of the firms regarded the continuance of the embargo as a serious impediment to their prospects of expanding their trade with China. An SBTC report concluded, 'It was instructive to note that a very wide range of the products in which the Mission was most interested were embargoed goods'. Officials at the UK Atomic Energy Authority expressed the opinion afterwards, 'There may be a substantial market in China for radio-isotope for agricultural purposes and that the visits enhanced the business prospects for these products'.[98] All in all, Dr Ji's mission was widely regarded in Britain as one of the most important events for the business community in 1957.

For overall Sino–British commercial relations, the year 1957 ended on a fairly positive note. The Chinese statistics show the total volume of trade between China and Britain as US$102 280 000, including US$43 930 000 for exports to Britain, and US$58 350 000 for imports from Britain. The total Chinese trade volume for the year was US$3.103 billion, and the British share was thus 3.29 per cent of that total.[99] Later in 1957, Chinese Premier Zhou Enlai stressed to F.J. Erroll and other British visitors the country's shortage of foreign currency as being the main economic factor which would militate against a greatly expanded trade with Britain during the Second Five Year Plan. The difficulty in organising sufficient supply nationwide for exports was compounded by China's scheduled repayment of some of the Soviet loans and for the new projects in which the Soviet Union and other socialist countries were assisting her.[100]

In effect, the Chinese government was about to work out a revised plan to allocate a greater share of her resources to trade with Britain in return for the partial relaxation by the British government. A number of very large barter transactions were to be negotiated in 1958, and the overall trade volume was to increase further. There was also a decision to allow trade organisations to negotiate a greater number of provisional contracts for embargoed goods from Britain. From 1957 to 1958 British exports of electrical machinery to China doubled, other machinery went up four-fold, and iron and steel, five-fold.[101] The total volume of Sino–British trade amounted to US$203 950 000; Chinese export into Britain being US$75 730 000, and import into China US$128 220 000, an increase of 99.4 per cent over the 1957 figure. The total volume of China's foreign trade for 1958 was US$3.87 billion, and the British share amounted to 5.27 per cent of that figure, as shown in table 8.

The years 1959–60 saw the sale and beginning of delivery of six Vickers Viscount aircraft for China's national airline CAAC

Table 8   Sino–British trade and its share in China's foreign trade
(in millions of US dollars)

	China–UK Trade*	China's Total Foreign Trade**	Percentage Share
1950	73.51	1135	6.38
1951	35.07	1955	1.79
1952	25.81	1941	1.33
1953	97.04	2368	4.09
1954	70.68	2433	2.92
1955	104.63	3145	3.33
1956	112.50	3208	3.51
1957	102.28	3103	3.30
1958	203.95	3871	5.27

* *Almanac of China's Economy* (1982), VIII, p. 43.
** *Almanac of China's Foreign Economic Relations and Trade* (1987), p. 1123.

(negotiated by some members of SBTC), followed in subsequent years by sales of Trident airliners to China. Meanwhile a Chinese mission was invited by the British Aircraft Corporation to the Farnborough Air Show in the autumn of 1960.[102] All this seemed to be very realistic, sensible and benefitial to both sides.

In 1957 ten British companies were still operating in Shanghai, of which five had British managers. In contrast 74 British firms had been reported to exist in Shanghai in 1952. In about 20 cases British property was directly requisitioned by the Chinese authorities. In addition to any eventual claims in respect of British commercial interests in China, the outstanding debt on the previous Chinese government's sterling bonds according to a British estimate amounted to just over £60 million, on which no payment had been made since 1939. Interest over this period would have amounted to a further £40–50 million.[103] It would take another 30 years for the two governments to reach an agreement to settle the old claims from each side, including the properties requisitioned during the Korean war.[104]

In contrast to fairly active business exchanges, a cold atmosphere prevailed at the political level, characterised by low-key official contacts. If the Chinese, judging from official positions, press commentaries, and private indications of intentions, had acted on the presumption that they could influence British policy-makers in such a way as to drive a wedge between Britain and the United States – a policy which not doubt had its simplicity and appeal – they appeared by 1957–8 to have realised that such attempts had largely been ineffective in vital East–West issues. In particular the nature and intensity of the political differences between China and Britain had remained virtually unchanged, despite the Geneva talks and improved diplomatic channels. China was now set to take a long-term view by keeping the flow of bilateral relations running but within narrow banks, focusing on areas such as trade, where countries like Britain were seen to have been allowed to retain some autonomy from the United States, and from which China could expect to derive tangible benefits and even some goodwill for her efforts.[105] From the viewpoint of the top CCP leadership bigger issues, such as the domestic campaign of the Great Leap Forward, with its disastrous economic consequences and deep political ramifications, and the oncoming break with the Soviet Union, would soon occupy China's full attention.

7 Conclusion

China's commercial relationship with Britain from 1949 onwards began with the CCP's policies and actions regarding private British interests inside Chinese territory. It is best viewed initially in the context of Beijing's efforts to reverse the historical trend by restoring Chinese control over institutions and practices which had been identified as manifestations of Western encroachment of the nation's sovereign rights and independence. These represented the first element embodied in the concept of national liberation: the power and ability to eliminate foreign domination over the key sectors of government and of the country's economic life. The British government at first hoped that the Chinese communists might face insurmountable economic weaknesses which the West could utilise to their advantage. The recognition that Britain lacked strong cards in this respect, combined with the policy of containment which was gaining currency following the start of the Cold War, led Britain to an increasing reliance on the multi-layer regime of export restrictions as political tension mounted.

The other necessary component of China's national self-assertion was a desire to be able to defend itself against foreign military action. That went beyond the removal of foreign nationals from the service of Chinese maritime customs, the nationalisation of inland shipping and commodity inspection, as well trade and financial controls. Primarily it underscored a concern over the country's national security. Judging from the *Amethyst* episode and the ensuing American-inspired blockade, the line must have struck the CCP leadership as being very thinly drawn indeed between the traditional version of 'gunboat diplomacy' or encirclement on the one hand, and an outright naked use of force on the other.

The danger of a national crisis became real as General MacArthur's forces marched towards the Yalu River. The sense of national heroism in China was heightened by the magnitude of a convulsion so close to the two wars prior to it, and by the fact that the enemy was inherently superior in force and power. While the Americans proved themselves pertinacious – though not invincible – combatants, the Chinese tasted the full flavour of an allied relationship with the Soviet Union long after the war ended.

Above all, national liberation in the Chinese context demanded a recognition from other governments of China's equality with all others, and of the right to dictate its own terms for the manner and shape of its foreign relations. If it was possible that a sense of vengeance engendered by the *Amethyst*'s escape in the summer of 1949 produced a political ripple, it was far more likely that the real reason for the deliberate delay in Sino–British diplomatic negotiations after Britain granted Beijing recognition was a combination of Beijing's doubt about British sincerity and its displeasure at London's reservation over the CCP's claim to exclusive representation of the Chinese nation in world affairs. The issue became a flashpoint of tension over China's seat in the United Nations, and over Chinese properties stranded outside its jurisdiction. The interposition of the American seventh Fleet in the Taiwan Straits at the outbreak of the Korean conflict was seen by Beijing as an American ploy to deny the PRC government of its authority to do what it wanted with any part of Chinese territory. The British attitude on the status of Taiwan was ambiguous and opportunistic, which contributed to the decision by the CCP leadership to minimise official contact with Britain. The diplomatic stand-off particularly infuriated the British mission in Beijing, some of whose members tended to show their resentment by counselling confrontation. Private British businesses and individuals, despite repeated assurances from the Central People's Government that their legitimate interests and personal safety would be duly protected, suffered the inevitable consequence of political isolation.

Thus the CCP's notion of national liberation in terms of what had happened in the past was not separable from the immediate diplomatic issues bearing on the present situation and future events. The history of British presence in China and the existing foreign policy position of the British government towards Beijing were two salient points in a continuous political spectrum. History might indeed be capable of repeating itself even under changed circumstances, what with the classic elements of trade, the national flag, and diplomacy on the coast – in spite of a *de jure* recognition from the British government this time, and in spite of renewed offers of sympathy and goodwill to the Chinese people by private British traders and managers.

It was no accident that commercial activities between China and Britain continued to be overshadowed by international politics, which may well have been an extension of the entangled past relationship. Side by side with China's disillusionment with the West was Beijing's ideological conviction that only from within the international communist movement could China find political recognition and material support. Beijing was more embarrassed than troubled by the bossy behaviour of the Soviet leadership of the day. While China's socialist programme enhanced the sense of solidarity between Beijing and other 'People's Democracies', the realities inside the country clashed with Western perception and antagonised British political opinion.

No matter how insensitive the CCP leadership might then have been to Western public opinion, it may readily be appreciated that the country's self-interests alone would have compelled the government to refrain from taking action to imperil the entire British commercial presence as a pre-requisite to socialism. At least during the period of recovery and material preparation, British capital and expertise could be useful for regenerating productivity and growth. In 1949 British banks and merchant houses proceeded to undertake specialised business operations with government blessing. Hong Kong never posited as a possible target of a forcible takeover; branches of the Bank of China continued to function in London and later in other Western financial centres. The PRC however refused to compromise on the question of previous foreign debt and loans as it was such a politically charged issue, nor did it see a necessary connection between this and China's prospect of doing trade with the same credit countries. It was in the 1980s that the insistence of the Bank of England on such a linkage, combined with China's practical desire to secure a foothold in the world capital market, finally brought Beijing to negotiate with London a lump-sum settlement of the old claims, without making concessions over its principle against the 'odious debt'.

There is no evidence to suggest that the CCP actually envisaged nationalisation of Western firms and expulsion of Western nationals after the founding of the People's Republic. In spite of some latter-day assertions to the contrary, there are persistent claims that the actual implementation of a 'sweep-the-house-clean' policy – if not its very utterance – was not confirmed officially until late 1950.

All available evidence points to the efforts of the CCP authorities after the 1949 revolution to prevent foreign capital, equipment and skills from leaving the country, in addition to preparations by the Foreign Enterprises Bureau for introducing new legislation on joint ventures, intended for use for years to come. Some commentators point to the government's centralised control over foreign exchange and trade, as well as efforts to delay the departure of foreign technicians and managers, as evidence of coercive measures to preserve the existing fragile economic structure; if these measures were considered excessive at times, perhaps their harshness was not deliberately intended. Again, while there are bound to be suggestions that local authorities pressured British firms to remit funds from Hong Kong and Britain in order to exact the historical 'pound of flesh', the immediate challenge to the nation, as seen by the top PRC leadership at the time of a nationwide depression, must have been to get the machines running on the factory floor rather than revenge.

The deflationary measure and labour militancy, it is true, caused great hardships to private interests, foreign and Chinese alike, aggravated at times and in places by stringent taxation and acute shortages of supply. But it would be fair to say that the government's central concern went beyond a mere vindication of ideological principles, especially if peaceful construction were to be allowed. The Korean war heightened the political tension between China and Western governments, and the Chinese government's primary concern for national security made whatever restraint had hitherto been needed for preserving British capital and expertise less urgent.

China's import offensive in the second half of 1950, coupled with a realistic adjustment of the government's industrial policies, alleviated the difficulties of British businesses. The Korean conflict rendered the desirability of regulated Western investment and possible joint ventures a moot issue, while Britain's summary deprivation of Chinese property rights triggered off Chinese retaliations. With the benefit of hindsight, it may be suggested that the British government probably could have avoided running the hare unnecessarily, unless the rationale was one of helping oneself *pour encourager les autres*.

Meanwhile, British firms found themselves being ground between Chinese restrictions on the one hand and the enforced embargoes of the British government on the other. As far as was allowed under the circumstances, the Chinese authorities followed the general guideline for a gradual process of socialisation of the domestic economy. This meant avoidance of massive closures of private businesses for the sake of production and social security, coupled with a policy to restrict the profit margins of private property owners and rent takers in deference of new ethical values. The old, decadent metropolises had to go, together with their racecourses, mile-long bars, stock exchanges and taipans' clubs, and in their place would rise new industrial centres, puritanical and egalitarian, drawing strength not from the Bund or the Nanking Road, but from the militant tradition of the working class.

A resolve to cut losses and to 'stop pumping in good money after bad' led the British firms to withdraw from China on the formula of the Yee Tsoong settlement. The Chinese government for its part refused to allow simultaneous closures, apparently for fear of disrupted production and aggravated unemployment. Whether or not the delay in the official processing of closure applications was centrally orchestrated, the effect for some firms was an accumulation of their liabilities in unpaid wages and taxes, which were then used to offset their assets upon their withdrawal. In the absence of agreed procedures, the Chinese were seen to have followed the same instinct to outwit their business opponents for the best bargain possible as in any other kind of wheeling and dealing, except that in this case time and the laws were on their side. While Soviet-supplied plants predisposed the Chinese to some extent to forfeit potential benefits from Western commercial presence, in many cases the disposal of British assets created gaps in industry and services which remained unfilled for years to come. For those British firms who tried to hang on, their ability to supply equipment and parts from the West was substantially curtailed by the ongoing embargo.

The Western embargo forced Beijing to seek new channels of trade, principally from Eastern Europe. CNIEC's various deals with British businessmen in Moscow, Beijing and East Berlin were shrewd moves to beat the sanctions and princely '*hongs*' commission-taking from the sidelines, although the efforts to cheapen import costs were partially offset by other departments underpricing Chinese exports to Eastern Europe in return for industrial supplies. Marginal utility in this case was not determined by free-market conditions, but by a political decision to choose between the devil of enforced scarcity and the deep blue sea.

From the outset, British strategic export controls on China hinged on the presence of a Soviet connection and on a pragmatic concern to avoid antagonising Beijing. Faced with a dilemma, Britain endeavoured at first to maintain a façade of legalistic correctness, combined with an under-the-counter administrative control. Paradoxically Whitehall felt less restrained legally and morally after the adoption of the UN embargo resolution, and set out to upgrade the level of the controls and to branch away into new areas of supplementary devices: transhipment, voyage licensing, bunkering, TAC and IC/DV, well beyond the explicit mandate of the United Nations. The CG–COCOM machinery admittedly was largely of America's making; its effectiveness was in direct proportion to the willingness of other members to follow the American lead, or to be compelled by ECA and Battle Act conditionality. Britain for her part played the role of a reliable partner once the rules of the game were agreed, and the force of inertia thus generated made it difficult for the authorities to turn around in the wake of the Korean armistice and the Geneva conference.

After fiddling the books for some time by means of exceptions procedures, CHINCOM members gathered enough courage to break ranks with the US by abolishing the China Differential. Britain did not join the mutiny without paying a price, which was a tacit commitment to a US lead in the China policy for the Western world for the next decade or more.

Anxious to maintain a veneer of dignity and justification, the British government appeared most touchy at the mere mention of its embargo policy being prolonged with little common sense. This in part explains Whitehall's resentment towards BCPIT and the '48' Group, and was an underlying factor in Trevelyan's refusal to consider the possibility of entering into a trade agreement with China during the Geneva trade talks, for fear of giving the Chinese a convenient peg on which to hang possible arguments against the trade restrictions. In the background was always a concern for American sensitivity, to the extent that considerable pains were taken to create a fiction about the Geneva trade talks, and to make sure that Britain would not go forward to upgrade her diplomatic relations with Beijing without first checking with the United States.

The Chinese government did not completely free itself from the problem of potential claims from private British individuals to their property rights in China, although the authorities did take care to avoid future entanglements by settling the assets and liabilities strictly according to legal rules. The Chinese experience shows that, unlike foreign films and other forms of popular culture which could in principle be replaced cost-free with a different ideological model, foreign ownership in tangible assets inside the host country can either be accommodated or disposed of by official action or inaction, which entails government responsibilities giving a reason for diplomatic representation by countries of which the property owners concerned were nationals. This is a question worth pondering both in assessing historical events and for the benefit of future policies on the part of capital importing and exporting countries. Britain's official representation for her nationals in the 1950s was weak, largely owing to anomalies in bilateral political relations. Nor does it necessarily mean that a repetition of that history may be affordable in future for either of the two countries. Suitable legal frameworks, standardisation of contract terms, and mutually acceptable levels of taxation and wage scales fall into the related category of conditions of entry, in addition to other business incentives from the host country, designed to make capital ventures attractive and worthwhile to foreign investors.

In the field of trade, China finally saw the emergence of a more equitable relationship with Britain. China's trade with most other countries was regulated by government or quasi-government agreements, but Britain resisted the idea in favour of private initiatives and *laissez faire* tradition. What business arrangements had been agreed between CNIEC, BCPIT and the '48' Group tended to be wide of the target in actual implementation, as China's bilaterally planned trade with the West at times appeared less stable and more subject to erratic fluctuations than had been expected. That does not mean that China's trade arrangements with British groups did not have their stimulating effect on Sino–British trade as a whole, particularly in view of the greater potential that did become discernable on both sides once trading conditions improved. In this respect, it is believed that the newcomers on the British side may have deserved a good deal more recognition from the government for their contribution throughout the years than they actually received. This was not possible at the time when not a few among government and business circles wished either to see that side of the trade perish or even to kill it.

Politicised trading tended to cut both ways. On the Chinese side, the negative effect tended to be exacerbated by centralised bureaucratic control. The Chinese admission that they could curtail domestic consumption for the sake of exports genuinely shocked the British (they still do), but the larger problem was that, given the built-in continuity in the purchasing pattern of a State trading partner such as China – which in turn generated an inertia against supply diversification – once initial business opportunities were lost to other competitors in the market such as Japan and continental Europe, traditional trading partners such as Britain tended to face an uphill task of launching into new products and even new sectors, with higher risks and opportunity costs. This might be true for imports as well as exports, given the inconvertibility of the *Renminbi*, which perpetuated a Chinese element of barter trade.

Both in the case of the negotiations for the release of the *Amethyst*, and of those for better diplomatic and commercial relations with Britain, the Chinese proved to be tough and subtle negotiators, who were seen always to proceed from the larger political framework and to seek a linkage between substance and symbolism, principles and formality, focus and perspective, immediate concerns and related issues. The British demonstrated a significant degree of flexibility at times, especially when encouraged or pushed by Parliamentary politics and public opinion. Both countries worked hard to advance their own best interests, whereas neither side was prepared to compromise without conditions. Painstaking efforts were required to reach some basic understanding about each other's intentions, so as to avoid or minimise potential conflict of interests. While trade developed steadily if slowly through the rest of the 1950s and 1960s, disagreement in their political commitments tended to pull the two countries in opposite directions. It took the Vietnam war and a major strategic realignment between China and the United States in the 1970s to usher in a real rapprochement between China and Britain. There is little doubt that throughout the period of reforms and openness from the late 1970s to the 1980s, the normalisation of Sino–British relations immeasurably improved the environment in which various forms of cooperative endeavours flourished. But to turn that political advantage into serious commercial benefit requires further imaginative efforts to overcome the effects of historical handicaps and contemporary differences in order to create more opportunities for many years to come.

Notes and References

1 China and Britain: A Theme of National Liberation

1. G.C. Allen and Audrey G. Donnithorne, *Western Enterprise in Far Eastern Economic Development: China and Japan*, 1954, pp. 265–68; Cheng Yu-kwei, *Foreign Trade and Industrial Development of China*, 1956, p. 8.
2. Wu Chengming, *Di Guo Zhu Yi Zai Jiu Zhong Guo De Tou Zi* (The Investments of Imperialists in Old China), 1958, p. 41.
3. Jerome Ch'en, *China and the West*, p. 207. See also W. Willoughby, *Foreign Rights and Interests in China*, vol. 2, 1927, pp. 544–77, 595–8, 602–13.
4. Treaty of Tientsin, Art. XXXVII, in William F. Mayers, *Treaties Between the Empire of China and Foreign Powers*, 1906, p. 17.
5. *Shang Hai Gang Shi Hua* (Historical Accounts of the Shanghai Port), 1979, pp. 36–7.
6. See Zhao Shu-min, *Zhong Guo Hai Guan Shi* (History of China's Maritime Customs), 1982, pp. 22–46. With reference to the Chinese authorities' agreement to foreign inspectorate, see W. Willoughby, *op.cit.*, vol. 2, pp. 769–70.
7. See S.F. Wright, *China's Struggle for Tariff Autonomy*, 1938; Zhao Shu-min, *op. cit.* pp. 27–38.
8. See Liu Kuang-chiang, *Anglo–American Steamship Rivalry in China, 1862–1874*, 1962; Charles Drage, Taikoo, 1970; Colin N. Crisswell, *The Taipans, Hong Kong Merchant Princes*, 1981. See also *Historical Accounts of the Shanghai Port*, pp. 193–240; *Archives of the China Merchant's Steam Navigation Company*, Maritime Transport Administration Bureau of the Ministry of Transport, Shanghai.
9. Chi-ming Hou, *Foreign Interests and Economic Development in China, 1840–1937*, 1965, pp. 17–18. Chinese Marxist economists subdivide 'direct investment' into 'productive capital–assets' and 'landed property'; and 'loans' into 'direct borrowings' and 'Boxer Indemnity payments', arguing that no direct foreign capital investment was involved in foreigners' land speculation and Chinese payments of war indemnities. Their figures, as a result, have come out somewhat differently. See Wu Chengming, *op.cit.* pp. 52, 64.
10. Harold C. Hinton, *China's Turbulent Quest*, 1970, pp. 11, 17; E. LeFevour, *Western Enterprise in Late Ch'ing China*, 1968, p. 49. D.K. Fieldhouse (ed.), *The Theory of Capitalist Imperialism*, 1967, p. 93.
11. Cheng Yu-Kwei, *op.cit*, pp. 48–9, 89–90; Zhang Zhongli, 'The Development of Foreign Enterprises in Old China and Its Characteristics – The Case of the British–American Tobacco Company', in *SASS Papers*, 1986, pp. 132–73, at 134; Zhang Zhongli and Chen Zengnian, *Sha Xun Ji Tuan Zai Jiu Zhong Guo* (The Sassoon Group in Old China), 1985, pp. 56–9.

12. See A.K. Cairncross, *Home and Foreign Investment, 1870–1913*, 1953, p. 235.
13. Mao Zedong, 'On New Democracy', *SW*, 2:354.
14. See Robert F. Dernberger, in D. Perkins (ed.) *China's Modern Economy in Historical Perspective*, 1975, pp. 19–35; Mark Elvin, *The Pattern of The Chinese Past*, 1973, p. 298; E. LeFevour, *op.cit.*, pp. 2, 130–1.
15. R. Dernberger, *op.cit.*, 30–5; John G. Gurley, *China's Economy and the Maoist Strategy*, 1976, p. 98; for counter-arguments, see E. LeFevour, pp. 4, 131. See also Lan Yiqiong, *Jie Kai Di Guo Zhu Yi Zai Jiu Zhong Guo Tou Zi De Hei Mu* (Unveil the Medusa of Imperialist Countries' Investment in Old China), 1962, pp. 34–5, 49–55; Wu Chengming, *op.cit.* pp. 5–6.
16. 'Treaty between the Republic of China and the United Kingdom and India for the Relinquishment of Extra-territorial Rights in China and the Regulation of Related matters' (With Exchange of Notes and Agreed Minute), signed at Chungking, 11 Jan. 1943; ratification was exchanged at Chongqing, 20 May 1943. Yin-Ching Chen, *Treaties and Agreements Between the Republic of China and Other Powers 1929–1954*, 1957, pp. 140–8; Wesley R. Fishel, *The End of Extraterritoriality in China*, 1952, pp. 210–12.
17. Aron Shai, *Britain and China, 1941–47*, 1984, p. 22.
18. *Aide Memoire* prepared for Sir William Strang, 10 Jan., *CA: M & C*, vol. I, no. 49/G/2; A. Shai, *op.cit.*, p. 21.
19. E. Luard, *Britain and China*, 1962, p. 57. See also FO371/279, 280 and 281 for Chinese and British positions on various points during the negotiations.
20. *Historical Accounts of the Shanghai Port*, pp. 153–8; *Aide Memoire* by the British Embassy at Nanking to the Chinese government, on the question of re-opening Yangtze ports to foreign flag vessels, 12 May 1947, F7458, FO371/63275; Extract from Issue no. 131 of News Messages from Nanking, 14 March 1947, F3753, FO371/63275; a report by Commercial Journal 30 Jan. 1947, in F2454, FO371/63374. The pressure was said also to have come from the Communists, see accounts of a conversation between Stevenson and Chiang, letter from R.S. Stevenson to M.E. Dening, 29 Jan. 1947, F2645, FO371/63274.
21. Statement by Lord Ailwyn, House of Lords, 1947, cited in letter from G.V. Kitson to G.A. Wallinger, Nanking, 12 Feb. 1947, F1407, FO371/63274. See also Nanking to FO No. 001, 17 June 1947, F9104, FO371/63276; L.H. Lamb to FO, 9 Aug. 1947, F11937, FO371/63726.
22. *Historical Accounts of the Shanghai Port, op.cit.* pp. 105–7.
23. BoT to Shanghai, No. 1 Askew, 18 Nov. 1946, BT11/3390.
24. Shanghai to BoT, No. 11 Askew, 24 March 1947, *ibid.*
25. A.L. Scott (FO) to L.H. Lamb (Nanking), 2 Sept. 1947, BT11/3390.
26. Note of a BoT meeting, 19 Oct. 1948, BT11/4139; H.O. Hooper to A.S. Gilbert, 8 Sep. 1947, F12378/37/10, FO371/63308.
27. A. Shai, *op.cit.* p. 149; Allen and Donnithorne, *op.cit.* p. 263. See also Parliament question, 8 May 1950, FC1106/106, FO371/83347.
28. J.C. Hutchison (Commercial Minister at Shanghai), 1947, BT11/3390. Information received from about 40 firms suggested that approximately

£7 million would be required to replace war damage to their physical assets. Shanghai to BoT, No. 11 Askew, 24 March 1947, *ibid.*

29. Parliament question, 8 May 1950, FC1106/106, FO371/83347; R.S. Stevenson to Dr Wang Shih-chieh, Nanking, 12 July, 1948, BT11/3390.

30. Note by MoT, in Roland Liem to Bottomley, letter dated 14 Oct. 1947, BT11/3406.

31. The British estimates appear to be at variance with the Chinese statistics, probably owing to a difference in ways of calculation. The total amount of British capital based on Chinese figures was US$1 095 337 000 in 1941 and US$1 033 674 000 in 1948, which, at the exchange rate of $4.03, would be £271 795 780 and £256 494 790. These then broke down into four sub-figures for each year, including Enterprise Investment (US$545 859 000 and US$393 752 000 for 1941 and 1948 respectively, or £135 448 800 and £97 705 211), Real Estate (US$219 504 000 and US$321 763 000, or £54 467 494 and £79 841 936), Loans (US$314 438 000 and US$318 159 000, or £78 024 318 and £78 947 643), and Boxer Indemnity Payment (US$15 536 000, or £3 855 087, for 1941 alone). Wu Chengming, *op.cit.* p. 52.

32. E.G. Price (B & S) to J.C. Hutchison, 24 Dec. 1947, BT11/3406; *Historical Accounts of the Shanghai Port, op.cit.* pp. 154–8.

33. Printed letter despatch from Shanghai to Nanking, 28 Jan. 1948, BT11/3406. These were admitted by British officials to have constituted a disguised form of encroachment upon China's navigation rights.

34. 'British Shipping Interests in the China Trade', Jan. 1949, FO371/75864.

35. *Financial Times* (China) 21 March 1949, *Archives of the China Merchant Steam Navigation Co.*, File No. 502/634, Shanghai.

36. Zhao Shu-min, *op.cit.* p. 50.

37. Wu Chengming, *op.cit.* p. 59.

38. Memorandum on the position of British banks in China, encl. in Nanking to FO, 9 Jan. 1948, F1771, FO371/69617. See also Nancy B. Tucker, *Patterns in the Dust*, 1983, p. 117.

39. Wu Chengming, *op.cit.* p. 68; p. 52.

40. According to British officials, high in this roll of dishonour stood the names of the shipping and other transportation interests such as those controlled by Tu Yueh-sheng and Li Yun-liang, both being officials of the National Federation of Shipping Guilds, and having ample connections with the government. L.H. Lamb to P.W.S.Y. Scarlett (FO), 30 June 1948, BT11/3406. See also I.C. Mackenzie to BoT, 6 Oct. 1948, F15619, FO371/69619.

41. J.R. Hobhouse to Major General R.C. Money (MoT), 29 July 1948, BT11/3406; John Gittings, *The World and China*, 1974, pp. 123–4, 128; Lands and buildings occupied by American military forces were exempt from rent and other charges. Lan Yiqong, *op.cit.* pp. 73–5.

42. As John King Fairbank wrote, 'having backed the [Guomindang] government increasingly since 1937, we [the Americans] could not in the Chinese view divest ourselves of responsibility for its evils . . .' John K. Fairbank, *The United States and China*, 1979, p. 348.

43. Mao, 'Introducing *The Communist*', *SW*, 2:289.

44. Mao, 'Chinese Revolution and Chinese Communist Party', *SW*, 2:313, 318–320.
45. Mao, *Ibid.*, 309–10; 'On New Democracy', *SW*, 2:341.
46. Mao, 'Chinese Revolution and Chinese Communist Party', *SW*, 2:315, 318. This is also in line with Lenin's idea: for Lenin, as for the Chinese Communists, salvation of the nation was not merely the basis for tactical manoeuvres, but was a virtue in itself. Fairbank and Feuerwerker (eds) *CHC*, vol. 13, p. 837.
47. Mao, 'On New Democracy', *SW*, 2:355.
48. *Ibid.*, 2:353.
49. 'Chinese Revolution and Chinese Communist Party', *SW*, 2:327. Mao wrote – during the heyday of the anti-Japanese war – that the new-democratic revolution 'aims at the nationalization of all the big enterprises and capital of the imperialists, traitors and reactionaries'. A similar statement was contained in the Constitutional Guidelines of the Soviet Republic of China, adopted by the Worker–Peasant–Soldier Representative Congress in Jiangxi in November 1931.
50. 'The CCP Central Committee Directive on the Work of Foreign Affairs', 18 Aug. 1944. In addition Mao was reported to have told US diplomat John Service in August 1944 and in March 1945 that China would need foreign, and especially American, capital in the post-war period. *FRUS 1944*, 6:613, *FRUS 1945*, 7:272–8, cited in Beverley Hooper, *China Stands Up*, 1986, p. 65.
51. 'The CCP Central Committee Directive on the Treatment of Foreign Nationals in China', 7 Feb. 1948.
52. The CCP Central Committee Directive on the Work of Diplomatic Affairs of 19 Jan. 1949.
53. Mao, *SW*, 4:370.
54. Han Nianlong *et al.* (eds) *Dang Dai Zhong Guo Wai Jiao* (China Today: Diplomacy), 1987, pp. 18–19; John Gittings, *The World and China 1922–1972*, 1974, pp. 178–9.
55. See Foreign Affairs College, *Zhong Hua Ren Min Gong He Guo Dui Wai Guan Xi Shi* (History of Foreign Relations of the PRC), 1964, p. 217; Jin Licheng *et al.*, *Shang Hai Gang Shi* (History of the Shanghai Port), 1986, pp. 18–23. See also Shanghai MCC's Provisional Regulations for Foreign Shipping, Enclosure, BBC Monitoring, 24 June 1949, in F9420/127/10, and F9653/1271/10, FO371/75919.
56. See F3385/1271/10, FO371/75918. The instructions about the change came directly from the North China Ministry of Communications in Beijing, see Stevenson (Nanjing) to FO, 19 July 1949, F10894/1271/10, FO371/75919. According to British law (Section 74 of the Merchant Shipping Act, 1894), the master was liable to a fine for not flying the national flag while the ship might not be underwritten should any incident occur in foreign territorial waters involving arrests or damages.
57. Report by L.V. Rowe, Master of *s.s.Hunan*, 3 March 1949, F6865/1271/10, FO371/75919; J.A. Blackwood to John Swire and Sons, 10 June 1949, F9658/1271/10, FO371/75919.
58. T.L.C. 'Report on Annual Accounts for 1949', 217 *JSS*, VII 3/7, 1949,

SOAS; FO Minute (P.D. Coates), 10 March 1949, F3462/1271/10, FO371/75918.

59. See Foreign Affairs College, *op.cit.*, p. 216–7. Up to Nov. 1949, 109 foreigners were said to remain in the service of Chinese Maritime Customs, of whom three-quarters were British subjects. They received their emoluments partly in the form of local pay, on the same scale as Chinese members of the Service, and partly in the form of sterling allotments. The Chinese authorities indicated their intention that at some point in time foreign Customs employees should be paid solely at Chinese rates. P.W. Scarlett to Mitchell, 10 Nov. 1949, *CA: FO Correspondence File* (1945–49), SOAS.

60. These laws and regulations are contained in Victor F.S. Sit (ed.), *Commercial Laws and Business Regulations of the People's Republic of China 1949–1983*, 1983, pp. 357, 378 and 414.

61. Letter from Tianjin Commodities Inspection Bureau to all the Appointed Banks, 29 Sept. 1949. The two British firms involved were the Borrows & Co. (cargo surveyors, marine measurers, fire adjusters and inspectors of export produce), and William Forbes & Co. Ltd. (Lloyd's agents conducting surveys required in connection with adjustment of losses insured by Lloyd's subsidiaries). The Swiss firm was Messrs. Liebermann Waelchli, which had acted as approved analysts for the British Ministry of Food in connection with the imports of Chinese eggs and other products. British Consul-General in Tianjin to FO, 4 May 1950, FC1106/95, FO371/83347; *CA: M & C* 50/G/36, 11 May 1950, *M & C*, 1950, SOAS. See also SASS, *Shang Hai Jing Ji* (Shanghai's Economy), *vol. I: 1949–1982*, 1983, p. 704.

62. R.Y. Frost (Shell), notes on trading conditions in North China, 9 July 1949, F10174/1121/10, FO371/75856; Michael Lindsay's memorandum, appendix to *CA: M. & C.* 1949, no. 49/E/15, 1 Nov. 1949.

63. *CA: Bull.* No. 35, 49/M/4, 20 April 1949; FO minute (E. Dening), 9 May 1949, F7350/1116/10 and FO minute 11 June 1949, F8403/1116/10, FO371/75851. In Shanghai, all the American banks were included. Among the British owned ones, notable omissions were the Mercantile Bank of India and the E.D. Sassoon Banking Company. FO agreed that the list of appointed banks in Shanghai showed no evidence of discrimination on a national basis, but the FO was visibly unhappy that American banks were better favoured. See Shanghai to FO, no. 444, 10 June 1949, and FO to Shanghai, no. 302, 16 June 1949, F8466/1116/10, FO371/75851.

64. H.F. Morford (Chartered Bank) to C.E. Loombe, BoE, 21 March 1949, F4953/1116/10, and HSBC (Tianjin) to Hong Kong (A. Morse), 2 May 1949, F8596/1116/10, FO371/75851.

65. See L.G. Frost (Jardine, Matheson & Co.) to the People's Bank of China, Tianjin, 31 December 1949, *HKBGA: SHG II*, 222. See also Temporary Regulations for Foreign Exchange Control for East China, *RMRB*, 11 June 1949, p. 2.

66. Circular Letter from BoC Foreign Dept to Appointed Banks, 11 July 1949, *HKBGA: SHG II*, 275.

67. W.R. Connor Green, Consul (Commercial, Tianjin) to J.C. Hutchison

(Shanghai), 8 May 1949, F8969/1121/10, FO371/75854; P.E. Scarlett to G.E. Mitchell, 20 Dec. 1949, F17859/1116/10, FO371/75852.
68. BCC Shanghai to CA no. 17, *CA: M & C*, 1949, no. 49/G.75, 28 Nov. 1949; Hughes and Luard, *The Economic Development of Communist China, 1948–1958*, 1959, pp. 23–6.
69. *CA: Bull.*, no. 42, 49/M/13, 20 Nov. 1949; R.Y. Frost's notes on trading conditions in North China, 9 July 1949, F10174/1121/10, FO371/75856; *RMRB*, 13 May 1949.
70. For reference on British remittances, see *CA: M. & C*, 1949, no. 49/F/15, 20 July 1949; memorandum by BCC Shanghai, *CA: M. & C*, 1950, no. 50/E/17, 13 Nov. 1950. The matter of dislocated exchange rate was also discussed between John Keswick and the Director of the Foreign Affairs Bureau Zhang Hanfu, J. Keswick's report from Shanghai, 29 Aug. 1949, enclosed in W.J. Keswick to Dening 28 Sept. 1949, F14852/1153/10, FO371/75867.
71. See SASS, *Shang Hai Jing Ji* (Shanghai's Economy), *op. cit.*, p. 807.
72. See Liu Binglin, *Jin Dai Zhong Guo Wai Zhai Shi Gao* (Draft History of Modern China's Foreign Debt) 1962; Carl F. Remer, *Foreign Investments in China*, 1933; *A Study of China's External Debt on January 1st, 1934, with a tentative scheme for the liquidation of the unsecured or insufficiently secured part of the said debt* (unsigned), dated 20 Feb. 1934, SASS collection.
73. '113th Annual Report of the Council of the Corporation of Foreign Bondholders', 1986. According to the report, between 1898 and 1936, there were 3 Customs Loans, 5 Salt Loans, 10 Railway Loans, plus the 8 per cent Skoda Loan of 1925. Willoughby classifies the loans into: (1) War and Indemnity Loans; (2) General or Administrative Loans; (3) Industrial, i.e. Railway and Mining Loans. Willoughby, *op.cit.*, vol. 2, pp. 978–1011.
74. Wu Chengming, *op.cit.* p. 77.
75. Liu Binglin, *op.cit.* pp. 13–19, 96–105. The Anglo–German Loan of 1898 had an issue price of 90, yielding 83 to the Chinese. With regard to the forms of discounting and their percentages, see Frank H.H. King, *The History of The Hongkong & Shanghai Banking Corporation, vol. 1, 1864–1902*, 1987.
76. Wilhelm Kuhlmann, *China's Foreign Debt 1865–1982*, 1982, p. 4; interview with the Bank of England, June 1987.
77. *Financial Times*, 6 June 1987.
78. W. Kuhlmann, *op.cit.*, pp. 9–11; '113th Annual Report . . .', *op. cit.*, pp. 27–8; R.S. Stevenson to Dr Wang Shih-chieh, Nanking, 12 July, 1948, BT11/3390. See also Letter from Earl of Bessborough, Chairman of the Chinese Bondholders' Committee, to Chinese Minister of Finance, Nanking, 3 Oct. 1947, BT11/3390; A.A.E. Franklin (FO) minute, 18 March 1950, FC1112/6, FO371/83361. The unpaid interests added another £162 million at the end of 1985, according to British negotiators.
79. Aide Memoire prepared for Sir William Strang, 10 Jan. 1949, *CA: M & C*. vol. 1, no. 49/G/2.
80. The amount of the 1941 credit agreement was £5 million. See draft letter from the Comptroller-General, BoT-ECGD, to PRC Minister of Finance,

25 Aug. 1950, FC1112/13, FO371/83361; Cf. Wilhelm Kuhlmann, *op.cit.* p. 6.

81. H. Somerville Smith (Comptroller-General, BoT) to PRC Minister of Finance, 24 Aug. 1950, FC1112/16, FO371/83361.

82. FO to Beijing, No. 75, 7 March 1950, FC1112/5, FO371/83361; CO to Hong Kong (Sir A. Grantham) no. 399, 21 March 1950, FC1112/5, FO371/83361. The amount of compensation claimed by Britain for the official *bona fide* loans was reported to have totalled over £35 million by 1985.

83. PRC-MFA, *Zhong Guo Wai Jiao Gai Lan* (A Survey of China's Diplomatic Relations) 1987, p. 455; *RMRB* (overseas ed.) 6 June 1987; *Financial Times*, 6 June 1987.

84. The texts of the three treaties are reprinted in *Guang Jiao Jing* (Wide Angle) Publishing House, *Xiang Gang yu Zhong Guo – Li Shi Wen Xian Zi Liao Hui Bian* (Hong Kong and China – A Collection of Historical Documents and Papers), vol. 1, 1984, pp. 168–82. See also G.B. Endacott, *A History of Hong Kong*, 2nd ed., 1973; Peter Wesley-Smith, *Unequal Treaty 1898–1997 China, Britain and Hong Kong's New Territories*, 1980.

85. H.C. Bough (Reuter) confidential memo. F124/1016/10, FO371/75779; Consul-Gen. (Peiping) to Secretary of State, telegram 27 Sept. 1949; *FRUS* (1949), 8:539, cited in Steve Tsang, 'Hong Kong Constitutional Development, 1949–52', D.Phil dissertation Oxon. 1986, pp. 124, 190.

86. Interview with Huan Xiang, Beijing, 27 July 1987; interview with Huang Hua, Beijing, 3 Sept. 1987.

87. *RMRB* editorial 8 Aug. 1963 and *Peking Review*, 15 March 1963; Chinese Mission to UN (Huang Hua) to the UN Special Committee on Independence for Colonial Countries and Peoples, letter 8 March 1972, UN Doc. A/AC.109/396.

88. The initialled text was published in 1984 (Beijing: Foreign Languages Press). The signing took place in Beijing on 19 Dec. 1984 by Zhao Ziyang and M. Thatcher, and ratifications were exchanged on 27 May 1985. See also Han Nianlong *et al.* (eds) *op. cit.*, 1987, pp. 378–83. The initialled text of the Joint declaration between China and Portugal on the question of Macao was carried in *RMRB* (overseas ed.) 27 March 1987.

2 New China: Diplomacy and Trade

1. Some of the works by Western writers in this field include Harrison Forman, *Blunder in Asia*, 1950; Ezra F. Vogel, *Canton under Communism*, 1971; Noel Barber, *The Fall of Shanghai*, 1979; Kenneth G. Lieberthal, *Revolution and Tradition in Tientsin, 1949–1952*, 1980; Nancy B. Tucker, *Patterns in the Dust*, 1983; Beverley Hooper, *China Stands Up*, 1986.

2. Mao, 'Report to the Second Plenary Session of the Seventh Central Committee of the Communist Party of China', 5 March 1949, *SW*, 4:370–1; Zheng Weizhi, 'Independence is the Basic Canon', *Beijing Review*, 7 Jan. 1985, p. 16; The common Program of the Chinese

People's Political Consultative Conference was more specific on existing treaty relations: the new government 'shall examine the treaties and agreements between the Kuomintang and foreign governments, and shall recognize, abrogate, revise, or re-negotiate them according to their respective contents'. *XHYB*, no. 1, 1949, pp. 8–10; *Documents of the First Plenary Session of the Chinese Political Consultative Conference*, 1949. No official record is available to show the exact occasion(s) on which the two principles were first advanced, whereas Zheng attributes them to the 2nd Session of the 7th CCP Central Committee.

3. Stevenson to FO, no. 368, 30 March 1949, F4793/1023/10, FO371/75808.
4. Tianjin to Nanjing, letter dated 23 May, 1949, F9115/10137/10, FO371/75808.
5. See Attlee's remarks, 26 April 1949, *PD*, 1948–9, Vol. 464, col. 26.
6. Stevenson to FO, no. 139, 1 Sept. 1949, F13102/1023/10, FO371/75814; and no. 1534, 19 Sept. 1949, F13268/1023/10, FO371/75815.
7. Stevenson to FO, no. 368, 30 March 1949, F4793/1023/10, FO371/75810; No. 685, 21 May 1949, F7514/10223/10, FO371/75811. Old memories were also revived at FO of the difficulties their 'ancestors' had in obtaining access to Chinese officials in the nineteenth century. FO minute (Coates) 29 April 1949, F5972/1023/10, FO371/57810.
8. Stevenson to FO, no. 530, 27 April 1949, F5917/1023/10, FO371/75810. *Cf*. B. Hooper, *China Stands Up*, 1986, pp. 171–2.
9. See, for instance, 'The Orientation of the Youth Movement', 4 May 1939, *SW*, 2:243–4; 'On the People's Democratic Dictatorship', *SW*, 4:415.
10. 'Report to the Second Plenary Session of the Seventh Central Committee of the Communist Party of China', *SW*, 4:371. See also *SW* of Zhou Enlai, Vol. I, p. 323.
11. Mao, 'Address to the Preparatory Meeting of the New Political Consultative Conference', 15 June 1949, *SW*, 4:408. The American representative in Shanghai observed that the new government's foreign affairs personnel displayed an obsession with possible secret sellout clauses between the Guomingang government and foreign powers, which was enhanced by their 'woeful lack' of archives because Guomindang officers had evacuated or destroyed their archives, including certified copies of treaties ratified by China. Shanghai 5200, 13 Dec. 1949, McConaughy to Secretary of State, *FRUS* (1949) 8:627–8.
12. The statement was drafted by Mao himself on 30 April 1949, *SW*, 4:401–3. See also Kang Maozhao, 'Hong Dong Yi Shi De Ying Jian Chang Jiang Shi Jian' (The British warship incident on the Yangtze which stirred public opinion), *SJZS* 1988, 8:25–6, 10:22–3, 11:22–5. For British accounts, see Attlee's remarks, 26 April 1949, *PD* 1948–49, Vol. 464, cols. 26–35; Lawrence Earl, *Yangtze Incident*, 1973; C.E. Lucas-Phillips, *Escape of the Amethyst*, 1957. Trivett, Dean of the Cathedral in Shanghai, wrote of a memorial service in Shanghai for those killed in 'the lower Yangtze fracas', letter dated 16 May 1949, contained in CA to Scarlett (FO), 31 May 1949, CA: *Foreign Office Correspondence File (1945–49)*.
13. Battersby (Admiralty) to Wood (MoD), letter dated 3 May 1949, F6522/

1219/10, FO371/75891; FO notes in connection with James Harrison's questions in Parliament of 22 April 1949, PREM 8/944.

14. Speech by W. Roberts, 5 May 1949, *PD* 1948–49, Vol. 464, cols. 1252–4. Cf. Vice-Admiral Taylor's retorted in a typical colonial fashion: 'Surely the action of the British gunboats has been against Chinese pirates, and has been welcomed by everybody except those pirates'. *Ibid.*, col. 1254.

15. Shanghai to FO, No. 533, 6 July 1949, F9856/1219/10, FO371/75893.

16. The initial claim in the Chinese press that the Battery troops mistook British ships as Guomindang ones up until the night of the 21 April was not followed up with any official substantiation. Cf. *RMRB*, 24 April 1949.

17. Battersby (Admiralty) to Wood (MoD), letter dated 3 May 1949, F6522/1219/10, FO371/75891. The British seemed never to have understood the initial salvos as the warnings the PLA claimed them to be, and even less were they prepared to change course and go back – it was certainly not provided for in their instructions.

18. The Chinese stressed this point to E. Youde (later Sir Edward) when he first contacted the local PLA command. Nanjing to Admiralty No. 240109, 24, April 1949, F6064/1219/10, FO371/75890.

19. Attlee's remarks, 26 April 1949, *PD* 1948–9, Vol. 464, col. 26. *Cf.* Guomindang's 'full knowledge and consent' alleged by Britain, see C.M. (49) 28th Conclusions, 26 April 1949, CAB 128/15 and related discussions in PREM, 8/944.

20. Message from the *Amethyst* 241049Z of 24 May 1949, F7550/1219/10; Stevenson to FO no. 750, 1 June 1949, F8040/1219/10, FO371/75892.

21. See F8841, 9430, 9450/1219/10, FO371/75893, and F10023, 10402/1219/10, FO371/75894; Message from *Amethyst* No. 221202Z, 22 June, and Instructions to *Amethyst* from C. in C. FES. 250801Z of 25 June 1949, PREM 8/944.

22. FO letter to Attlee, 1 June 1949, PREM 8/944; FO to Nanjing no. 614, 1 June 1949, F7440/1219/10, FO371/75892; Nanjing to FO, no. 777, 6 June 1949, F8225/1219/10, FO371/75892.

23. The Chinese initially agreed to accept nothing but Brind (C. in C. FES)'s signature as legally binding but later agreed that Captain Donaldson (Naval Attaché at Nanjing)'s signature could stand in stead. The exchange of instruments never took place.

24. See CM (49) 42nd Conclusions, Minute 7, 23 June 1949, CAB128/15. The CCP insisted that the British admit having entered the war zone 'indiscreetly' during the first stage of negotiations, leaving details of the circumstances and questions of compensation to a separate negotiation. See Mao, 'On the Outrages by British warships', 30 April 1949, *SW*, 4:401. See also General Yuan's reply in Messages from *Amethyst*, 180754Z and 180814Z of 18 May 1949, F7168/1219/10, FO371/75891; messages from *Amethyst*, 311149Z of 31 May 1949, and 221202Z of 22 June 1949, PREM, 8/944.

25. PLA's conflicting orders to let the ship go was cited as a significant factor which compromised the effectiveness of their interception. See Kang Maozhao, *op.cit.*; *SJZS*, 1988, 8:25–6, 10:22–3, 11:22–5. See also Yuan Zhongxian's statement in *RMRB*, 3 Aug. 1949, in which the escape was

condemned as an act of heartless breach of faith.
26. An internal appreciation report by the Military Commission of the CCP Central Committee of 28 April 1949.
27. 'On the People's Democratic Dictatorship', dated 30 June 1949, *SW*, 4:411–24.
28. The Soviet Union recognised the PRC on 2 October 1949. Ten other socialist governments also recognised the PRC right away, and diplomatic relations were established without negotiations. These were Bulgaria, Romania, Hungary, the Democratic People's Republic of Korea, Czechoslovakia, Poland, Mongolia, the German Democratic Republic, Albania and the Democratic Republic of Vietnam. Yugoslavia also recognised the PRC but diplomatic relations were not established until January 1955.
29. See R. MacFarquhar and J.K. Fairbank (eds) *CHC*, 1987, vol. 14, pp. 265–70.
30. For one thing, all three countries kept considerable armed forces stationed in China during the civil war – warships, military aircraft and marines. See Mao, 'On the Outrages by British Warships', 30 April 1949, *SW*, 4:402.
31. Zhou Enlai mentioned this to a visiting African delegation on 5 September 1963, and again on 30 April 1965. On the latter occasion – to a different African delegation – Zhou said that this message was conveyed by Stuart through Mr Lo Longji.
32. Sir O. Franks (Washington) to FO, 12 May 1949, F6894/1023/10, and Stevenson to FO, no. 653, 17 May, F7089/1023/10, FO371/75811. See also R. MacFarquhar and J.K. Fairbank, (eds) *CHC*, vol. 14, pp. 262–3; Edwin W. Martin, 'The Chou démarche', *Foreign Service Journal*, Nov. 1981, pp. 13–6, 32; Shaw Yu-ming, 'John Leighton Stuart and US–Chinese Communist Rapprochement in 1949', *China Quarterly*, 89, March 1982, pp. 74–96; its translation in *Dang Shi Tong Xun* (Party History Circulars) nos 9 and 10, 1985.
33. Mao, 'Farewell, Leighton Stuart!', 18 August 1949, *SW*, 4:433–40. Referring to the US, Mao wrote, 'Money may be given, but only conditionally. What is the condition? Follow the United States . . . they have cast the line for the fish who want to be caught. But he who swallows food handed out in contempt will get a bellyache'. *Ibid.*, p. 437.
34. Dening's Minute, 28 July, F11392/1153/10, FO371/75866. The American support to the blockade was confirmed in Telegram from Shanghai to FO no. 694, 18 Aug. 1949, in Annex B to CP (49) 180, 23 Aug. 1949, CAB129/36. See also Mao, 'Friendship or Aggression?' 30 August 1949, *SW*, 4:449; *FRUS*, 1949, 8:448, 457.
35. The Foreign Affairs College, *Zhong Hua Ren Min Gong He Guo Dui Wai Guan Xi Shi* (History of the Foreign Relations of the PRC), 1964, p. 187.
36. 'On the People's Democratic Dictatorship', *SW*, 4:417.
37. Urquhart (Shanghai) to FO No. 586, 21 July 1949, PREM 8/943. See also 'On the People's Democratic Dictatorship', *SW*, 4:416, in which Mao described British imperialism as 'an old hand at trickery and deception'.
38. CP(48) 72, 3 March 1948, CAB29/25. On 8 May 1950, Bevin talked

about the need to 'withstand the great concentration of power now stretching from China to the Oder', quoted in Ritchie Ovendale, *The English-Speaking Alliance*, 1985, front page. See also *ibid.* p. 160, where the British Defence Co-ordination Committee in the Far East was quoted as having suggested the urgent need for diplomatic, economic and military action 'to form a containing ring against further Communist penetration'. Sir William Strang reported to the Cabinet after his tour in Southeast Asia early in 1949 that the darker side in the Far Eastern picture included 'the revolution in China and the menace that it brings for South-East Asia with its great Chinese communities and for foreign interests in the whole area'. CP(48) 67, 17 March 1949, CAB129/33.

39. CP(49) 120, 23 May 1949, CAB129/35.
40. CM(49) 38th Conclusions, Minute 3, 26 May 1949, CAB128/15.
41. See CP(48) 299, 9 Dec. 1948, CAB129/31; CP(49) 180, 23 August 1949, CAB129/36.
42. CP(49) 180, 23 August 1949, CAB129/36, Annex A. See also CP(49) 248, 12 Dec. 1949, CAB129/37.
43. The policy was first put forward in CP(48) 299, 9 December 1948, CAB129/31, and was essentially followed through by later Cabinet decisions. One may even trace the origin of the policy to early 1947, when E. Dening suggested that Britain's assets and advantages could not be exploited to the full until she had completed her 'industrial re-conversion' and revived her economy for active competition in the China market. The government's policy therefore should be to keep 'a commercial foothold in China until better days come'. Memorandum by E. Dening, F2612/2612/10, FO371/63549.
44. CP(49) 180, 23 August 1949, CAB129/36, Annex A; CP(49) 214, 24 Oct. 1949, CAB129/37; CM72 (49), Minute 3, 15 Dec. 1949. CAB128/16. Those departments which supported early recognition were FO, CRO, and MoT. CRO pressed it because of the possibility of early recognition by other Commonwealth governments, notably India. MoT was mainly concerned with British shipping interests in China. See FO371/75824. The others, such as the Treasury, BoT, MoD, and CO, were brought in later on.
45. FO to Nanjing, 1 Feb. 1950, FC1022/173, FO371/83283.
46. See FO minute (P. Scarlett), 17 Feb. 1949, F3305/1023/10, FO371/75810. 'The British Government should not appear to be unduly precipitate in recognising the Communist regime and give the impression that when British interests are at stake we are perfectly prepared to swallow our principles.' See also Record of a Meeting between Acheson and Bevin, Washington, 13 Sep. 1949, F14109/1-023/10G, FO371/75815.
47. At their first meeting on 3 March 1950, Vice Foreign Minister Zhang Hanfu spoke to Hutchinson about the issues which China wanted Britain to clarify before the establishment of diplomatic relations could be considered. Beijing to FO, 3 March 1950, FC1022/228, FO371/83285.
48. See Immanuel C.Y. Hsu, *The Rise of Modern China*, 3rd ed., 1983, pp. 660–1. Re. CCP's legal arguments on recognition, see Zhou Gengsheng, *International Law*, vol. I, 1975, pp. 132–4; see also Ti-chiang Chen, *The International Law of Recognition*, 1951. Andrew Franklin (FO) minuted

that it was reasonably clear during the negotiations in Beijing that 'the Chinese have been largely insincere'. 13 May 1950, FC1022/319, FO371/83288.

49. The Chinese commented, 'Thus the British imperialist elements do not in the least conceal their instinctive enmity towards the Chinese People's Republic'. *XHYB*, vol. I, no. 4, 15 Feb. 1950, pp. 850–1.

50. CP(49) 244, 26 Nov. 1949, CAB129/37. See Foreign Affairs College, *op.cit.*, pp. 189–90; *PD*, 24 May 1950, vol. 475, col. 2083. This seems to fit one of the hypotheses on misconception suggested by Robert Jervis. Actors rarely believe that others may be reacting to a much less favourable image of themselves than they think they are projecting. George Kennan also criticised the tendency 'to attach to its own cause an absolute value which distorts its own vision of everything else'. James N. Rosenau (ed.) *International Politics and Foreign Policy*, 1969, p. 253.

51. See E. Luard, *Britain and China*, 1962, p. 86. Luard suggested that while Britain's decision to maintain a consulate at Tamsui was no doubt designed to secure protection for British trading and other interests in Taiwan, it was possible that some less formal arrangements, for example by asking US consulates to look after British interests in Taiwan as Britain looked after US interests in China, would have been more easily overlooked by the Chinese government. Hutchinson in an oral communication on 17 March 1950 tried to explain the political motive behind the British vote by saying that it was because 'there was at that time no likelihood of a majority decision and it was consequently premature for the question to be raised'. FC1022/518, FO371/83295.

52. CM19 (50), 6 April, 1950, CAB128/17, Minute 2.

53. Humphrey Trevelyan, *Worlds Apart*, 1971, pp. 131–2.

54. Pryor (KMA Tianjin) to Nathan, 10 Jan. 1949, F5066/1153/10, F0371/75865; Rae-Smith of Butterfield & Swire, Notes on his visit to Tianjin, 15 Feb. 1949, encl. in Mitchell (CA) to Scarlett (FO), 22 Feb. 1949, F2803/1271/10, FO371/75918.

55. Stevenson to FO no. 1253, 16 Aug. 1949, F12452/1261/10, FO371/75906; Admiralty to Cin CFES 211933A, 21 June 1949, F9112/1261/10, 75900; Urquhart (Shanghai) to FO no. 1030, 30 Nov. 1949, F18017/1261/10, FO371/75915. The bombing of the *Anchises* was the subject of a Cabinet memorandum, see CP(49) 133, 22 June 1949, CAB129/35, and CM42 (49)/6, CAB128/15. It was suggested that the continuation of the blockade would mean death sentence for half the British firms and for the remainder a sentence of extinction as their reserves ran out. Shanghai to FO, No. 58, 21 July 1949, PREM 8/943.

56. A BAT report, enclosure in FO minute (Scarlett) of 26 July 1949, F11173/1153/10, FO371/75866; Urquhart (British Consul-General at Shanghai) to FO, no. 115, 22 Feb. 1949, F2748/1153/10, FO371/75864; Pryor to Nathan, 10 March 1949, F5066/1153/10, FO371/75865.

57. Letter from C. Mackenzie (Shanghai) to S.O. Gray (BoT), 24 Feb. 1949, F5286/1123/10, FO371/75859.

58. S.L. Burdett (British Consul-General at Tianjin) to L.H. Lamb (Beijing), 8 May 1949, F7904/154/10, FO371/75933; J. Keswick's reports on these interviews, encl. W.J. Keswick to Dening, 28 Sept. 1949, F14852/

1152/10, FO371/75867. With reference to contacts with Chinese local authorities, also see Stevenson to FO No. 1381, 1 Sept. 1949, F13149/1123/10, FO371/75860.

59. Shanghai to FO no. 632, 2 Aug. 1949, F11489/1153/10, FO371/75866; no. 945, 5 November, 1949, F16653/1153/10, FO371/75868. John Keswick delayed making the trip to Beijing, admittedly 'from consideration of his firm's interests elsewhere'. See also B. Hooper, *op. cit.* p. 101.

60. A Lopato report dated 5 July 1949, enclosed in Loudon of BAT to Scarlett (FO) 11 July 1949, F10443/1153/10, FO371/75865, alleged that the Harbin authorities levied discriminatory taxes on British enterprises.

61. See Chen Shou-chi, 'On Foreign Trade Policy', in the Economist Supplement of *Guang Ming Ri Bao* (Guang Ming Daily) Beijing, 29 July 1949, encl. F13021/1123/10, FO371/75859.

62. As a British businessman later wrote, 'During the years when all victorious nations had to exercise the strictest economy with their foreign assets, [the Guomindang government] carried the idea of free trade to absurdity, contrary to the well being of the nation, and almost exclusively to fill the pockets of a few individuals. After such a display of inefficiency and lack of discipline, it is not surprising that the new regime should remove foreign trade from private initiative and manipulation'. 'Mao Tse-tung's Foreign Trade', a private study, appendix to *CA: M & C*, 1950, Bulletin No. 46 50/M/3, 20 March 1950.

63. Enclosures to Circular to Consuls no. 46 of 9 April 1949, F5286/1123/10, FO371/75859.

64. 'Temporary Measures Governing the Control of the External Trade of the North China Area', 15 March 1949, Article 7, F5286/1123/10, FO371/75859, encl. 3; SASS, *Shang Hai Jing Ji* (See note 1, chapter 1, p. 188) (Shanghai's Economy), *vol. I, 1949–82*, p. 665. See also *RMRB*, 10 July 1949, p. 2. With regard to cancellation of permits, see *CA: Bull.* no. 53, 50/M/12, 20 Oct. 1950.

65. R.Y. Frost (Shell's APC), notes on trading conditions in North China, 9 July 1949, F10174/1121/10, FO371/75856.

66. *CA: M & C*, no. 49/G/86, 30 Dec. 1949.

67. See 'Regulations Governing the Cigarette Industry in Manchuria (the Northeast)', attached to letter from Richard Price, Shanghai, to Lamb, Nanjing, 9 March 1949, FO371/75865. See also G.E. Mitchell to member firms, 1 March 1949, *CA: M & C*, No. 49/F/5., 1949.

68. Memo. from BCC Shanghai, *CA: M & C*, no. 50/E/17, 13 Nov. 1950.

69. *CA: M & C*, no. 49/G/86, 30 Dec. 1949.

70. See Michael Lindsay's memorandum on Shell's experience with a Tianjin statistical officer, appendix to *CA: M & C*, no. 49/E/15, 1 Nov. 1949.

71. Memorandum by BCC Shanghai, *CA: M & C*, no. 50/E/17, 13 Nov. 1949.

72. Tianjin to FO, 26 Oct. 1949, and attached memorandum from BCC Tianjin on the supply of egg products and soya beans, F17578/1123/10, FO371/75860; Memorandum from BCC Shanghai, *CA: M & C*, 1950, no. 50/E/17, 13 Nov. 1950; *CA: M & C*, no. 49/G/86, 30 Dec. 1949.

73. *CA: M & C*, no. 49/G/86, 30 Dec. 1949.

74. H.J. Collar (ICI), Hong Kong, to G.E. Mitchell, 11 July 1949, *CA:*

M & C, no. 50/G/53, 18 July 1950. On the need to avoid 'exploitation by intermediaries', see Chen Shou-chi, 'On Foreign Trade Policy', *op. cit.*, encl. F13021/1123/10, FO371/75859.

75. Extract from an article in the *FEER*, 31 Sept. 1950, appendix to *CA: M & C*, Bulletin No. 52, 20 Sept. 1950. See also *CA: M & C*, no. 50/G/19, 23 Feb. 1950. Judging by the very great volume of trade which was recorded in 1950 especially, it was suggested that all *bona fide* merchants must have derived considerable profits from doing business with China.

76. R.Y. Frost (Shell's APC), notes on trading conditions in North China, 9 July 1949, F10174/1121/10, FO371/75856. It was noted that the new government in this instance had given permission for foreign ships to fly their national flags on entering and leaving port and had withdrawn the cabotage restrictions because of the 'emergency'.

77. W.P. Montgomery (UK trade Commissioner to HK) to A.S Gilbert (BoT), 11 Mar. 1949, F4352/1121/10, FO371/75853.

78. Notes by the Shipping Sub-committee of the BCC Tianjin , 20 May 1949, F10174/1121/10, FO371/75856. The procedure involved the navigation bureau, water police at Tianjin and Taku, customs, quarantine service, police headquarters, local area police station, public utilities service, and Bank of China. When entry slips were issued by the navigation bureau, it was the responsibility of the shippers to inform all other departments concerned.

79. W.P. Montgomery to BoT O.T.B. 332, 12 Oct., F17650/1121/10, FO371/75858; *Cf.* Heilongjing People's Publishing House, *Dong Bei jie Fang Qu Cai Zheng Jing Ji Shi Gao* (A Draft History of the Finance and Economy of the Northeast Liberated Area) 1987, pp. 414–6.

80. W.P. Montgomery to BoT OTB332, 12 Oct., F17650/1121/10; OTB336, 17 Oct., F16759/1121/10; OTB353, 2 Nov. 1949, F17650/1121/10; OTB409, 5 Dec. 1949, F19040/1121/10, FO371/75858. The British shipping agents involved included Mollers Ltd., Jardine, Matheson & Co., Lom Kee S.S. Co., Butterfield & Swire, Sanson Shipping Co., Holly S.S. Co., Mollers (HK) Ltd., Winly & Co., Lu On Co., Ta Hing Co., Gt Southern S.S. Co., and Roland & Co. Orders of some commodities such as copper wire and rubber tyres were of a size for which it was believed there was no demand in China proper, and were therefore suspected as being for other destinations via the China route. One theory concerning rubber, prevalent in Malaya, was that much of this was forwarded with or without trans-shipment to the US on Second Bills of Lading in order that the owners might benefit by the US dollars so acquired. Another possible destination was the Soviet Union. The local conditions of shipping trade can also be glimpsed from *XHYB*, on North China, vol. I, no. 1, pp. 124–6; on the port of Tianjin, vol. I, no. 5, p. 1175; and on the port of Shanghai, vol. I, no. 5, p. 1176.

81. *CA: M & C*, no. 50/E/17, 13 Nov. 1950; Beverly Hooper, *op. cit.* p. 86.

82. W.R. Connor Green (Tianjin), to J.C. Hutchison (Shanghai), no. 41, 8 May 1949, F8969/1121/10, FO371/75854; R.Y. Frost, notes on trading conditions in Tianjin, 9 July 1949, F10174/1121/10, FO371/75856.

83. *Ibid.* See also 'Provisional Regulations Governing Commodity Tax in North China', 21 Sept. 1949, *XHYB*, vol. I, no. 1, pp. 140–1.

84. Memorandum by Michael Lindsay, appendix to *CA: M & C*, no. 49/ E/15, 1 Nov. 1949; Telegram from BCC Shanghai, 12 July 1949, *CA: M & C*, no. 49/F/13, 14 July 1949. The tax authorities grouped the firms of similar businesses and sizes and made each group collectively responsible to make sure that every individual member paid his fair due, *CA: Bull.* no. 38, 49/M/8, 20 July 1949.
85. 'Provisional Measures on Business Tax in Shanghai', 12 Aug. 1949, *XHYB*, vol. I, no. 1, pp. 141–5, 147.
86. *CA: Bull.* no. 39, 49/M/9, 20 Aug. 1949, and no. 40, 49/M/10, 20 Sept. 1949.
87. Memorandum by BCC Shanghai, 20 Feb. 1950, FC1106/40, FO371/83345.
88. BCC Tianjin, 29 March 1950, FC1106/79, FO371/83350.
89. *XHYB*, vol. I, no. 5, 15 Feb. 1950, pp. 1155–60.
90. *Ren Min Shou Ce* (The People's Handbook) 1950, Sec. V, pp. 1–3. It was said that in 1950 more than 40 per cent of the national deficit was financed by the bond issues. R. MacFarquhar and J. Fairbank (eds) *CHC*, vol. 14, p. 151.
91. *CA: Bull.*, no. 49, 20 June 1950; memorandum by BCC Shanghai, *CA: M & C*, 1950, no. 50/E/17, 13 Nov. 1950. See also Hughes and Luard, *The Economic Development of Communist China*, 1959, pp. 26–8; *Manchester Guardian*, 14 Aug. 1950.
92. Cui Jingbo, 'How Should We Look at Taxation?' *XHYB*, vol. I, no. 5, 15 Feb. 1950, pp. 1160–3. The author's citation of Coleridge (which appears at the beginning of the present chapter) is in Barbara E. Rooke (ed.) *The Collected Works of Samuel Taylor Coleridge The Friend* (I), 1969, pp. 228–44.
93. The Foreign Office did not agree with the Chartered Bank in Tianjin that the levy of 2.9 per cent on the banking group could be termed 'crippling'. *CA: M & C*, 1949, no. 49/G/42, 15 July 1949; Justin Littlejohn, 'China and Communism', printed pamphlet attached to *CA: M & C*, 1951, no. 51/G/8, 27 Feb. 1951; *International Affairs* vol. XXVII, no. 22, April 1951.
94. Mao, *SW*, 5:64.
95. Noel Barber, *The Fall of Shanghai*, 1979, p. 227; *XHYB*, vol. I, no. 5, 15 Feb. 1950, pp. 1155–60. The catering business in general, be it owned by British or Chinese, faced the same problem of deliberate government disincentive. Harrison Forman, *Blunder in Asia*, pp. 132–3.
96. R. MacFarquhar and J.K. Fairbank (eds) *CHC*, vol. 14, p. 75.
97. Shipping Sub-Committee of BCC Tientsin, notes on North China shipping, 20 May 1949, F10174/1121/10, FO371/75856. See also extract from an article from *FEER*, 1 Sept. 1949, *CA: Bull.* no. 40, 20 Sept. 1949; B. Hooper, *op.cit.* pp. 88–9.
98. Liu Shaoqi, 'Address at a Meeting with Capitalists of Tianjin's Industry and Commerce', 25 April 1949; 'Address at a Conference of Staff Representatives in Tianjin', 28 April 1949, in Yu Zhenzhou et al. (eds) *Zhong Gong Dang Shi Jiao Xue Can Kao Zi Liao* (Background Documents on the History of CCP: A Collection for Teaching Purposes) 1980, pp. 371–82, 394–405. See also *The Listener*, 14 April 1949; *Manchester Guardian*, 30 June 1949.

99. *Da Gong Bao*, 19 Aug. 1949, cited in B. Hooper, *op.cit.* p. 91.
100. W.H.E. Coates (YTT Tianjin) to W.B. Christian (YTT Shanghai) 13 June 1950, SASS, *Yee Tsoong Files*, Box no. 7, 180; FAB Shanghai, 'An Investigation Report on the Yee Tsoong Tobacco Company', Nov. 1950, SASS, *Yee Tsoong Files*.
101. Memorandum by BCC Shanghai, *CA: M & C*, no. 50/E/17, 13 Nov. 1950.
102. According to one estimate, the government was financially responsible for 7 million military, political, administrative and educational personnel in 1949 in the whole country, and 9 million in 1950. Fan Shouxin, 'Jian Guo Chu Qi Tong Yi Cai Zheng Jing Ji, Wen Ding Wu Jia De Dou Zheng' (The Strive for a Unified Fiscal Management and Price Stability During the Initial Period of the Founding of the PRC), in Chinese People's University (ed.) *Zhong Guo She Hui Zhu Yi Ge Ming He Jian She Shi Jiao Xue Yan Jiu* (Teaching and Reasearch in the History of Socialist Revolution and Construction in China), 1985, p. 40. See also *SW of Zhou Enlai*, vol. II, pp. 3, 6.
103. Zhou Enlai, 'A Report on Peaceful Negotiations', 17 April 1949, *SW of Zhou Enlai*, vol. I, p. 324; Liu Shaoqi, 'Address at a Meeting with Capitalists of Tianjin's Industry and Commerce', 25 April 1949, Yu Zhenzhou et al. (eds) *op.cit.* pp. 371–82.
104. This information was leaked out at the time and was picked up by a financial newspaper in London, presumably from Hong Kong. Tiencken to Winmill, 22 Dec. 1950, Fc1103/7, FO371/92259.
105. See Wei Zichu, *Ying Guo Zai Hua Qi Ye Ji Qi Li Ruen* (British Enterprises in China and their Profits), 1951; Wei Zichu, *Di Guo Zhu Yi Yu Kai Luan Mei Kuang* (Imperialism and the Kailan Mines), 1954; Wei Tsu-chu, an article on British industrial interests in China in *FEER*, 5 June 1952.
106. J.W. Breen of Shanghai Insurance, 31 May 1950, FC1109/1, FO371/83355.
107. Despite labour regulations, British and other Western employers continued to experience strident demands and occasional lock-ins by employees. It is also suggested that both the Labour Bureau and the People's Court tended to resolve the overwhelming majority of disputes in the workers' interests. B. Hooper, *op.cit.*, pp. 91–2.
108. See Kenneth G. Lieberthal, *Revolution and Tradition in Tientsin, 1949–1952*, 1980, pp. 85, 88.
109. Tianjin to FO, 26 Oct. 1949, F17578, FO371/75860.
110. See Hsueh Mu-chiao, Su Hsing and Lin Tse-li, *The Socialist Transformation of the National Economy in China*, 1960, pp. 184–219; Liu Chaojin, *Dui Wai Jing Ji Guan Xi Yu Ye Wu Shi Jian* (Foreign Economic Relations and Business Practice) 1985.
111. SASS, *Shang Hai Jing Ji, op. cit.*, pp. 62, 665.
112. Mao Zedong to Liu Shaoqi, 6 March 1948, the Research Office of Historical Papers of CCP Central Committee (ed.) *Mao Zedong Shu Xin Xuan Ji* (Selected Letters of Mao Zedong), 1983, p. 296; Ren Bishi, 'Address at the Enlarged Conference of the Battle Front Committee of the Northwest Field Corps', 12 Jan. 1948, Yu Zhenzhou et al.

(eds) *op.cit.*, pp. 63–4; Xi Zhongxun to Mao 4 Jan. 1948, *ibid.*, p. 44.
113. Mao, 'Don't Hit out in all Directions', 6 June 1950, *SW*, 5:33–6.
114. Ygael Gluckstein, *Mao's China*, 1957, pp. 192–9.
115. Liu Shaoqi, 'On the Socialist Transformation of Capitalist Industry and Commerce', 16 Nov. 1955, *SW of Liu Shaoqi*, vol. II, pp. 177–9.
116. R. MacFarquhar and J.K. Fairbank (eds) *CHC*, vol. 14, p. 92, 152–3. Mao was credited with a development theory to the effect that economic growth could be attained by increasing the amount of labour, capital goods, and land used in production, by improving the quality of these factors of production, by combining them in more efficient ways and inspiring labour to greater efforts, and by taking advantage of economies of scale. See John G. Gurley, *China's Economy and the Maoist Strategy*, pp. 17, 24, 29.

3 The Korean War Period

1. A Hong Kong newspaper report on 26 May 1950, excerpted in *CA: Bull.* no. 49, 20 June 1950. See also a copy of an unsigned letter from CA to J.S.H. Shattock, 5 June 1950, *CA: Cresta File*.
2. Quoted in *CA: Bull.* no. 49, 20 June 1950.
3. Nikita Khrushchev, *Khrushchev Remembers*, 1971, p. 332 f. See also Peter Lowe, *The Origins of the Korean War*, 1986, pp. 150–7; Karunker Gupta, 'How Did the Korean War Begin?' in *China Quarterly*, VIII 1972, pp. 699–716.
4. Dean Acheson, *Present at the Creation* (London, Hamish Hamilton) 1969, p. 356, f.; William Stueck, 'the Soviet Union and the Origins of the Korean War' in *World Politics*, June 1976, p. 632, cited in D.B.G. Heuser, *Yugoslavia in Western Cold War Policies, 1948–1953*, unpublished D.Phil dissertation Oxon., May 1987.
5. Philip Noel-Baker, 11 May 1953, *PD*, vol. 515, 1952–3, col. 901.
6. R. MacFarquhar and J. Fairbank (eds) *CHC*, vol. 14, 1987, pp. 271–2. Chinese Premier Zhou Enlai also stressed this in his telegram to UN Secretary-General Lie on 6 July 1950.
7. CP(50) 3 July 1950, CAB129/41, including Annex A containing the declaration of 28 June 1950 by Zhou Enlai.
8. M.L. Dockrill, 'The Foreign Office, Anglo–American relations and the Korean war, June 1950–June 1951', in *International Affairs*, no. 3, 1986, p. 462.
9. R. Ovendale, *The English-Speaking Alliance*, 1985, p. 217.
10. CP(50) 220, 6 Oct. 1950; New York to FO, no. 1156, 22 Sept. 1950, attached in CP(50) 216, 26 Sept. 1950, CAB129/42.
11. Mao, two telegrams dated 2 and 13 October 1950 on the entry of the Chinese People's Volunteers in the Korean war, *SW* 5:61; *CHC*, vol. 14, 1987, pp. 274–5. Zhou Enlai, in his talks with Julian Nyerere during his visit to Tanzania 4–8 June 1965 also related that Mao had believed that should no decisive determination be made at that crucial moment, not only would Korea be occupied but China's own construction would become impossible.
12. CM 63 (50)/4, CAB128/18, 9 Oct. 1950. See also Bevin to Nehru,

28 Sept. 1950, FK/1023/11, FO371 84109; Pannikar's reports on his meeting with Zhou, New Delhi to CRO, 3 Oct. 1950, FK1023/17G, FO371 84109. Esler Dening said that Pannikar was apt to exaggerate, but there were usually grounds for his reports and this one had to be treated 'with some seriousness'. R. Ovendale, *op.cit.*, p. 217.

13. CM 73(50)/2, CAB128/18, 13 Nov. 1950; CM, 78(50)/1, CAB128/18, 29 Nov. 1950.

14. A Chinese delegation finally managed to visit New York in late November and made their case with regard to Taiwan and Korea in the Security Council on 28 November, but the GA resolution of 14 December was adopted without Chinese representation. See Wu Xiuquan, *Zai Wai Jiao Bu Ba Nien De Jing Li* (Eight Years in the Ministry of Foreign Affairs) 1983, p. 39.

15. This and the indefinite postponement of the objective of liberating Taiwan owing to the interposition of the US Seventh Fleet are considered by some as among the negative effects of China's intervention in Korea, outweighing the bonus of domestic political consolidation. R. MacFarquhar and J.K. Fairbank (eds), *CHC*, vol. 14, 1987, pp. 276–7. Cf. C.P. FitzGerald, *Mao Tse-tung and China*, 1976, pp. 106–7.

16. Hutchison to Bevin, with the enclosed memorandum on the Central People's Government of the PRC as seen from Peking, FO Despatch no. 72 of 22 February 1951, FC10120/1, FO371/92220.

17. Dening to R.H. Scott, 16 April 1951; A.S. Campbell minute, 18 May 1951; S.J.L. Oliver minute, 14 June 1951; FC10120/1, FO371/92220.

18. Lamb to FO, no. 522, 27 June 1952, FC1051/13, FO371/99271; Lamb to R.H. Scott, 2 April 1952, FC1025/13, FO371/99260; Prepared answers to Parliament question, FC1051/13, FO371/99271.

19. See various cases in FO371/99243, 99244 and 99272. The British and Hong Kong governments eventually decided that Hong Kong water police should be given full authority to return fire for self-defence in case Chinese frontier guards resorted to the use of firearms. CO to HK (Sir A. Grantham) no. 475, 8 May 1952, FC1055/1, FO371/99275.

20. The government's announcement in the House of Commons on 21 March 1951 that consulates-general or consulates at Chongching, Kunming, Hankou, Nanjing, Qingdao and Xiamen were to be closed gave rise to grave concern to members of China Association, Mitchell to FO, 12 April 1951, *CA: Cresta File*; see also another letter from CA to FO re British decision to close the consulate-general at Guangzhou, 4 Feb. 1952, *ibid.*

21. BBC Shanghai, Annual Report for 1950, 17 April 1951, FC1103/63, FO371/92262.

22. *CA: M & C*, no. 50/E/17, 13 Nov. 1950.

23. 'The China Engineering Quarterly Review' for Dec. 1950, FC1103/17, FO371/92259.

24. BBC Shanghai, Annual Report for 1950, 17 April 1951, FC1103/63, FO371/92262. Prices were forced up not only because the immediate demand for them was increased by the war and by Western rearmament, but also because, for fear of another world war, the United States, and other countries to a lesser extent, began 'stock-piling' potentially scarce

materials of strategic importance. This led to a very sharp rise in their price, greatly aggravated by speculative buying in anticipation of still higher prices to come. G.D.H. Cole, *The Post-War Conditions of the British Economy*, 1956, p. 191.

25. S.L. Burdett (Tianjin) to FO, 19 April 1950, FC1122/28, FO371/83373; Shanghai to FO, no. 525, 19 May 1950, FO371/83348; Hutchison (Beijing) to FO, no. 1781, 9 Nov. 1950, FC1106/237 FO371/83353. A Chinese estimate indicated the volume of trade as worth some US$130 million for the East China region from July to November, covering both exports and imports.
26. Shanghai to FO, no. 1046, 22 Nov. 1950, FC1122/57 FO371/83374.
27. Hong Kong Governor (A. Grantham) to CO, no. 1323, 5 Dec. 1950, FC1122/63, FO371/83374.
28. Shanghai to FO, no. 1147, 23 Dec. 1950, FC1122/68, FO371/83374.
29. Mitchell (CA) to Shattock (FO), 26 Feb. 1951, *CA: Cresta File*; see also FC1121/121, FO371/92276.
30. Shanghai to FO, no. 44, 22 Jan. 1951, FC1345/15, FO371/92294.
31. Minutes of a meeting of the CA General Committee, 10 Jan. 1951, *CA: M & C*, no. 51/G/4, 12 Jan. 1951.
32. London Chamber of Commerce (A. de V. Leigh) to BoT President, 22 Jan. 1951, *CA: M & C, Bull.*, no. 57, 20 Feb. 1951. See also Hughes and Luard, *The Economic Development of Communist China, 1948–1958*, 1959, pp. 123–4.
33. G.E. Mitchell to Shattock, 26 Feb. 1951, *CA: Cresta File*; L.H. Lamb to R.H. Scott, 26 May 1951, with enclosures, FC1103/76, FO371/92262.
34. G.E. Mitchell to Johnston, 9 July 1952, *CA: Cresta File*; see also the record of a meeting between Lord Reading, FO officials and representatives of British firms, 25 July 1952, *ibid*, in which it was suggested that the BoT might find it difficult to accept direct responsibility but that a form of words could be used to attribute it generally to British governmental policy.
35. *The Trade of U.K.*, vols. 1949–1955 (London: HMSO); *CA: Bull.*, no. 58, 20 March 1951.
36. After a decline in exports to China, Hong Kong still relied heavily on imports from China. For developments in the 1960s and 1970s, see Xui Tiandong and Hu Dun-ai, *Xiang Gang Yu Nei Di Mao Yi* (Hong Kong's Trade with Mainland China) 1984, pp. 7–9, 17–18.
37. The Editorial Board of the Almanac of China's Economy, *Almanac of China's Economy*, 1982, VIII, pp. 34, 35, 42, 43, 45, 46.
38. See J. Wilczynski, *The Economics and Politics of East–West Trade*, 1969, pp. 47–9.
39. Shih I-t'ao, 'It is Time to Call off the "Embargo"', cited in Ygael Gluckstein, *Mao's China*, 1957, p. 71. See also Hughes and Luard, *op.cit.*, p. 125.
40. W.P. Montgomery (Hong Kong) to W.O. Newsam (BoT), 4 Dec. 1950, FO371/83386. Before World War II, the agents in Shanghai of UK manufacturers had predominance in the field of railway material. In addition, several of the trunk lines were engineered and financed by British interests. As a result, a preponderance of the requirements, including replenishments, was supplied by UK manufacturers through

their Shanghai agents, notably Jardine Engineering Co., the Pekin Syndicate, Ltd, and Arnhold Trading Co., Ltd. During the UNRRA Relief Programme for China, the UK share consisted substantially of some millions of pounds worth of locomotives and rolling stock which were, in the main, imported into China through Hong Kong. It was believed that the Chinese government, given the choice, would wish to pay for British supplies of railway material as a more attractive source of replenishments.

41. Hughes and Luard, *op.cit.*, p. 126.
42. The Editorial Board of the Almanac of China's Economy, *op.cit.*, VIII, pp. 38–41.
43. The Editorial Board of the Almanac of China's Foreign Economic Relations and Trade, *1987 Almanac of China's Foreign Economic Relations and Trade*, Beijing: Chinese Prospect Publishing House, 1987, p. 1123.
44. The company has since changed its name into the Chinese–Polish Joint Stock Shipping Company. See the PRC-MFA (ed.) *Zhong Guo Wai Jiao Gai Lan* (A Survey of China's Diplomatic Relations) 1987, pp. 225, 233.
45. Seventeen shareholders' meetings were held between 1951 and 1984. See *The Company's 35th Anniversary Commemoration Book*, by the Editorial Staff of CHIPOLBROK, Shanghai, 1986.
46. According to a Polish officer's memoirs, the detained Polish members of the crews were said to have staged a protest hunger strike in Taiwan and, thanks to intervention from the International Committee of Red Cross, were later released and returned to Poland. The Chinese members of the crews were held *incommunicado* in Taiwan and many are unaccounted for. Interviews with CHIPOLBROK officials, Shanghai, 1987. See also SASS, *Shang Hai Jing Ji* (Shanghai's Economy), *vol. 1, 1949–82*, 1983, p. 474.
47. Chancery, Warsaw, to FO, 22 Sept. 1953, M349/313, FO371/105883.
48. The likelihood of China's exposure to Soviet overpricing appeared to be compounded by China's differential in the level of Western embargoes in comparison with the Soviet union; according to one calculation, China had to pay an extra US$940 million during 1955–9 for shipments of western products resold by the Soviet Union, although it was admitted that the amount of this terms-of-trade loss could not be accounted for with any precision. See Alexander Eckstein, *Communist China's Economic Growth and Foreign Trade*, 1966, pp. 171–2; Chin-Yuen Chen, 'American Economic Policy Towards Communist China, 1950–70', unpublished Ph.D. thesis, Columbia University, 1972, pp. 93–102.
49. Wu Xiuquan, *Eight Years in the Foreign Ministry*, 1983, p. 17.
50. Peter J.D. Wiles, *Communist International Economics*, 1968, pp. 250–3, in which Wiles cited the argument by Feng-hwa Mah in *China Quarterly*, Jan.–Mar. 1964. See also R.F. Mikesell and J.N. Behrman, *Financing Free World Trade with the Sino-Soviet Bloc*, 1958.
51. Interview with Herbert G. Samuel of Delbanco Meyer & Co. Ltd, London, 1986. See also G.E. Mitchell (CA) to Percival (BoT) 22 Oct. 1951, *CA: M & C*, no. 51/G/41; Mitchell to Foreign Secretary 15 April 1954, *CA: Cresta Files*.
52. H.J. Collar (ICI) to Allen (FO) and Percival (BoT), 21 Jan. 1954, and

C.T. Crowe (FO) to H.J. Collar, 1 Feb. 1954, *CA: Cresta Files.*

53. Ygael Gluckstein, *op.cit.*, p. 71.
54. With regard to Soviet industrial construction assistance and financial help, see Macfarquhar and Fairbank (eds) *CHD*, vol. 14, pp. 281–3. Also the PRC-MFA (ed.) *Zhong Guo Wai Jiao Gai Lan* (A Survey of China's Diplomatic Relations), 1987, pp. 224, 227; Roy Medvedev, *China and the Superpowers,* 1986, pp. 22–8.
55. Peter J.D. Wiles, *op.cit.*, p. 496.
56. With regard to US freezing of Chinese assets and US government Transportation Order T-1 as communicated to the FO, see FC1121/11, FO371/92272. With regard to Chinese control of American companies and US assets, see generally FC11345, FO371/92294.
57. CM, 23 (51)/4, CAB128/19, 2 April 1951; CM, 24 (51)/2, CAB128/19, 5 April 1951. The Chiefs of Staff thought that so long as she remained in harbour in Hong Kong, the tanker would be a continuing irritant to local Chinese opinion.
58. *RMRB*, 30 April 1951; Colonial Secretariat, Hong Kong, *Economic Bulletin* no. 30, 15 May 1951, FC1121/200, FO371/92280. See also remarks by R.H. Scott (FO), Minute by G.E. Mitchell, undated, *CA: Cresta File.*
59. Foreign Affairs College, *History of Foreign Relations of the PRC*, 1964, p. 220; interviews with Shanghai officials, 1987. See also *RMRB*, May 4, 6, 8, and 17, 1951. On 21 June Bates wrote to FAB Director Huang Hua, expressing on behalf of his London principals a deep regret that 'as a firm with old and friendly associations of trade with China and notwithstanding the Company's full conformance with such regulations (issued by the CPG) . . . it has been necessary to apply their requisitioning Order to the Company's properties and equipment'.
60. The formal exchange of notes concerning the transfer of requisitioned physical equipment in the East China region took place in July 1953 between Dr Kang-Chi Cheng and Mr Wang Yihua of the Shanghai Military Control Commission. Dr Cheng was Chargé d'Affaires in Canberra, Australia, during the war, director of the Shanghai Office of the Ministry of Foreign Affairs of the Guomindang government till 1949, and then acted as foreign affairs adviser to Communist Mayor Chen Yi until he was employed by Shell, with government blessing. When Pattern left China he was succeeded by Dr Cheng as general manager in Shanghai. Dr Cheng died in 1957 and was succeeded by Christopher Powell, with Cheng's widow Nien Cheng as adviser. Interview with C. Powell, London, 27 Jan. 1989; Nien Cheng, *Life and Death in Shanghai*, 1986, pp. 13–14, ff.
61. Price's (China) Ltd, which was incorporated in Britain on 12 Oct. 1912, was successor to the property of Price's Patent Candle Co. Ltd which had been in Shanghai since 24 July 1913. Historically it did business both in soap and candles. Since 1923 Shell Co. of China Ltd had been general managing agents for all Price's (China) Ltd's activities in China in return for commission, including the supply of raw materials, sales of candles, remission of proceeds of sales. Its factory had not been in operation since V.J. Day. On 1 Aug. 1950 most of the candle factory premises were let to

the China Food Corporation for a period of three years. Shell included Price's requisitioned properties into its claim, submitted to the British government in 1986.

62. Letters from Shell management to Commissioner Moh dated 27 Sept. and 12 and 21 Nov. 1951.

63. One account claimed that up until 1949, Shell operated some 30 depots and 1000 filling stations throughout China. Brian Leung, 'The Road to Eminence', *Shell (Hong Kong)* (an in-house magazine), Nov.–Dec. 1988, pp. 16–19. Some earlier cases of government control of Shell's properties were reported in J.N. Bates to C.M. Vignoles, message from Shanghai Consul to FO, no. 1108, 8 Dec. 1950, FC1106/244, FO371/83353. The company originally had a workforce of 963 men in Shanghai. The majority had been dismissed in Jan. 1951, and 397 were retained. A further reduction of 33 guards was made at the time of the requisition.

64. See Nien Cheng, *op. cit.* There were then 48 staff members and one retired pensioner. Shell does not seem to have incurred other liabilities.

65. These aircraft had originally been purchased by the China National Aviation Corporation (CNAC) and the Central Air Transport Corporation (CATC) under American lend-lease. The CNAC was incorporated in China in 1945 as a civil aviation enterprise and was governed by a Memorandum & Articles of Association. Article 5 provided that the Chinese government (through the Ministry of Communications) was to subscribe for 80 per cent of the shares and Pan-American Airways the remaining 20 per cent. Of its nine Board directors, seven were nominated by the Ministry of Communications and two by Pan-Am. CATC, on the other hand, was never formally incorporated but was an agency of the then Guomindang government set up in 1942. *Hong Kong Law Reports*, vol. XXXIV, 1951, pp. 365–6; CP (50) 61, 3 April 1950, CAB129/39, Annex A.

66. The managing directors of the two companies flew to Beijing – with 12 aircraft – to consult with the CPG as to the ways and means of bringing back the remaining 71 aircraft and parts, as well as maintenance and repairs plants, with an estimated total value of some US$40 million. On 12 November, Zhou Enlai issued a directive to the managing directors, declaring the two corporations to be the property of the new government and replacing the previous management with newly appointed directors. On 3 December he issued a public statement, *inter alia*, that the right of the Chinese government to the properties of the two companies in Hong Kong deserved respect and proper protection from the Hong Kong authorities. On 23 December 1949, the head of the Civil Aviation Bureau of the PRC government issued a public statement declaring the transactions with CAT as legally null and void, and specifically brought the British government's attention to PRC claims. On 13 January 1950, the head of the new Civil Aviation Bureau of the CPG issued instructions to the companies' new general managers to take over all the assets of CNAC and CATC. See Foreign Affairs College, *The History of Foreign Relations of the PRC*, 1964, p. 191.

67. House of Lords Judicial Committee, *The Law Reports* 1953 (mode of citation: [1953], AC), pp. 83–5. There is suggestion that CAT was a CIA

proprietary company. See Myron J. Smith, Jr, *The Secret Wars*, vol. II, Santa Barbara, Cal.: ABC-Clio, Inc., 1981, p. xxx (Chronology).

68. Charles Loseby (ed.) *The Hong Kong Law Reports*, vol. XXXIV, 1951, at 358, ff.

69. *Hong Kong Law Reports, op. cit.*, at 358 and 386, ff.

70. CP, (50) 61, 3 April 1950, CAB 129/39; CM 24 (50), 24 April 1950, CAB128/17.

71. CM 19 (50), 6 April 1950, CAB128/17.

72. CM 24 (50), 24 April 1950, CAB128/17.

73. See Foreign Affairs College, *op. cit.*, p. 220. This was foreseen by the British Foreign Office. For British views of their dilemma, see J. McKenzie, minute 24 June 1952, FC1121/48, FO371/99312. See A. Grantham, *Via Ports: From Hong Kong to Hong Kong*, 1965, p. 162, cited in James T.H. Tang, 'Diplomatic Relations with a Revolutionary Power: Britain's Experience with China, 1949–1954', unpublished Ph.D. thesis, LSE, University of London, 1987, p. 381.

74. See House of Lords Judicial Committee, *The Law Reports*, London (1953) AC, pp. 70–95, and Charles Loseby (ed.) *The Hong Kong Law Reports*, vol. XXXIV, 1951, pp. 302–7. In addition to these 71 aircraft, another seven were blown up by KMT saboteurs on 2 April 1950. The pro-PRC employees who were guarding the planes at Kai Tak airport were later accused by the Privy Council of acting against the law of Hong Kong.

75. Shanghai to FO, no. 223, 15 Aug. 1952, FC1461/17, FO371/99345; *Jie Fang Ri Bao* (Liberation Daily) 16 Aug. 1952.

76. C.H. Johnston to L.H. Lamb 22 Aug. 1952, FC1461/16, FO371/99345. The Shanghai Dockyards were said to have lost £70 000 in 1951. J. McKenzie (FO) minute 18 Aug. 1952, *ibid.*

77. Lamb to FO, no. 881, 22 Nov. 1952, FC1461/46; local newspaper cuttings, FC1461/63, FO371/99346.

78. D. Buchan to F.C.B. Black (HK) 21 May 1952, HK: *HKBGA*, GHO 154, Shanghai Office 1945–57, Box no. 1860; G.W. Aldington to Johnston, 3 Dec. 1952, FC1461/57, FO371/99346; CA to W.D. Allen, 14 Sept. 1952, *CA: Cresta Files*.

79. *Jie Fang Ri Bao*, 21 Nov. 1952; J.M. Addis to the Salvage Association, Lloyds, 9 Oct. 1952, FC1461/37, FO371/99346.

80. S.L. Burdett, Consul in Shanghai, to FO, 17 Jan. 1951, FC1102/2, FO371/99258; Foreign Affairs College, *op. cit.* p. 221.

81. The ceremonies for handing over the inventories were held with solemnity and respect. At the early stage of the requisition, Gadsby and his colleague Henry of the Gas Co. had been found destroying company documents and were promptly stopped.

82. Lamb to FO, no. 945, 19 Dec. 1952; Shanghai Consul to FO, no. 291, 15 Dec. 1952, FC1461/58, FO371/99346.

83. The Shanghai Gas Co. was incorporated in 1862, and its plant began to supply gas in 1865. The Shanghai Waterworks was started in 1881 and began to supply water in 1883. The British Tramway began operating its first line in 1908, and later expanded to include buses and trolley buses.

84. See SASS, *The Economy of Shanghai, op. cit.*; FO files FO371/83353 and

92258. It was estimated that the British Tramway's indebtedness to the People's Bank of China in 1950 stood at £140 000, in addition to another £103 000 to the American-owned Shanghai Power Company for power supply, equal to approximately three months' total revenue. *Annual Report*, 18 Sept. 1950, FC1106/232, FO371/83353. The accumulated loss of the Shanghai Waterworks at the end of 1950 was £256 540, not including the loss of £5575 on the Shipping Consumers' Account. *Director's Report*, 28 June 1951, FC1102/6, FO371/92258. The Shanghai Gas Co. suffered a loss of HK$1 722 808.47 in 1950, the total debit was brought to HK$3 095 379.08. *Company Report* for 1950, dated 22 Aug. 1951, FC1102/9, FO371/92258.

85. The management of the Gas Co., for instance, was criticised for unduly increasing the salaries of senior and foreign personnel in spite of the financial strains experienced by the firm, and for selling by-products at a greater discount than necessary, thereby causing the company great losses. There were also complaints about anomalies in the company's bookkeeping.

86. See J. Gadsby of the Gas Co., remarks at a general meeting of the company, FC1106/232, FO371/83353; FC1102/2, 9, FO371/92258, quoted at the beginning of this chapter.

87. Lamb, no. 774 to FO, 4 Oct. 1952, FC1461/36(A), FO371/99346.

88. The crews of the five vessels, that is s/s *Yu Jing, Yu Yang, Yu Lian, Yu Pu* and *Yu Qong*, announced their allegiance to the Beijing government on 29 March 1950. Their former owner was the Board of Trustees for Rehabilitation Affairs (BOTRA), a special agency of the Guomindang government. See J.S.H. Shattock (FO) minute, 17 March 1953, FC1461/34, FO371/108088; *RMRB*, 27 Feb. 1953.

89. The last Court decision was taken on 31 Jan. 1953, to award the *Yu Qong* to BOTRA. See FO brief for Lord Reading, 21 March 1953, FC1121/61, FO371/108083. See also Foreign Affairs College, *op.cit.*, p. 221.

4 Trade Restrictions and Embargoes

1. Minute by S.M.B. Green, 24 Dec. 1948, FO371/75864.

2. CP (49) 39, 4 Mar. 1949, CAB129/32; Memorandum by the Foreign Secretary, 23 Aug. 1949, and Annex A, CP (49) 180 CAB129/36; G. Adler-Karlsson, *Western Economic Warfare 1947–67*, 1968, p. 40.

3. A memorandum entitled 'Foreign Sales of Arms: Application of Reciprocity Principle' (DO (48) 44), 19 July, 1948.

4. In March 1948 the Department of Commerce established two categories of countries: 'R' category included all European countries, and 'O' category comprised all other destinations. The US required export licences for all goods exported to the R group of countries, and this was called the R procedure. Yoko Yasuhara, 'Japan, Communist China, and Export Controls in Asia, 1948–52', *Diplomatic History*, vol. 10, no. 1 (winter 1986), p. 76. The classified strategic lists were known as the IA List and IB List. The IA list included items of the highest military significance, other than arms and munitions. The IB List included machine tools and other equipment and materials for more

generalised industrial purposes. Licences for shipments to ECA countries freely were granted, and licences for the Soviet Union and Soviet allies denied, without disclosing the criteria upon which the licensing system operated.

5. EPC (49) 8th Meeting, Minute (2); report by the Security Export Control Working Party (SECWP), Joint War Production Staff, MoD, 23 June 1950, UR3437/16G, FO371/87211. These were introduced under the Export of Goods (Control) Orders 1948, no. 2778, as amended in 1949, nos 384, 515 and 652. In addition, licenses were required for exports of a fairly large number of short supply items, some of which were on the US 1B List. *FRUS*, 1949, 9:861.

6. CP (49) 39, 4 Mar. 1949, CAB129/32.

7. Minutes of a meeting held by the SECWP, composed of representatives of the Treasury, BoT, Ministry of Fuel and Power, CRO, CO and MoT, 13 Apr. 1949, F5766, FO371/75865; R. Stevenson (Nanjing) to FO, 22 Apr. 1949, F5746, FO371/75865. See also Ritchie Ovendale, *The English-Speaking Alliance*, 1985, pp. 7, 16, 186–7, 229.

8. See FO371/75853; NSC41, 28 Feb. 1949, *FRUS*, 1949, 9:826–34; R. Stevenson (Nanking) no. 467 to FO, 22 Apr. 1949, F5746, FO371/75865.

9. See FO371/75854-75857; *FRUS*, 1949, 9:847–9, 851, 861–3, 869.

10. SECWP Report, 2 July 1949, F10972/1121/10, FO371/75856. There was agreement on five areas where controls might be usefully applied on China. Record of the 3rd meeting, 22 June 1949, F9124/1121/10. FO371/75855.

11. SAC (49) 6th Meeting, Minute 1, in CP (50) 157, 3 July 1950, CAB129/41.

12. CM (48)/3, 13 Dec. 1948, CAB128/13; General Headquarters Far East Land Forces to Ministry of Defence, 27 June, 1949, F8592/1121/10, FO371/75854. See also *FRUS* 1949, 9:1016–18; FO to Washington no. 7428, 28 July 1949, F8844/1121/10, FO371/75854.

13. Acheson to US missions, 11 Oct., *FRUS*, 1949, 9:883.

14. Acheson to US missions, 11 Oct., *FRUS*, 1949, 9:881; NSC41/1, 7 November, *ibid.*, 9:894; 'Present Provisional United States Licensing Policy for Far Eastern Destinations', enclosed in F.P. Bartlett (US Embassy London) to Tomlinson (FO) 22 Dec. 1949, F19382/1121/10, FO371/75858.

15. See FO371/83364; *FRUS*, 1949, 9:887–8, 906. The Canadian government passed an Order in Council, dated 9 December 1949. The object was to exercise control over commodities corresponding to American 1A and 1B Lists with respect to China and Korea.

16. JWPC(WP)/M (49) 18, 117D WP, minutes of a meeting, 21 October 1949, F1550/1121/10, FO371/75857; See also FC1121/7A, FO371/83364.

17. Engineering Industries Division, Ministry of Supply, to Johnson and Phillips, Ltd, 2 October 1950, M349/247, FO371/105879.

18. M.M. Cohen, Acting Secretary of BCC in Shanghai, to G.E. Mitchell (CA), 24 July 1951, FC1121/308, FO371/92284. See also Homewood of BoT to G.E. Mitchell, 10 August 1951, *ibid.*

19. SECWP report, 26 July 1950, FE (O) (50) 41, CAB134/290.

20. Draft paper on East–West trade, 2 May 1950, UR3437/16, FO371/ 87211.
21. FO to Sir O. Franks (Washington) no. 897, 7 July 1950, UR3437/45G, FO371/87212; Working Party report 26 July 1950, FE (O) (50) 41, CAB134/290.
22. Summary of decisions 9–20 Jan. 1950, UR348/13, FO371/87186. See also *American Foreign Policy Current Documents*, 1956, pp. 1072–3; and Margaret P. Doxey, *Economic Sanctions and International Enforcement*, 1977, pp. 22–5.
23. Circular letter to Britain's OEEC posts, 14 April 1950, UR3437/11, FO371/87211.
24. CM 46 (50) (2), 17 July 1950, CAB128/18; Bruce to Acheson, telegram 283, 17 July 1950, *FRUS*, 1950, 6:650.
25. Outward telegram from CRO, no. 189, 19 July 1950, FC1121/12, FO371/ 83364; H. Gresswell (MoD) to J.A. Turpin, UK Del to OEEC, 18 July 1950, UR3437/48, FO371/87212.
26. CP (50)201, 31 August, 1950, CAB129/42. The Cabinet's Conclusions are in CM, 55(50)/7, 4 September, 1950, CAB128/18.
27. These items included construction and conveying machinery, precision instruments, transportation equipment, chemicals, steel mill products, non-ferrous metals and their manufactures, electric power generating and distributing apparatus, and other miscellaneous items.
28. SECWP Report on export to China, 23 January 1951, FC1121/146, FO137/92277. See also FO brief for the debate on export of heavy machine tools and strategic raw materials, 18 Sept. 1950, UR3437/75, FO371/87213; CM 55(50)/7, CAB128/18.
29. Annex C to the Report on London Tripartite talks, Tri/31 (Final), agreed on 20 Nov. 1950, UR3437/92G, FO371/87214; Foreign Secretary's circular despatch on East–West trade policy, 5 Oct. 1950, UR3437/78G, FO371/87214. UK recommended to COCOM on oil embargo on or about 18 July and COCOM agreed on 24 July. Gray to Acheson telegram 429, 24 July 1950, *FRUS*, 1950, 6:655.
30. G.E. Mitchell (CA) to Laver, 6 Nov. 1950, FC1126/2; Memorandum by BCC Shanghai, Shanghai to FO no. 974, 30 October, 1950, FC1126/1, FO371/83377.
31. FO to China Association, 19 Dec. 1950; FO to Beijing, no. 2204, 19 Dec. 1950, FC1126/3, FO371/83377. N.C.C. Trench wrote to W.O. Newsam at BoT that he found some of the remarks made by the China Association 'surprisingly naive'.
32. *The Current Export Bulletin*, no. 596, 7 Dec. 1950, cited in *American Foreign Policy Current Documents*, 1956, pp. 1086–7. See also *FRUS*, 1950, 6:684, 7:1907–11, 7:1926.
33. SECWP report, FC1121/146, FO137/92277; Minutes of meetings, CAB134/292.
34. Treasury minute (A.J. Phelps), 11 Jan. 1951, FC1121/22, FO371/92273.
35. Telegram no. 814 saving from FO to Washington, 17 Feb. 1951, annex B to Memorandum by the Foreign Secretary, CP (51) 100, 3 Apr. 1951, CAB129/45.
36. CM, 34 (51) Minute 2, 7 May 1951, CAB128/19; US 82nd Congress, 1st

Session, House Report no. 464; *The Economist* 19 May 1951. In the background were also the allegation of a new offensive by the Chinese in Korea, a recent letter from US Secretary of State pressing Britain for drastic punitive measures against China, and the criticisms in the House of Commons concerning reported shipments of rubber to China in spite of the further controls on rubber to China adopted on 6 April.

37. CM, 34(51) minute 2, 7 May 1951, CAB128/19; the UN resolution of 18 May 1951. UN Document A/1805.

38. The remarks were attributed to UK delegate to UN, Sir Gladwyn Jebb, made on 14 May 1951, see M.A. Fitzsimons, *The Foreign Policy of the British Government 1945–1951*, 1953, p. 148.

39. CP(51) 100 3 Apr. 1951, CAB129/45.

40. Adler-Karlsson in his comment on the UN resolution of 18 May 1951 suggested, 'It is in this context, as a way of justifying a doubtful policy with a sanction from the United Nations, and in that way getting Western public opinion favourably inclined to embargo activities, that the United Nations embargo resolution on China must be understood'. G. Adler-Karlsson, *Western Economic Warfare, 1947–1967*, 1968, p. 30.

41. *Board of Trade Journal*, vol. 160, no. 2844, 23 June 1951, pp. 1321–2.

42. FO paper, May 1951, FC1121/196, FO371/92279; COCOM Doc. 402, 3 July 1951, M3415/122, FO371/94296; FO Minute (R.M.K. Slater) 21 June 1951, FC1121/245, FO371/92281.

43. Tokyo (H.H. Thomas) to the Department of Treasury (N.E. Young), 15 Jan. 1951, FC1121/46, FO371/92274. With regard to US controls over the shipping of commodities to Hong Kong, see Sir A. Grantham to CO no. 31, 9 Jan. 1951, FC1121/15, FO371/92272, and nos 40 and 46, 11 Jan. FC1121/25, FO371/92273.

44. These included steel helmets, military type water bottles and radio sets. The Hong Kong authorities obviously were in a rush to impose new controls in order to meet the American demand. Sir. A. Grantham to CO, 26 Jan. 1951, FC1121/57, FO371/92274.

45. Hong Kong Saving no. 113 to CO, 1 Aug. 1951, FC1121/313, FO371/92284.

46. Shell for instance, totally depended on US supplies of certain oil products which were not forthcoming. Ministry of Fuel to Washington, 2 Feb. 1951, FO371/92275. See also generally FO371/93374, 93376.

47. Hong Kong Export Controls, FO to Washington, no. 600, 14 Feb. 1951, FC1121/10, FO371/92276. An earlier version is in FC1121/68, FO371/92275.

48. Sir A. Grantham to CO, no. 922, 28 Aug. 1951; J.J. Pasken (CO) to R.H. Scott (FO) 29 Aug. 1951, FC1121/321, FO371/92285.

49. Trench (FO) to H.E.G. Barrett (MoF), 28 Oct. 1951, FO371/83386.

50. C.J. Homeward to R. Anderson (MoS), 28 May 1951, FC1121/202, FO371/92280.

51. JWPC, SECWP, SX/P (53) 36, 28 Jan. 1953, M349/10, FO371/105869; minutes in M349/219, FO371/105875.

52. A. Rumbold, minute, 4 May 1951, M3415/88, FO371/94293; CM, 34(51), Minute 2, 7 May; CM, 35 (51), minute 4, 10 May, CAB128/19.

53. Minutes of a meeting called by C.R. Attlee, 17 May 1951, FC1121/
1193; FC1121/187E, FO271/92279.
54. Sir O. Franks to FO, no. 346, 3 Feb. 1951, FC1121/69; Grantham to
CO, no. 142, 6 Feb. 1951, FC1121/70, FO371/92275. See also *FRUS*,
1951, 7:1976–7, 1897–8, 1918–19; M.E. Lashmore, Staff Officer (Intelligence) Hong Kong, report in Admiralty to FO, 4 April 1951, FC1121/
147, FO371/92278. For a list of main items in her cargo, see FC1121/
125, FO371/92276.
55. BoT Note on export of streptomycin to China, 14 May 1953, M3415/25,
FO371/106001; Governor of Hong Kong to CO, saving no. 113, 1 Aug.
1951, FC1121/313, FO371/92284; COCOM Doc. 368, 28 Apr. 1951,
M3415/79, FO371/94292.
56. COCOM Doc. 490, 9 Oct. 1951, M3415/230, FO371/94302; China
Committee document CH/44 (53), M3414/15; CH/202 (53), 30 Oct.
1953, M3414/36, FO371/106001.
57. FO371/94299-94307-318, C (52)1, 1 Jan. 1952, and C(52) 7, 17 Jan.
1952, CAB129/49; the Cabinet decisions are in C.C. 1 (52)/1, 3 Jan.
1952, and C.C. 4 (52)/4, 17 Jan. 1952, CAB128/24; *American Foreign
Policy Current Documents* (1956) pp. 1605–6, and 1067–71. For a
comparison with the ILs I–III, see FO letter to Singapore (F. Bren-
chley), 27 May 1953, M349/117, FO371/105874.
58. FO to Copenhagen, no. 155, 21 July 1951, M3415/146, FO371/94297;
and files in FO371/94298. The French proposal and declaration are in
Consultative Group Paper no. IV.B., M3415/162, FO371/94299.
59. See M3415/162, FO371/94299.
60. COCOM Doc. 785, 17 June 1952, M3410/73, FO371/100225.
61. H.B. Shepherd (Paris) to R.M.K. Slater (FO), 27 Oct. 1951, M3415/
234, FO371/94302; COCOM Doc. 519, 3 Nov. 1951, M3415/245 and
COCOM Doc. 533, 26 Nov. M3415/251, FO371/94303.
62. Re. List II, see COCOM Doc. 659, 27 Mar. 1952, M3410/43; re List III,
see COCOM Doc. 723, 22 Apr. and 2 May 1952, M3410/62,
FO371/100224.
63. COCOM Doc. 785, 17 June 1952, M3410/73, FO371/100225. A UK
statement in the Consultative Group pressing for the adoption of the
UK Supplementary List is in Annex D to C.G. IX, 18 July 1952,
M3410/106, FO371/100227.
64. COCOM Doc. 495, 25 Sep. 1951, M3415/210; H.B. Shepherd to
R.M.K. Slater (Paris) 6 Oct. 1951, M3415/216, FO371/94301. See also a
note prepared by the SECWP, 24 July 1952, M3410/113, FO371/100227.
65. Sir E. Hall Patch (Paris) Savingram no. 392, 26 June 1952, M3410/75,
FO371/100224; FO minute (R. Arculus) 6 June 1952, M3415/100225.
The British were complaining that the Americans were 'working behind
our backs in Tokyo to influence the Japanese Government'.
66. Record of a meeting between US and UK officials at MoD, 3 July 1952,
M3410/97, FO371/100227.
67. Washington to FO saving no. 761, 15 July 1952, M3410/99, FO371/
100227; Washington to FO no. 1441, 28 July, M3410/112. The package
deal with Japan included an explicit Japanese guarantee to the US that
the Japanese would separately control their export items on the US lists

and some additional items found to be readily determinable as of strategic importance to China. Ryuii Takeuchi, chief of Japan's Overseas Agency in Washington, protested and was compelled to agree to the relevant exchange of letters at 2 a.m. early on 1 August. He was greatly disturbed and said that his instructions were 'primitive' and that in doing so he was acting in a large degree upon his own responsibility. *FRUS*, 1952–4, 14:1332.

68. CO saving no. 1346 to Hong Kong, 11 Aug. 1952, M3410/118, and the Consultative Group Resolution on the China Committee, FO371/100228. See also Yoko Yasuhara, *op.cit.* p. 88.

69. UK Delegation Paris Comm'd, 2 Jan. 1953, M349/3, FO371/105869; a draft paper, enclosed in letter from H. Gresswell to Arculus, 27 Feb. 1953, M349/40, FO371/105870; FO to Washington (Strang) no. 1374, 24 March 1953, M349/60, FO371/105871.

70. See FO371/105877 and 105878.

71. Remarks by Chancellor of the Exchequer R.A. Butler 30 July 1953, *PD*, vol. 518, 1952–3, cols. 1558–60.

72. *American Foreign Policy Current Documents*, 1956, pp. 1080–2. The revised lists came into effect on 16 Aug. 1954. The position on China control was expounded by W. Churchill in Feb. 1954 when he called for a substantial relaxation of the Soviet embargo.

73. FO Circulars no. 035 (Anthony Eden) 15 Mar. 1954 and no. 061 (Harold Macmillan) 23 July, 1955, respectively in M341/51, FO371/111208 and M341/137, FO371/111210; Brief by BoT 'Trade with China' 13 June 1956, CAB130/113, GEN.518/6/4b.

74. Hong Kong (Grantham) to CO, no. 658, 2 July 1949, F9607/1121/10, FO371/75855; E.H. Jocobs-Larkcom (UK Consul at Tamsui) to Shattock, FO, 13 Aug. 1951, FC1121/315, FO371/92285. US Senator McCarthy alleged that two British owned Panamanian ships carried Chinese troops along the China coast in 1951 and 1952. Ministry of Transport (G.R.W. Brigstocke) to CO (C.G. Gibbs), 22 July 1953, M349/162F, FO371/105876.

75. UK Delegation to UN (Sir B. Jebb) to FO, 9 June 1951, FC1121/218, FO371/92280.

76. Re UK IC/DV system, see doc. no. Sub-C (51) 1, 8–19 Sept. 1951, M3415/209, FO371/94301.

77. The COCOM IC/DV system was inaugurated on 15 July 1951. COCOM doc. 445, 19 July 1951, M3415/138, FO371/94297. Re extension of the UK system, see COCOM, Doc. 755, 23 May 1952, M3410/64, FO371/100225.

78. SX/P(53) 61, 23 Feb. 1953, M349/80B, FO371/105872.

79. CRO Outward Telegram, no. 60 Presse, 13 Mar. 1953, M349/82U, FO371/105873. The British announcement was made on 7 March, see the communiqué of 7 Mar. 1953, *American Foreign Policy, 1950–1955, Basic Documents*, pp. 1702–4.

80. Doc. CH/78 (53), 17 Apr. 1953, M349/76A, FO371/105872; *Board of Trade Journal*, 28 Mar. 1953, p. 624; Hong Kong (Grantham) to CO, no. 349, 7 May 1953, M349/163A, FO371/105875.

81. CO to Hong Kong, Singapore and Aden, no. 421/319/317, 26 Apr. 1953, M349/82Wi, FO371/105873.
82. F.A. Kendrick (MoD) to R. Arculus (FO), 16 Apr. 1953, M349/125, FO371/105875; FO minute (R. Arculus) 2 Apr. 1953, M349/123, FO371/105874. Indonesia regarded the new British measure as outside the scope of UN resolution and would not commit itself with regard to the bunkering services of the Royal Dutch–Shell Group operating in Indonesia, especially in cases where a stranded ship needed bunkering in an Indonesian port. Djakarta, no. 47 to FO, 25 Apr. 1953, M349/141, FO371/105875. For reference to the *Falaise* incident, see Paris (Dunnett) to FO (Arculus), 28 Oct. 1953, M349/330, FO371/105884.
83. China Doc. CH/328/ (54), 1 Dec. 1954, M3443/12, FO371/111303.
84. Memo by MoT and Civil Aviation (Harold Watkinson) 4 Jan. 1956, M3426/8, FO371/121939.
85. FO Circular, no. 035 (Anthony Eden), 15 Mar. 1954, M341/51, FO371/111208.
86. Copy of a letter from CO to MoD, SX/P(58) 31, 22 July 1958, DEFE10/341.
87. *PD*, vol. 478, 1949–50, cols. 951, 1126 and 1153.
88. Ritchie Ovendale, *The English-Speaking Alliance*, 1985, the front page, and pp. 207, 213, 237.
89. Ministry of Transport Note (W.P.S. Ormonds), 16 Jan. 1951, FC1121/20, FO371/92273.
90. MoT (B.P.H. Dickinson) to FO (R.S. Crawford), 27 Feb. 1954, M3443/2, FO371/111303.
91. See Sir A. Grantham (HK) to A.M. Kackintosh (FO) 15 Oct. 1955 re remarks by D'Orlandi, former COCOM chairman, M3444/52, FO371/116020.
92. G. Adler-Karlsson, *op. cit.*, pp. 45–6.
93. Roger Makes (FO) minute, 9 July 1951, M3452/14, FO371/94329.
94. Re air compressors, see M349/2, 15 Dec. 1952 to 7 Apr. 1953, FO371/105869, and Doc. CH/188, 7 Oct. 1953, M349/291, FO371/105882; re grinding machines, see China Committee Summary, no. 52, 22 June 1953, M349/204, FO371/105877; re lorries, see telegram no. 75 from Consul in Macao to FO, 11 June 1953, M349/207, FO371/105877; re dosimeters, Nov. 1953, M349/289, FO371/105881; re iron and steel products, see SX/P(53) 201, 15 September, 1953, M349/301A, FO371/105882.
95. T.M. Pink at COCOM to FO (J.E. Coulson), 21 Feb. 1953, M349/38, FO371/105870. The French delegate, Charpendier, attacked the UK position towards control of antibiotic drugs for China as 'scandalous and hypocritical', and alleged that 'the only reason why we [the British] were insisting on such a wide Embargo List was because we had such an efficiently organised contraband system through Hong Kong'. The UK delegate fought back, saying that these adjectives, if they were to be used, 'might with more justice be applied to the line taken by [the French] government'. He also said that the suggestion that there was a large contraband trade through Hong Kong was constantly being

brought forward but was never substantiated 'although we had challenged our critics to produce their evidence'.

96. FO circular, no. 035 (Anthony Eden), 15 Mar. 1954, M341/51, FO371/111208.
97. BoT memo. 13 June 1956, GEN.518/6/4B, CAB130/113.
98. J.F. Dulles to H. Macmillan 16 Nov. 1955, M3444/52 (A), FO371/116020. Lord Reading wrote, 'I suppose that in all the circumstances we must agree', but 'The inescapable inference is that we are refraining under American pressure from taking a course which we ourselves believe to be reasonable and indeed advantageous'. 21 Nov. 1955, M3444/52(C), *ibid.*
99. A.J. Edden (FO) minute, 29 Nov. 1955; H. Macmillan to J.F. Dulles, FO to Washington, no. 5100 saving, 2 Dec. 1955, M3444/69, FO371/116021.
100. J.F. Dulles to H. Macmillan 12 Dec. 1955, M3444/73, FO371/116021. For the summit talks, see M3426/24, FO371/121939.
101. FO to Washington, no. 5101 saving, 2 Dec. 1955, M3444/69, FO371/116021; No. 6229, 30 Dec. 1955, M3426/3, FO371/121939.
102. D.I. Dunnett (Paris) to E.M. Smith (FO) 17 Mar. 1956, M3426/56(F), FO371/121941.
103. J.E. Coulson (Washington) to FO, 13 Apr. 1956, M3426/76, FO371/121942; NSC 269th meeting, 8 Dec. 1955, *FRUS*, 1955–7, 3:209–11. See also *The Economist*, 3 May 1956.
104. J.E. Coulson (Washington) to FO, no. 1003, 19 Apr. 1956, M3426/77(B), FO371/121942.
105. Eisenhower to Eden, 27 Apr. 1956, M3426/93, FO371/121943.
106. BoT memo. 13 June 1956, GEN.518/6/4B, CAB130/113. Dulles gave a news conference on 22 May. Sir R. Makins (Washington) to FO, no. 407 saving, 23 May 1956, M3426/110, FO371/121943.
107. Doc. CH/658(56), 12 June 1956, M3426/121, FO371/121944.
108. Report by the chairman of the Council on Foreign Economic Policy (Clarence B. Randall) Sept. 1956, *FRUS*, 1955–7, 9:28.
109. P.H. Gore-Booth (FO) minute 10 Jan. 1957, FC1121/1, FO371/127321.
110. UK Del. Bermuda to FO, no. 1 saving, 25 Mar. 1957, M3426/31, FO371/128299.
111. Doc. CH/1375(57), 9 Apr. 1957, M3426/55(E), FO371/128300; L.M. Minford (UK Del. Paris) to E.G. Rolleston (FO) 2 Apr. 1957.
112. Doc. CH/1375(57), 9 Apr. 1957, M3426/55(E), FO371/128300. See also a Parliamentary motion, 12 Apr. 1957, endorsing an appeal made to the government by FBI and other SBTC organisations, M3426/36, FO371/128300.
113. Doc. CH/1438 (57), 21 May 1957 M3426/101(B), FO371/128302. In particular Britain believed that a strict control was demanded by the US on those items on which there was a great pressure for relaxation from British trading interests, e.g. land rovers, heavy tractors, diesel engines, certain chemicals, locomotives, surveying instruments, ballbearings; and that certain items which could now be exported to China subject to notification would in future require the prior approval of CHINCOM, under a very strict procedure for consultation and justifi-

cation. This would cover items important for the UK trade: small generating sets, motor trucks, civil engineering and road-making equipment, some mining machinery, tyres for farm tractors, and rubber. FO to Washington, no. 2180, 14 May 1957, M3426/96, FO371/128302.

114. F.W. Glaves-Smith (BoT) to D.S. Laskey (FO) 18 Apr. 1957, M3426/71, FO371/128301. See also D. Eisenhower to H. Macmillan, letter dated 18 Apr. 1957, M3426/99, FO371/128301.

115. FO to Washington, no. 1053, 22 May 1957, M3426/110, FO371/128303.

116. Mutual Aid Dept (FO) brief, 28 May 1957, M3426/126(B) FO371/128304; FO to UK Del. Paris, no. 482, 22 May 1957, M3426/110, FO371/128303.

117. H. Macmillan to D. Eisenhower, 29 May 1957, M3426/157, FO371/128305; *PD*, vol. 571 1956–7, cols. 618–20; notes for Supplementaries, M3426/134, FO371/128304.

118. State Dept text of news release to the press, Washington to FO, no. 1195, 30 May 1957, M3426/132, FO371/128304; Eisenhower's press conference, Washington to FO, no. 310 saving, 5 June 1957, M3426/160, FO371/128305.

119. Beijing to FO, no. 248, 14 June 1957, M3426/140, FO371/128305; Con O'Neill (Beijing) to O.C. Morland (FO) 5 June 1957, FC1151/40, FO371/127354. Zhang Hanfu was said to have spoken very warmly about the British step.

120. Susan Strange, 'The Trade Embargoes: Sense or Nonsense?', *The Yearbook of World Affairs*, 1958, pp. 55–73, at 57. See also Suchati Chuthasmit, 'The Experience of the US and Its Allies in Controlling Trade with the Red Bloc, 1948–60', Ph.D. dissertation at the Fletcher School of Law and Diplomacy, Tufts University, 1961.

121. An FO memo, 20 Aug. 1957, FC1151/82, FO371/127355.

122. The two governments planned to set up a joint working group in Oct. 1957 to consider the criteria for strategic controls. Record of a conversation 25 Oct. 1957, UEE10447/2, FO371/127198.

5 The Departure

1. See Zhang Zhongli and Chen Zengnian, *Sha Xun Ji Tuan Zai Jiu Zhong Guo* (The Sassoon Group in Old China), 1985, pp. 153–9.

2. Hutchinson to FO, 19 May 1950, FC1106/126, FO371/83348.

3. Re confiscation of the state capital controlled by the Guomindang government, see Hsueh Mu-chiao *et al.*, *The Socialist Transformation of the National Economy in China*, 1960, pp. 26–8, 33.

4. Memorandum by Gutierrez, 22 June 1949, FO 371 75866; Daily Press Bulletin, Shanghai, 15 July 1949, 'Local Trade Firm Forms Automobile Company', enclosed in F16098/1153/10, FO371/75867; Shanghai to FO, 9 Feb. 1950, FO371/83344.

5. Chi-ming Hou, *Foreign Investment and Economic Development in China 1840–1937*, 1965, pp. 73–6; Wei Zichu, *Di Guo Zhu Yi Yu Kai Luan Mei Kuang* (Imperialism and the Kailan Mines), 1954; G.C. Allen and A.G. Donnithorne, *Western Enterprises in Far Eastern Economic Development: China and Japan*, 1954, pp. 153–5.

6. See BT11/3390; F5066/1153/10, FO371/75865. The CCP also condemned the Guomindang authorities for giving approval to the 1934 agreement, in particular, Mr Chen Gongbo (Ch'en Kung-po), then Minister of Industries of the Guomindang government, for rushing through the case in an act of national betrayal. See Lan Yiqong, *Jie Kai Di Guo Zhu Yi Zai Jiu Zhong Guo Tou Zi De Hei Mu* (Unveil the Medusa of Imperialist Countries' Investment in Old China), 1965, p. 93.
7. FO minute (Trench), 2 Apr. 1951; J.S.H. Shattock to E.J. Nathan (CEM's Chairman) 25 Apr. 1951; Fitzmaurice minute 6 Apr. 1951, FC1103/25, FO371/92260.
8. FO minute (Trench), 2 Apr. 1951. Pryor, a Managing Director of KMA, sent this letter. See also conversation with the FAB Secretariat of the Tianjin Municipality, enclosed in Nathan to Scarlett, 6 Apr. 1949, F5056/1153/10, FO371/75865.
9. Stevenson (Nanjing) to FO no. 655, 18 May 1949, PREM8/945; S.L. Burdett (Tianjin) to L.H. Lamb (Beijing) 8 May 1949, F7904/154/10, FO371/75933.
10. It was suggested that (after Pryor left) the assets in China were no longer in the possession of the Chinese Engineering and Mining Co. As it would seem impossible to give a monetary value to the chance of recovering their value, or any part thereof, no figure could be set in the Balance Sheet in respect of these assets. Opinion by John Foster (Legal Counsel) 1951, FC1103/197, FO371/92267. See also Report of Proceedings at the 40th Annual General Meeting, 18 June 1952, FC1105/321, FO371/99293.
11. Note of a discussion between FO and Nathan of KMA, 30 Mar. 1950, FO371/83345; interview with Wu Chengming, Beijing, 9 Sept. 1987.
12. See BT11/3390; J.R. Milligan (Shanghai) to the Pekin Syndicate, Ltd; London, 10 Mar. 1949, F5324/154/10; and P.D. Coates (FO) minute, 2 May 1949, FO371/75933. Some mines in Qingdao used to be under Pekin Syndicate's control but fell into controversy with the CCP government.
13. W.J. Keswick's interview with FO officials, 2 Feb. 1950, *CA: M & C*, no. 50/G/10, 6 Feb. 1950; *CA: M & C*, no. 50/G/26, 17 Mar. 1950.
14. Sir Esler Dening, minute 29 Apr. 1950, FC1106/90, and J.S.H. Shattock, minute 4 May 1950, FC1106/102, FO371/83347; *CA: M & C*, 1950, no. 50/G/29, 50/G/33.
15. FC1106/178 and 184, FO371/83350.
16. BCC Shanghai confidential memo. 29 Sept. 1949, *CA: M & C*, 1949, no. 49/G/66, 20 Oct. 1949.
17. Circular on the organisation of British commercial interests in China, *CA: M & C*, 1949, no. 49/G/72, 9 Nov. 1949. A memorandum written by Schlee of the China Association was attached to Circular 49/G/49 dated 17 Aug. 1949. Schlee's suggestion was intended to prevent Chinese Government agencies playing off one merchant against another; whilst still providing customary expert advice to foreign connections and meeting the Chinese half way by providing a convenient service, including financial facilities.

18. A paper prepared by John Kenyon of Patons and Baldwins, Aug. 1950, FC1106/210, FO371/83352.
19. Sir Esler Dening (Hong Kong) to Robert H. Scott (FO), 4 Nov. 1950, FC1106/238, FO371/83353.
20. K. Bumstead (Shanghai) to FO, no. 177, 26 May 1951, FC1103/67, FO371/92262; CP(51)123, 3 May 1951, CAB129/45.
21. Previously some business people had wanted to use the threat as a kind of pressure to bear upon the British government for accelerating the pace of political negotiations with Beijing leading to better commercial relations between China and Britain.
22. Lamb (Beijing) to FO, no. 1036, FC1103/68, FO to Lamb, letter 28 June 1951, FC1103/74, FO371/92262.
23. J.S.H. Shattock to Baron Alessandro Farace, Italian Embassy, London, 4 Sept. 1951. The text of Lamb's communication to Zhang Hanfu of the PRC–MFA is in FC1103/182, FO371/92266. The Counsellor of the Swiss Legations presented the director of the Western European Dept. of the MFA Huan Xiang with an *aide mémoire* and also took up cases involving Spanish, French and Italian nationals. Lamb to FO, no. 1388, 20 Aug. 1951, FC1103/118, FO371/92264.
24. FO to Brussels, no. 401 saving 20 Aug. 1951, FC1103/109, FO371/92264.
25. British officials in Singapore reported that all disabilities allegedly imposed by Chinese authorities on foreign nationals in China 'are now being suffered by Chinese nationals detained under emergency regulations in Malaya'. Singapore (M.L. MacDonald) to FO, no. 507, 21 Aug. 1951, FC1103/119, FO371/92264. See also Foreign Affairs College, *Zhong Hua Ren Min Gong He Guo Dui Wai Guan Xi Shi* (History of Foreign Relations of the PRC), 1964, p. 192.
26. See R.H. Scott (Permanent Under-Secretary) minute, in which he advocated retaliation through visa and other restrictions against the Chinese, 25 Jan. 1952, FC1025/9, FO371/99260. The fact that this policy had already been implemented was probably evidenced by British refusal of a visa for the UK to Li Yimang (Lee Yi-mang) on the occasion of a meeting of the Anglo–Chinese Friendship Association in 1951. L.H. Lamb to R.H. Scott, 21 June 1951, FC1052/16, FO371/92251. See also FC1103/145, FO371/92266, where the Head of the Asian Affairs Dept. of the PRC–MFA was reported as saying that the Chinese government purposely had not given publicity to the arrest of Americans and other nationals in deference to strong popular resentment towards Westerners.
27. C.(52)107, 8 April 1952, CAB129/51. With regard to CA's meetings with Lord Reading and the Foreign Secretary, see FC1105/59, FO371/99283; FC1105/114, FO371/99285.
28. FC1105/82, FO371/99284; CC 40(52)/3, 9 Apr. 1952, CAB128/24.
29. FC1105/130, FO371/99286; Press Release from CA, 19 May 1952, *CA: M & C*, 1952.
30. See 'Correspondence between the Government of the United Kingdom of Great Britain and Northern Ireland and the Central People's

Government of China on British Trade in China', Peking, 12 Apr.–5 July 1952, no. 4, in *CMD*, 8639, 1952, pp. 820–5.

31. Lamb (Beijing) to FO, no. 556, 8 July 1952, *CA: Cresta File*. Lamb also suggested that the Chinese argument 'seems to me to be less aggressive than usual and to lack appearance of conviction'. Some press interpreted the response as 'though argumentative in form, is conciliatory in content'. *The Times*, 22 July 1952. See also *RMRB*, 19 July 1952.

32. The Agreement of Assignment, 2 Apr. 1952, FO371/99286; K.C. Johnson-Hill (BAT Co. (Hong Kong) Ltd) to H.V. Tiencken, Shanghai, 8 Jan. 1952, *The Yee Tsoong Files*, SASS.

33. BAT came to China in 1902 to set up distributing and manufacturing operations. BAT Co. (China) Ltd was founded on 27 Feb. 1919. On 22 Sept. 1934 Yee Tsoong Tobacco Co. Ltd was founded to take over the properties of BAT (China), the latter moved to Hong Kong upon registration there in Dec. 1936. The Board of Directors of BAT Co. (China) Ltd. decided on 10 Nov. 1947 to transfer the registry of their Yee Tsoong Tobacco Co. Ltd, Yee Tsoong Tobacco Distributors Co. Ltd, Capital Lithographers Ltd, and Tobacco Development Co. Ltd, from China to Hong Kong, which was implemented on 22 Jan. 1948; on 23 Sept. 1948, the entire stock of BAT (China) shares was transferred to Yee Tsoong Tobacco Co. On 22 Mar. 1951 BAT Co. (China) Ltd. changed its name to BAT Co. (Hong Kong) Ltd. See *Ying Mei Yan Gong Si Zai Hua Shi Liao Hui Bian* (British American Tobacco Company's Enterprises in China: A Collection of Source Material) (4 volumes), ed. by Economic Research Inst., SASS, 1983.

34. Zhang Zhongli, 'The Development of Foreign Enterprises in Old China and Its Characteristics – The Case of the British–American Tobacco Company', in *SASS Papers*, pp. 134, 142–3.

35. The quotas were determined on a monthly basis and changed from season to season. For instance, Shanghai proposed at the time of the First All-China Rolled Tobacco Industry Conference in Beijing in July 1950, that Shanghai be allotted 45 000 cases per month, to be divided as follows: –

Government factories	(2)	9 720
Nanyang Bros.	(1)	2 500
Other Chinese Factories	(22)	22 960
Foreign Factories*	(2)	9 820

*YTT and Tobacco Products Corporation (American).

However the conference decided in the end that the allotment to the region be 87.2 per cent of the original figure, thereby reducing YTT's quotas to approx. 8570 cases, Richard Price to E.G. Langford, 5 July 1950; memo. by Ray Chang 4 Aug. 1950, FC1106/218, FO371/83352; Notes on YTT's quotas for the second half of 1950, 11 Sept. 1950, *The Yee Tsoong Files*, Shanghai.

36. A. Lopato and Sons Ltd. (Russian-owned) was founded in 1909, with its cigarette factory in Harbin. It passed into BAT control in 1914. In May 1952 the Chinese authorities formally took it over. 'A Brief History of the Lopato Cigarette Factory, 1904–1952', ed. by its succes-

sor Harbin Cigarette Factory (PC), 22 Jan. 1957 (unpublished); see also a paper prepared by John Kenyon of Patons and Baldwins, Aug. 1950, FC1106/210, FO371/83352.
37. H.V. Tiencken to T.F. Winmill, 21 July 1950, FC1106/195, FO371/ 83351. The maximum monthly production of YTT's Shanghai factories with labour was said to be 25 000 cases, whereas the maximum monthly production, operating all machines at present installed, was 37 000 cases, YTT to Shanghai Rolled Tobacco Industry Assoc. 30 June 1950, FC1106/218, FO371/83352. It was said that one of the conditions attached was that factories would have to employ a minimum of 40 workers per machine installed; surplus labour could not be discharged without agreement from the union, Richard Price to E.G. Langford, 5 July 1950, FC1106/218, FO371/83352.
38. F.S. Geldart (Shanghai) to the Ministry of Food Industry and the Foreign Investments Bureau of the Financial and Economic Commission of the central government, 4 Dec. 1950, FC1103/4, FO371/ 92259.
39. See files in FO371/92259, 92261, 92266.
40. J.M. Bescheremnih (YTT Tianjin) to R.J.E. Price (Shanghai), 7 Nov. 1950, *The Yee Tsoong Files*, SASS; notes on Chi-Tung Tobacco company, Ltd, Shenyang and Yingkou properties, 9 July 1951, FC1103/91, FO371/92263.
41. Tiencken to Oppenheim, message conveyed in Shanghai to FO no. 237, 16 July 1951, FC1103/95; Loudon to Shattock, 23 July 1951, FC1103/96, FO371/92263.
42. W.B. Christian (Shanghai) to A.J.H. Bowerman (Qingdao) 23 Sept. 1950, *The Yee Tsoong Files*, SASS.
43. Chronology of the BAT Co. (China) Ltd, *British American Company's Enterprise in China: A collection of source material*, 1983, vol. IV, at 1613.
44. FO officials believed that, 'We should not look for any signs of a firm policy by the Central People's Government in their handling of the Case of the YTT. . . . Their approach to the problem of the YTT may have been so empirical because crises in the affairs of the YTT were reached sooner than they wished'. J.S.H. Shattock to L.H. Lamb, 1 Dec. 1951, FC1103/199, FO371/92267.
45. Information derived from the final tabulation of YTT assets and liabilities, Apr. 1952, *The Yee Tsoong Files*, SASS.
46. H.V. Tiencken to T.F. Winmill, 21 July 1950, FC1106/195, FO371/ 83351.
47. James Tuck Hong Tang wrote some lucid comments on this conference in his 'Diplomatic Relations with a Revolutionary Power: Britain's Experience with China, 1949–1954', unpublished Ph.D. dissertation, LSE, University of London, July 1987, Chapter Six.
48. Appendix: List of Participants, Committee for the Promotion of International Trade, *International Economic Conference in Moscow*, Moscow, 1952, p. 311. The British Cabinet, in this connection, decided to dissuade Conservative MP G.B. Drayson from attending. CC 31(52)2, CAB128/24, 18 Mar. 1952.

49. Lei Zhenmin's statement on 7 Apr. 1952, *International Economic Conference in Moscow*, 1952, pp. 112–3, 115.
50. *RMRB*, 13 July 1952; Xu Ziqing, 'On the Question of Sino–British Trade', in *SJZS*, no. 30 (1952), p. 6.
51. 'Correspondence', *op.cit.*, *CMD*, 8639, Aug. 1952, no. 2, p. 3.
52. Zhang Hanfu's statement, in 'Correspondence', *op.cit.*, *CMD*, 8639, no. 4, pp. 4–6.
53. Memo. from BCC Shanghai for Head Offices in London and Hong Kong, encl. in J.O. Lloyd (FO) to G.E. Mitchell (CA), 20 May 1950, FC1105/180, *CA: Cresta File*.
54. Remarks by L.I. Ovadia, *CA: M & C*, no. 52/G/24, 16 June 1952.
55. See two telegrams from Beijing to FO (undated), telegrams no. 376 of 2 May and no. 410 of 14 May 1952, *CA: Cresta File*.
56. FO to Beijing, no. 554, 18 June 1952, *CA: Cresta File*.
57. Shanghai to Beijing, no. 92 saving, 24 Apr. 1952, *CA: Cresta File*.
58. Beijing to FO, no. 502, 20 June 1952, *CA: Cresta File*. See also Zhang Hanfu in his reply to Lamb's note of 19 May in 'Correspondence', *op.cit.*, *CMD*, 8639, Aug. 1952, no. 4, p. 6. Lamb also agreed that the Chinese government might be favourably disposed to proposed representative group in principle.
59. Shanghai to Beijing, no. 180 saving, 10 Sept. 1952, *CA: Cresta File*.
60. Beijing to FO, no. 739, 20 Sept. 1952, *CA: Cresta File*.
61. Shanghai to Beijing, no. 182 saving, 15 Sept. 1952; J.M. Addis (FO) to G. Mitchell (CA) letter d. 10 Dec. 1952, FC1105/430, *CA: Cresta File*.
62. Bumstead (Shanghai) to FO, no. 177, 21 June 1952, FC1105/242, FO371/99290. A list of firms which had notified the local authorities of their wish to withdraw as of 7 July 1952 is in J.M. Addis (later Sir John) (FO) to E.R. Price, 19 Aug. 1952, FC1105/315, *CA: Cresta File*. They included: Arnhold Trading Co., Ltd; Babcock and Wilcox Ltd; British General Electric Co. Ltd; Chartered Bank of India, Australia and China, Ltd; Holt's Wharf (B. and S.); Hongkong and Shanghai Banking Corporation; ICI; Jardine Matheson and Co. Ltd; Mackinnon, Mackenzie and Co. Ltd; Mercantile Bank of India, Ltd; Orient Paint and Varnish Co. (B. and S.); Richards Auto Works, Ltd; Star Laboratory; Swire and Maclaine (B. and S.); and Taikoo Sugar Refinery (B. and S.). An incomplete list of a number of important interests which had not taken action by then is in CA to J.M. Addis, 26 Aug. 1952, FC1105/315, *CA: Cresta File*. They included: B. and S. (that is the firm itself); China Navigation Co. (B. and S.'s shipping business); Shanghai and Hongkew Wharf Co.; Ewo Cotton Mills; Ewo Brewery; Ewo Silk Filature, and so on. (Above Jardine Matheson and Co.'s interests; possibly the firm's application covered everything); Moller Line (UK) Ltd; Shanghai Dockyards; Messrs. Patons and Baldwins Ltd; Calico Printers Association Ltd; the various interests of China Engineers Ltd; Mackenzie and Co.; Liddell Bros.; the Sassoons Group; and Dodwell and Co.. The information was given by the manager of Babcock and Wilcox Ltd.
63. Beijing to FO, no. 566, 8 July 1952, *CA: Cresta File*.
64. Beijing to FO, no. 621, 30 July 1952, *CA: Cresta File*.

65. Correspondence between Johnston (FO) and G.E. Mitchell (CA) 24–6 June 1952, FC1105/235, *CA: Cresta File.*
66. E.W. Jeffery (Consul in Tianjin) to C.T. Crowe (Beijing), 18 June 1952; C.T. Crowe (FO) to H.J. Collar (CA) 2 June 1954, *CA: Cresta File.*
67. E.W. Jeffery to C.T. Crowe, 1 Sept. 1952, FC1105/382, FO371/99295.
68. Contract of Transfer of Property between Jardine, Matheson and Co., Ltd Tientsin Branch, Jardine Engineering Corp. Ltd Tientsin Branch, and the Tientsin Real Estate Co., d. 17 June 1953, signed by A. Kidd, and Yang Cheng Ching, FC1102/97(A), FO371/108083; Lamb (Beijing) to FO, no. 843, 3 Nov. 1952, FC1105/400, FO371/99296; John Keswick (Hong Kong) to G.W. Aldington, 24 July 1953, FC1102/97(A), FO371/108083. See also Aron Shai, 'Imperialism Imprisoned: the Closure of British Firms in the People's Republic of China', *The English Historical Review*, vol. CIV, no. 410 Jan. 1989, p. 105.
69. See E.W. Jeffery to Crowe, 19 June 1952, FC1105/276, and the China and Korean Dept. (FO) to Beijing, 31 July 1952, FC1105/277, FO371/99291.
70. Properties taken over from British official possessions spread over 22 cities. In Nov. 1950 the Central Government promulgated 'Regulations Governing Land Reform in Cities and Suburban Areas', on which the British government reserved its position.
71. See David Sassoon and Co. Ltd (Director, M. Maynard) to C.H. Johnson (FO) 2 Sept. 1952, FC1105/349, FO371/99293. A list of British-owned real estate companies operating in Shanghai as of 1956 is in Shanghai to FO, 3 Oct. 1956, FC1151/72, FO371/120945. They included: Cathay Land Co. Ltd; Central Properties Ltd; Shanghai Estates and Finance Ltd. Other cases were San Sing Properties Ltd (leased to the government); E.D. Sassoon and Co. Ltd (dormant).
72. Veitch (Shanghai) to FO, no. 281, 19 Nov. 1952, FC1105/414, FO371/99296; *Butterfield & Swire 1867–1957* (a short history reprinted from the Blue Funnel Bulletin of Jan. 1957), London: SOAS, p. 11.
73. Shanghai People's Government Notification Characters Fu/Ti, no. 1020, *Ta Kung Pao*, 15 Dec. 1949. On 11 Aug. 1951 the Shanghai authorities promulgated 'Measures Governing Application for Registration of House and Land Property by Foreign Nationals'. For details, see W.T. Yoxall (HSBC Shanghai) to J.R. Jones (Hong Kong) 9 Nov. 1951, *HKBGA*: GHO 154 (Shanghai Office 1945–57), Box No. 1860.
74. The government promulgated 'Measures Governing Requisitioning of Land for National Construction', *Jie Fang Ri Bao* (the Liberation Daily) 6 Dec. 1953. On this decree Britain declared that she would reserve her position.
75. C.H. Scott (FO) to F.D. Bisseker on behalf of Eden, 25 Feb. 1952, FC1461/6, FO371/99345, re two lots of open land held in the name of Mrs Bisseker; C.H. Johnston (FO) to James Ness and Son, Glasgow, 12 May 1952, re the Alston House in Beidaihe (Peitaiho), FC1461/10, FO371/99345.
76. See Trevelyan and Veitch to FO 25–27, Nov. 1953, FC1461/67 and 68,

FO371/108088; W.T. Yoxall (HSBC Shanghai) to O. Skinner (HSBC Hong Kong) 20 Nov. 1953, HKBGA: GHO 154 (Shanghai Office 1945–57), Box no. 1860. The British officials in Beijing subsequently communicated to the Chinese government that the owners formally wished to reserve all British property rights affected by the Chinese authorities in Shanghai, and by the Tianjin government in similar cases. FC1461/5 re two diplomatic notes d. 10 Dec. 1953 and 28 Feb. 1954, *CA: Cresta File.* Requisitioned by the Shanghai authorities in Nov. 1953 were the Shanghai Club, Union Jack Club, Country Club and Race Club.

77. Record of a meeting between CA reps and Humphery Trevelyan, 22 Apr. 1954, *CA: Cresta File.*

78. The company was one of the firms which filed applications to close down in June 1952, including its offices in Shanghai, Tianjin, Qingdao, Hankou, Guangzhou, Xiamen and Fuzhou. R.J. Sheppard (ICI Shanghai) to British Consul (Shanghai) 11 June 1952, FC1105/315, FO371/99292.

79. A glimpse can be taken into the business operations of these and other British firms by going through their records of financial transactions with HSBC, *HKBGA:* SHG I(R) P, K9. files, Hong Kong.

80. C.T. Crowe to H.J. Collar, 2 June 1954, *CA: Cresta File.* See also J.M. Addis to S.H. Levine, 14 Apr. 1954, encl. a BoT draft Brief on China trade for the Geneva conference, FC1151/45, FO371/110288.

81. W.T. Yoxall (HSBC Shanghai) to Sir Arthur Morse (Hong Kong), 26 Dec. 1951, *HKBGA:* GHO 154 (Shanghai Office), Box no. 1860.

82. See Memorandum of HSBC's head office (Hong Kong) to FAB Shanghai, undated, in Closure File 15 Sept. 1951–15 Mar. 1954, *HKBGA:* SHG II, 615.

83. Yoxall to O. Skinner letters d. 29 Oct. 1953 and 25 Jan. 1954, *HKBGA:* GHO 154, Box no. 1860. Because the inspection coincided with the Three- and Five-Anti Movements, a large number of official queries were over sundry small commissions, interest, rentals and so forth collected abroad, all coming under the campaign and subject to possible penalties. No evidence has been found to suggest that any official accusations were made.

84. H. Trevelyan to C.T. Crowe, letter d. 24 Dec. 1953, FC1111/1, FO371/110265; Price (Beijing) to FO, no. 422, 9 July 1953, FC1113/71, FO371/108086.

85. Consul Shanghai to FO, no. 54, 20 Mar. 1954, FC1111/55, FO371/110266; W.T. Yoxall to O. Skinner, 18 Apr. 1955, *HKBGA:* GHO 154, Box no. 1860. Yoxall wrote of the lions, 'Old customs survive even in changing times. The paws get more wear and tear from stroking by passers-by than ever'. During the Cultural Revolution, the lions were removed and were seen no more.

86. W.R. Cockburn (Chartered Bank London) to C.H. Johnston (FO) 21 Aug. 1952, FC1105/324, FO371/99293; Yoxall to Morse, 8 Oct. 1952, *HKBGA* GHO 154, Box no. 1860.

87. *RMRB*, 20 Feb. 1953, encl. FC1113/13, FO371/108085. The Foreign Office's Legal Adviser (Sinclair) stated that it was doubtful if the

Chinese measures could be challenged in international law, although they were contrary to normal practices. FO minute of a meeting with reps of banks, 14 Mar. 1953, FC1113/17, FO371/108085.

88. F.C.B. Black (Hong Kong) to J.W.P. Perry-Aldworth (London) 30 Dec. 1955, *HKBGA*: GHO 154, Box no. 1860.

89. Federal Register, vol. 15, no. 245, 19 Dec. 1950, p. 9040.

90. Of this figure, HSBC had $7 095 629, the Chartered Bank had $1 683 156.06, and the Mercantile Bank of India had $497 240.90. J. Mark (Embassy in Washington) to B.R. Serpell (Treasury Chamber London) 11 June 1953, FC1113/62, FO371/108086.

91. FO to Washington, no. 2122 saving, 16 Apr. 1954, FC1111/99, FO371/110267; Eden (Geneva) to FO, no. 12 saving, 18 May 1954, FC1111/90, FO371/110266. The Chinese did propose some ways of getting around the problem (such as the suggestion that the banks put sterling or Hong Kong dollars with the Bank of China in place of the frozen US dollars), but the banks did not find them acceptable.

92. See *Aide Mémoire* by British embassy in Washington to US government 19 Mar. 1953, FC1113/121, FO371/108085; H.W. Hawkins (Mercantile Bank of India Ltd) to S.W.P. Perry-Aldworth, 30 May 1956, *HKBGA*: GHO 154, Box no. 1860.

93. R.H. Drake (Mercantile Bank of India, Ltd.) to C.T. Crowe (FO) 20 Apr. 1956, FC1113/12; Drake to A.L. Mayall (FO) 19 June 1956, FC1113/19, FO371/120941. The bank's manager in Shanghai, M.D.A. Smith, left China after the settlement.

94. T.C. Crowe to C.D. O'Neill (Beijing) letter d. 13 June 1956, FC1113/18, FO371/120941.

95. D. Buchan to Skinner, letter d. 16 Sept. 1955, *HKBGA*: GHO 154, Box no. 1860.

96. Beijing to FO 24 Sept. 1951, FC1103/183, FO371/92267. Yoxall admitted that to finance barter imports was certainly profitable, but argued that to do that would mean a big outlay in foreign currency to finance the imports which had to arrive first, and a considerable delay in getting documents for the counterpart exports, 'in other words, capitalising China trade in foreign currency, which I always explain, is contrary to the Bank's policy'. W.T. Yoxall to Sir Arthur Morse, 26 Dec. 1951, *HKBGA*: GHO 154, Box no. 1860.

97. The Chartered Bank seemed to have suffered particularly from this partially self-inflicted curtailment. W.T. Yoxall to Sir Arthur Morse, 26 Dec. 1951, *HKBGA*: GHO 154, Box no. 1860.

98. See Geng Biao, 'Hui Yi Xin Zhong Guo Jie Chu de Wai Jiao Jia Zhang Han Fu Tong Zhi' (In Memory of New China's Outstanding Diplomat, Comrade Zhang Hanfu), *RMRB*, 3 Sept. 1987, p. 5. See also Wang Haipo (ed.) *Xin Zhong Guo Gong Yie Jing Ji Shi* (History of Industrial Economy in New China), 1986, pp. 60–1.

99. Lamb charged that, 'The Unions have clearly been given a free hand to extort whatever they can and demands will not be moderated unless Chinese authorities intervene'. Lamb to FO, no. 679, 25 Aug. 1952, FC1105/326, FO371/99293. For allegations made by British officials against FAB in Tianjin, see Beijing to FO, no. 717, 9 Sept. 1952, *CA:*

Cresta File; Jeffery (Tianjin) to Crowe, 1 Sept. 1952, FC1105/382, FO371/99295.

100. Lamb to FO, no. 833, 30 Oct. 1952, with message by Shell's Guangzhou manager to Shell manager Shanghai, FC1105/396, FO371/99295. Interviews with Huang Hua, 3 Sept. 1987, and with Chinese Foreign Ministry officials, 5 Sept. 1987, Beijing.
101. See Beijing to FO, no. 679, 25 Aug. 1952, *CA: Cresta File*; E.W. Jeffery (Tianjin) to C.T. Crowe (Beijing), 19 Sept. 1952, FC1105/403, FO371/99296.
102. See Lamb to FO, no. 844, 3 Nov. 1952, FC1105/399, FO371/99296, proposing to enquire of the Chinese MFA whether there were any regulations forbidding the sale of foreign property. See also Addis to Mitchell, 10 Dec. 1952, FC1105/430; Alan Price to Zhang Hanfu (note no. 154), 2 July 1953, FC1102/86; FO to the Chinese Government (note no. 222) 3 Oct. 1953; FO to the Chinese Government (MFA, note no. 252) 3 Dec. 1953, *CA: Cresta File*.
103. This mill was founded in 1934, being the largest undertaking of the Baldwins in the Far East. In 1940 the mill had 12 000 looms and a workforce of over 1000, with a capacity of 3 000 000 pounds of woollen threads a year. It further expanded its operations in 1950. SASS (ed.) *Shanghai Jing Ji* (Shanghai's Economy), *vol. I, 1949–82*, 1983, p. 862.

6   A New Pattern of Trade

1. Han Nianlong et al. (ed.) *Dang Dai Zhong Guo Wai Jiao* (China Today: Diplomacy), 1987, p. 51. See also *SW of Zhou Enlai*, vol. II, pp. 52–3: Zhou stated in October 1950 that the US was following the logic of Japanese militarism since the war of 1895, that is. 'He who annexes Korea takes China's Northeast, and he who takes the Northeast conquers the whole of China'. The number of Chinese battle casualties up to 17 Oct. 1952, including killed and wounded, was estimated at 773 459, nonbattle casualties 189 606, POWs 20 900, totaling 983 965. This figure, while not confirmed by the Chinese, would more than double the total number of the UN and South Korean losses for the same period (estimated at 347 558). A MoD Memo. 5 Nov. 1952, C (52)392, CAB129/56. The financial cost of the war to the Chinese was estimated at US$10 billion. Yao Hsu, *Dang Shi Yan Jiu* (Studies of the Party's History), 1980, pp. 5, 13, cited in *CHC*, vol. 14, p. 278.
2. Wang Bingnan, *Zhong Mei Hui Tan Jiu Nian Hui Gu* (Nine Years of Sino–US Talks Recalled), 1985, pp. 4–5.
3. See H. Trevelyan, *Worlds Apart*, 1971, p. 71; MacFarquhar and Fairbank, (eds) *CHC*, vol. 14, p. 281.
4. Wang Bingnan, *op.cit.*, pp. 5–6.
5. See *SW of Zhou Enlai*, vol. II, p. 89; Su Chao, 'Zhan-Wang Zhong-Ying Guan-Xi' (An Overview of Sino–British Relations), *SJZS*, no. 17, 1954, pp. 10–11. The Chinese leadership noted the statement made by Winston Churchill during his visit to the United States in Jan. 1953 that the British government was opposed to an unlimited extension of the war into China.

6. Trevelyan to FO, no. 231, 5 Apr. 1954, FC1051/7, FO371/110245. The Chinese government had hitherto treated Trevelyan strictly as 'U.K. representative for negotiations' (Ying-Guo Tan-pan Dai-biao), rather than *de facto Chargé d'Affaires*.

7. Trevelyan, *op.cit.*, p. 79. The meetings started on 26 Apr. 1954, and Dulles stayed on till 2 May. *FRUS*, 1952–4, 16:7.

8. C.T. Crowe (FO) minute, 24 May 1954, FC1051/13, FO371/110245; 396.1FE/5–154: Telegram Secto.67 Dulles, Geneva, 1 May 1954, *FRUS* 52–4, 16:648.

9. C.T. Crowe (later Sir Colin) (FO) minute 12 June 1954, FC1051/31, FO371/110246. A Labour Party delegation headed by Aneurin Bevan and Clement Attlee was scheduled to visit China in August 1954 and was to be received by Mao Zedong.

10. Eden to FO, no. 693, 13 June 1954, FC1051/23, FO371/110245.

11. Eden (Geneva) to FO, no. 752, 16 June 1954, FC1051/29, FO371/110245; Winston Churchill's statement 17 June 1954, *PD*, vol. 528, 1953–4, col. 2275; *The New York Times*, 27 June 1954.

12. Trevelyan, *op.cit.*, pp. 107–8; Trevelyan to FO, letter 24 Sept. 1954, FC1014/3, FO371/110207; Con O'Neill to C.T. Crowe, letter 28 July 1955, FC1051/14, FO371/115061.

13. Resolution adopted by the Plenary session 12 Apr. 1952, Committee of the Promotion of International Trade, *International Economic Conference in Moscow*, 1952.

14. LEC, *Two Decades with People's China 1952–1972 The Story of London Export Corporation*, London, 1972, pp. 4–6. Other members of the IIC included Dr Ji Chaoding and the principal chairmen of the conference, M.V. Nesterov, President of the USSR Chamber of Commerce, and Dr Oskar Lange of Poland.

15. These included Shi Zhi-ang, who later participated in the trade talks in Geneva in 1954 and was killed in Sarawak in 1955 in a plane crash caused by Guomindang sabotage – the *Kashmir Princess* Incident.

16. LEC, *Two Decades*, p. 7.

17. G.E. Mitchell to R.H. Scott (FO) 16 Jan. 1952, *CA: Cresta File*. Mitchell suggested that there was no wish on the part of (British) business that Britain should take any line which would cause a serious disagreement between Britain and the US. Mitchell also suspected that Buckman was a Communist and he wrote to Scott asking 'whether M.I.5 have run across him'.

18. R.H. Scott to G.E. Mitchell 25 Feb. 1952, FC1152/1G, *CA: Cresta File*. Scott confirmed Mitchell's assumptions about Buckman as 'entirely correct', as 'Buckman has been known to the authorities for many years'.

19. Mitchell to Scott, 3 Mar. 1952, *CA: Cresta File*.

20. Mitchell wrote that Buckman initially suggested that 'All we would be required to do would be to find our way to Helsinki, whereafter we would be the guests of the Russian government'. In the end Buckman was said to have realised that 'little good would be served by pursuing us [the China Association] further. . . . It remains to be seen whether we have shaken him off'. Mitchell to Scott, 3 Mar. 1952, *CA: Cresta File*.

21. *RMRB*, 15 May 1952, FC1122/18 FO371/99313; interview with Wu Chengming, 9 Sept. 1987, Beijing.
22. Eden's statement, 6 Nov. 1953, PD vol. 520, 1953–4; his written answer, 18 Nov. 1953, *ibid.* pp. 164–5; Sir Peter Tennant's Notes (undated, probably 1980), SBTC: *Matheson Memorandum*.
23. R.H. Scott (FO) minute, 29 July 1952, FC1105/298, FO371/99292.
24. R.H. Scott minute, 29 July, FC1105/298, FO371/99292. See also BOT to FO, 30 Aug. 1952, FC1152/91, and Charles Johnson (FO) minute, 4 Sept. 1952, FO371/99320; F.S. Tomlinson (British Embassy in Washington) to C.H. Johnson 22 Oct. 1952, FC1152/102, FO371/99321.
25. S.H. Levine (BoT) to R.D.F. Marlow, 23 June 1954, FC1151/101B; H. Collar (CA) to C.T. Crowe (FO), 8 June 1954, FC1151/99, FO371/110290.
26. LEC, *Two Decades*, pp. 9–10.
27. Memo. by the Secretary of State for Foreign Affairs and the President of BoT, 3 Feb. 1953, C (53)37, CAB129/58. Memo. 3 Feb. 1953, C (53)37, CAB129/58; Minute 7, 5 Feb. 1953, CC7(53)/7, and Minute 7, 10 Feb. 1953, CC8(53)7, CAB128/26.
28. J.S.H. Shattock (FO) to G.E. Mitchell (CA) 11 Apr. 1953, FC1153/37; G.E. Mitchell to J.S.H. Shattock, 21 Apr. 1953, *CA: Cresta File*.
29. The firms signing the Business Arrangement included Austin Motors, Brush Electrical Engineering, The China Engineers, Crompton Parkinson, Dominions Export, Enfield Cables, H.M.F. Faure, Harrisons (London), Harvey Main, Hirsch So and Rhodes, Kreglinger and Fernau, LEC, The Oil Cakes and Oil Seeds Trading Co., Rubery Owen and Co., together with their consultant Roland Berger. The signatory on the Chinese side was the general manager of CNIEC, Lu Xuzhang. Hence the 17 signatories. Reference from an article for *British Business*, June 1988, reprinted by the '48' Group.
30. Hao Shuyun, 'Ying Guo Si Shi Ba Jia Ji Tuan Qing Kuang Jian Jie' (A Brief Introduction to the British '48' Group), *Guo Ji Mao Yi Xiao Xi* (International Trade News), Supplement, 17 Sept. 1982. See also a report of a meeting convened by LEC, 9 Dec. 1953, SBTC: *Archival Material File* ex. *CA: M & C*, 1954.
31. 'Questions Asked and Answered in Parliament', 9 July 1953, *Board of Trade Journal*, 165/2952, 18 July 1953, p. 111.
32. *The Times Supplement*, 21 Mar. 1973, p. vi; interview with Roland Berger, 9 Nov. 1986, London.
33. J.B. Scott (Crompton Parkinson and Co. Ltd) to H.E. Percival (BoT) 19 Jan. 1954, FC1151/16, FO371/110287.
34. CA: minute of a meeting between FBI, LCC and CA, 3 Mar. 1954, SBTC: *Archival Material File*. The withdrawing firms include Austin Motors, Brush Electrical Engineering, Crompton Parkinson and Enfield Cables.
35. Interview with S. Gordon Sloan, 4 Jan. 1989, London. Eden was reported as having referred to BCPIT as 'Commies', and told him, 'You can't touch pitch without being defiled'. Sloan subsequently conveyed the message from his company chairman Alfred Owen (Sir) to Eden to

the effect that 'If you take care of the politics, we will take care of the trade'.

36. The '48' Group: LCM, 26 May, 10 June 1954.
37. F.B.W. Harrison, (UK Trade Commissioner in Hong Kong), to S.H. Levine (BoT) 6 Jan. 1954, FC1151/14; M.M. Mocatta (BoT) to C.T. Crowe (FO) 13 Feb. 1954, FC1151/16, FO371/110287.
38. J.M. Addis (FO) minute 1 Dec. 1953, FC1151/2A; S.H. Levine to C.T. Crowe 3 Feb. 1954, FC1151/4, FO371/110287.
39. CA: minute of a meeting, 3 Mar. 1954, SBTC: *Archival Material File* ex *CA: M & C*, 1954; Text of a letter dated 29 Mar. 1954, signed by W.C. Cockburn of CA, Sir Harry Pilkington of FBI, and Lord Luke of Pavenham, LCC, D/3015A, FBI, SBTC: *The Orr File*.
40. See FC1151/43B, FO to Beijing, no. 168, 26 Mar. 1954, Beijing to FO no. 217, 29 Mar. 1954, FO to Beijing, no. 180, 1 Apr. 1954, FC1151/34, FO371/110288.
41. C.T. Crowe (FO) minute, 3 May 1954, FC1151/46A, FO371/110288.
42. C.T. Crowe to Trevelyan (Geneva), 4 May 1954; FO to Berne, no. 72, 4 May 1954, FC1151/46, FO371/110288; interview with Sir Peter Tennant, 9 Sept. 1988.
43. See P.F.D. Tennant, Notes on Talks on Trade with China, May 6–7 1954, SBTC: *Archival Materials File*.
44. Record of a meeting 7 May 1954, FC1151/50A, FO371/110288. The British list was published in *Board of Trade Journal*, 12 June 1954, pp. 1271–2. The Chinese complained that the British lists made no mention of industrial electrical equipment and vehicles, non-ferrous metals, train engines, and vessels, which their industrial development most needed.
45. Eden (Trevelyan) to FO, no. 164, 6 May 1954, FC1151/48, FO371/ 110288.
46. 'F.B.I. Discussions on Expansion of Trade with China', *Board of Trade Journal*, 12 June 1954, p. 1271; the text of the Chinese press release was attached to H. Trevelyan to C.T. Crowe, 11 June 1954, FC1151/92; see also Combs (Beijing) to FO, no. 362, FC1151/87, FO371/110290.
47. Trevelyan to FO, no. 478, 13 July 1954, FC1151/118, FO371/110291; 'A comprehensive report of China's foreign trade practice', Trevelyan to FO no. 90E, 1120/7/55, dated 21 Apr. 1955, FC1124/8, FO371/115091.
48. Harold Anthony Caccia, Deputy Under-Secretary at the Foreign Office, knew Peter Tennant well and promised him in Geneva that the government would issue 20 visas to the Chinese mission and that uncourteous procedures by (security–intelligence) people would be eschewed while the Chinese were in Britain. Interview with Sir Peter Tennant, 9 Sept. 1988, England.
49. Minutes of the 1st meeting, 11 June 1954, and minutes of a meeting 17 June 1954, SBTC: *Archival Files*; Notes on the origins of SBTC, SBTC: *Matheson Memorandum*.
50. It was stated that ABCC had a membership of 100 Chambers of Commerce throughout Britain, with a total membership of 70 000 merchants and manufacturers. LCC itself had 13 000 members, and 45

Notes and References

affiliated trade associations comprising over 50 000 individual members. FBI, which represented manufacturing interests, had a membership consisting of 6800 firms and 285 trade associations, while the individual firms belonging to these trade associations totalled over 40 000. NUM was a nationwide organisation with 5500 members and 72 affiliated trade associations. FBI and NUM together could, it was stated, fairly claim to cover every product manufactured in the United Kingdom and both had regional offices throughout the country. Harry Pilkington to Cao Zhongshu, letter 30 July 1954, SBTC: *The Orr File*. These latter two bodies through subsequent changes evolved into The Confederation of British Industry (CBI).

51. Trevelyan to Crowe, 11 June 1954, FC1151/92, FO371/110290. S. Gordon Sloan of the '48' Group sent a cable to Shi Zhi-ang in Geneva to suggest further discussions between the Chinese mission and the association in London, and Shi cabled back signaling pleasure in meeting the '48' Group when the group was in London. LCM, 10 June 1954.

52. C.T. Crowe (FO) minute 12 June 1954; FO to Geneva (UK delegation) no. 1075, 12 June 1954, FC1151/87, FO371/110290.

53. Eden to FO No. 715 14 June 1954; No. 730, 15 June 1954, FC1151/89, FO371/110290.

54. *Quarterly Review* issued by the China Engineers, Ltd., No. 67, Sept. 1954, SBTC: *The Orr File*; *The Times* and *Financial Times*, 10 July 1954. In respect of the so-called 'Gilbertian episode', see Tennant to Sir Alfred Le Maitre (MoT & Civil Aviation), 25 June 1954, FC1151/100, FO371/110290.

55. SBTC report on the visit of the Chinese mission; Notes distributed by the Chinese trade mission for general discussion with SBTC June 1954, SBTC: *The Orr File*.

56. *Quarterly Review* issued by the China Engineers, Ltd, no. 67, Sept. 1954, SBTC: *The Orr File*. These activities upset some people in SBTC. See Personal Note from Peter Tennant to FBI President, 2 July 1954, FC1151/111, FO371/110290; Peter Tennant to Colin Crowe (FO), 8 July 1954, FC1151/116, FO371/110291.

57. This was calculated to preempt BCPIT from reaping a windfall in the next trip in early 1955. C.T. Crowe (FO) to S.H. Levine (BoT) 25 Oct. 1954, FC1151/143, FO371/110292.

58. Firms represented included the following: Dawe Instruments, Ltd, Overseas Egg and Produce Co. Ltd, T. and H. Smith Ltd, Union International Co. Ltd, Harry Wicking and Co. Ltd, Gordon Woodroffe and Co. Ltd, ICI, M.W. Hardy and Co. Ltd, Fuerst Bros. Ltd, Glaxo Laboratory Ltd, J.H. Little and Co. Ltd, the China Engineers Ltd, H. Kunstlinger and Co., Biddle Sawyer and Co. Ltd, Askinex Ltd, M.D. Ewart and Co. Ltd, Harlow and Jones Ltd, Harvey Main and Co. Ltd (Hong Kong), GEC, Leyland Vehicles Ltd, the Marconi Co. Ltd, Chartered Bank of India, Australia and China, Shanghai and Hongkong Banking Corporation, Arnhold Trading Co. Ltd, Lamet Trading Co., Matheson and Co. Ltd, Wu Shaw Trading Co. Ltd.

59. Trevelyan (Beijing) to Eden (FO) 21 Dec. 1954, FC1151/2, FO371 115107. The largest business was probably done by Jardine (including a

large contract for Belgian sulphate of ammonia), Biddle and Sawyer, and Swire and Maclaine. Union International did not enter into any contract but obtained from China preemptive rights on Chinese frozen egg exports for 1955 and 1956. It was reported that 'LEC seems to be less in favour since Swires were told [by the Chinese] their quotations for wooltops and offered business at the same price'. Trevelyan (Beijing) to FO, no. 1005 7 Dec. 1954, FC1151/173, FO371/110292.

60. Trevelyan (Beijing) to FO, no. 1005 7 Dec. 1954, FO371/ 110292; Trevelyan (Beijing) to Eden (FO) 21 Dec. 1954, FC1151/2, FO371/115107. See also *Financial Times*, 24 Dec. 1954; 'Report on the group visit of British businessmen to Peking, Nov./Dec. 1954', FC1151/ 1, FO371/115107. The latter report, while it admitted that it was always difficult to assess to what extent a reception of this nature was dictated by political rather than commercial motives, cited specific cases as indications that 'the political objectives did not take a primary place'.

61. See files in FC1151/25, FO371/115108. See also *The Financial Times*, 23 Feb. 1955; *CA: Circular*, no 55/G/5, 25 Feb. 1955. Trevelyan (Beijing) to FO no. 196, 22 Feb. 1955, FC1151/11, FO371/115107.

62. LCM 31, Dec. 1954, 18 April 1955. See also LCM, 3 June 1955.

63. SBTC (R.D.F. Marlow, Co-ordinating Secretary), 'A Summarised Report of the Second Group Visit of Businessmen to Peking March/ April 1955', 20 June 1955, FC1151/31, FO371/115108.

64. Trevelyan (Beijing) to FO, no. 415, 23 April, FC1151/23F, FO371/ 115107. In addition, it was suggested at the time that the 2nd SBTC group visit compared unfavourably with that of the 1st group in leadership and secretarial organisation, which 'was particularly unfortunate having regard to the success of the BCPIT mission under Berger's expert guidance'. The timing of the trip, right after Berger's group, was also blamed for the small volume of business done. Report of a meeting of the Working Sub-Committee (Acting Executively), 15 June 1955, SBTC: *Minutes* 1954–64.

65. SBTC (Marlow) 'A Summarised Report', 20 June 1955, FC1151/31, FO371/115108.

66. LCM, 8 Sept. 1955; Notes of a meeting with CNIEC, Leipzig, LCM, 27 Feb. 1956; minutes of the 48 Group meeting, LCM, 16 Mar. 1956.

67. SBTC, Notes for the Information of S.T. Hsieh (Xie Shoutian, Chinese Commercial Counsellor in London), FC1151/51, FO371/115109; E.H. Osborne (ECGD), to J.G. Owen (Treasury) 13 June 1957, FC1151/42, FO371/127354.

68. J.E. Galsworthy (FO) minute 23 Apr. 1955, FC1151/25, FO371/115108.

69. P. Wilkinson (FO) minute 7 Dec. 1955, FC1151/42 FO371/115108; C.T. Crowe to S.H. Levine, 25 Oct. 1954, FC1151/143, FO371/110292. See also S.H. Levine of BoT, 'Note of an interview with Garett and Sloan', 10 Aug. 1956, FC1151/63, FO371/120945.

70. P. Wilkinson minute, 7 Dec. 1955, FC1151/42 FO371/115108. See also SBTC to Crowe 16 June 1955, FC1151/30, FO371/115108. Opinions within the government were by no means uniform, especially with regard to requests for assistance from individual British firms, but most in the FO agreed that the use of HM's Chargé d'Affaires in Beijing as

an intermediary should be denied the '48' Group because the latter refused to drop Berger. See minutes by A. Leavett and by J.E. Galsworthy 13 July 1955, FC1151/42, FO371/115108.

71. Galsworthy called Berger's statement in Tokyo after the Blott party early in 1955 'undisguised Communist propaganda', and stated that 'the short lead [the Liaison Committee said they were keeping on Berger] had not prevented the dog from making a pretty good mess on the carpet and that I should be interested to see how the Committee proposed to clean it up'. J.E. Galsworthy minute of a meeting with SBTC, 23 Apr. 1955, FC1151/25, FO371/115108.

72. A memo. 19 Aug. 1954, SBTC: *Minutes 1954–64*. See also minutes of a meeting with the representatives of the '48' Group, 11 July 1955, SBTC: *Minutes*, 1954–64.

73. LEC received business with China amounting to £6 million in 1955, more than one-sixth of the Sino–British trade volume for that year (£34 million, estimated by the Chinese). For the first half of 1956, LEC's business with China further increased to 30 per cent of the British total of £21 million. Amongst the various products traded in both directions, 90 per cent of China's purchase of British wooltops was done through LEC, which caused the envy of other wooltop merchants, even colleagues within the '48' Group. Note of five meetings between Chinese Foreign Trade Ministry officials and LEC delegation July–Aug. 1956, Beijing. See also Miss Mocatta (BoT), Note of a talk between J.A. Blott and UK Trade Commissioner in HK (File C.37/8/2), FC1151/15, FO371/115107.

74. A delegation of LEC executives was in Beijing during July–Aug. 1956 for a series of exchanges of view with Chinese trade officials. See also: A letter to confirm a conversation between H. Flint (SBTC) and Huan Xiang (Chinese Chargé d'Affaires in London) London, 2 Aug. 1956, SBTC: *Minutes* 1954–64; Huan assured SBTC that British firms needed not employ the medium of the LEC but should feel free to negotiate direct with Chinese trading organisations if they so wished. See also C.T. Crowe to Con D.W. O'Neill (Beijing) letter, 9 Aug. 1956, FC1151/59, and John Addis (Beijing) to Crowe, 25 Sept. 1956, FC1151/69, FO371/120945.

75. On the Chinese reaction to the Taiwan crisis and the Kawloon riots, see Wai Jiao Xue Yuan (College of Foreign Affairs), *Zhong Hua Ren Min Gong He Guo Dui Wai Guan Xi Shi* (History of the Foreign Relations of PRC), 1964, pp. 150–1. On the effects of the Suez crisis on Sino–British trade, see LCM 7 Jan. 1957, in which it was suggested that the serious view of the crisis taken by China was the major factor in disrupting trade and creating anomalies in freights to and from China. 'For the moment it seemed the fresh proposals submitted by the '48' Group were in cold storage'.

76. FO to Beijing, no. 1017, 15 Nov. 1954, FO371/110292; Trevelyan (Beijing) to FO, no. 976 30 Nov. 1954, FC1151/163, FO371/110292; report on the group visit of British businessmen to Peking Nov.–Dec. 1954, FC1151/1, FO371/115107; record of a meeting, in Collar to Crowe (FO) 5 Jan. 1955, FC1151/1A. FO371/115107.

77. Trevelyan (Beijing) to FO, no. 90E 1120/7/55, 21 Apr. 1955, FC1124/8, FO371/115091; A.D. Macay (Associated British Engineering Co. Ltd) statement 20 Feb. 1955, FC1151/52, FO371/115108.
78. Cao Zhongshu (CNIEC) to SBTC, letter 16 Sept. 1955, FC1151/51, FO371/115109; LCM 27 Feb. and 27 April 1956. See also F.W. Dawe, to MoS, 21 Feb. 1955, M3444/9, FO371/116017.
79. A meeting with metal manufacturers and merchants, LCM, 5 Sept. 1956.
80. Minutes by T.C. Crowe, 2 Feb. 1955 and P. Wilkinson, 21 Feb. 1955, FC1151/9 FO371/115107; report on discussions with CNIEC 2–13 April 1955, FC1151/28, FO371/115108; R.D.F. Marlow to C.T. Crowe, 26 Jan. 1956, FC1151/12, FO371/120943.
81. Notes for the information of Chinese commercial counsellor, meeting at Chinese Embassy, 15 Sept. 1955, SBTC: *Minutes* 1954–64. See also FO371/115109.
82. See *Zhong Guo Da Bai Ke Quan Shu: Fa Xue* (Encyclopedia Sinia: the Volume on Law), 1984, pp. 520–2, 808–9.
83. Notes for the information of Chinese commercial counsellor, meeting at Chinese Embassy, 15 Sept. 1955, SBTC: *Minutes*, 1954–64. See also FO371/115109.
84. Memorandum on the SBTC mission to China, in Trevelyan to Eden, letter 21 Dec. 1954, FC1151/2, FO371/115107.
85. H.J. Collar (CA) to FO, 13 Dec. 1955, *CA: Cresta File.*
86. The '48' Group: LCM, 16 March 1956. See also J.E. Chadwick (Tokyo) to C.T. Crowe (FO) 23 Feb. 1955, M3444/8, FO371/116016.
87. FO memo. 20 Aug. 1957, FC1151/82, 127355.
88. FO to UKDel/OEEC No. 132, 4 Apr. 1956, M3426/70, FO371/121941.
89. A.H. Campbell (Beijing) to W.F. Morris (ECGD) 27 July 1956, FC1151/52, FO371/120945.
90. *CA: Bull*, no. 126, 21 Nov. 1956; J.M. Addis (Beijing) to C.T. Crowe, 5 July 1956, re interview with MFT 3rd Dept. Deputy Director Chen Ming, FC1151/48, FO371/120944.
91. Record of conversations between Chen Ming and LEC officials July–Aug. 1956, Beijing; a MFT Directive dated 12 Apr. 1957, specifically bearing on enquiries directed to Hong Kong firms.
92. H. Flint (Chairman of SBTC) to Sir David Eccles (President of BoT) 23 Apr. 1957, SBTC: *Minutes*, 1954–64; SBTC: *Matheson Memorandum*.
93. Trevelyan, *The Worlds Apart*, pp. 120; P.H. Gore-Booth (FO) minute, 10 Jan. 1957, FC1121/1, FO371/127321. *PD*, vol. 571, 1956–7, cols. 618–9.
94. O'Neill to O.C. Morland (FO) 5 June 1957 FC1151/40, FO371/127354. O'Neill suggested that the Chinese warmth was mainly 'due to the belief that our step marks the beginning of a serious rift with the United States'.
95. O'Neill to O.C. Morland (FO) 5 June 1957 FC1151/40, FO371/127354.
96. E.A. Cohen (BoT) to Sir Paul Gore-Booth (FO) 18 July 1957, FC1151/64, FO371/127355. For general information of his visit, see other files in FO371/127355–127358. For Zhou Enlai's talks with Erroll,

see various telegrams by A.D. Wilson (Beijing) to FO on 31 Oct. 1957, FO371/127357.

97. The constituent organisations of the Sino–British Trade Committee appointed a Council chosen from leaders of industry, commerce and Finance. This step had the full support of the British government, which authorised the Council to be the officially recognised trade organisation to arrange for the visit of a Chinese technical mission to Britain. A written statement by Hugh Beaver, the Council's first President, 7 Oct. 1957, FC1151/131 FO371/127357.

98. The SBT Council: Report on a visit (6 Sept.–6 Dec. 1957), Feb. 1958, London, SBTC: *Minutes*, 1954–64.

99. *Zhong Guo Dui Wai Jing Ji Mao Yi Nian Jian* (Chinese Yearbook of Foreign Trade and Economic Relations), 1984, IV3, IV67.

100. A.D. Wilson (Beijing) to FO, no. 528, 31 Oct. 1957, FC1151/143, FO371/127357.

101. Tim Beal, *The China Trade*, 1982, p. 43.

102. SBTC: *Matheson Memorandum*.

103. A Note on British Interests in China (for the information of Erroll), R.H.V. Benson (FO), 11 Sept. 1957, FC1151/94, FO371/127356. The ten British firms were Bank Line (China) Ltd, Cathay Land Co. Ltd, Central Properties Ltd, Chartered Bank, Far Eastern Investment Co., Hongkong and Shanghai Banking Corporation, Lester Johnson & Morriss, Moller (China) Ltd, Patons and Baldwins Ltd, San Sing Properties Ltd, E.D. Sassoon and Co. Ltd., Sassoon Banking Co. Ltd, Shanghai Estates and finance, Shell Co. of China Ltd. H.J. Collar to Duncan Wilson, 25 June 1957, FC1151/28a, FO371/127353.

104. A lump-sum agreement was signed in Beijing on 5 June 1987, under which Britain would pay China $3.8m (£2.33m) and China would pay Britain £23.5m, thereby waiving Britain's claims for £61m of old Chinese bonds. China's claims against Britain would presumably cover the cargo of rubber on board the *Nancy Moller*, the requisitioned Yung Hao tanker, the five fishing trawlers, and all the aircraft of the two Chinese national airlines. See *RMRB* overseas ed. 6 June 1987; *Financial Times*, 6 June 1987; *RMRB*, domestic ed. 6 Dec. 1987, re PRC State Council's Public Notice dated 5 Dec. 1987 , and *The Independent*, 29 Feb. 1988, re The Foreign Compensation (People's Republic of China) Order 1987.

105. This guideline was attributed to Mao, who was quoted as having used the metaphor of 'narrow cold stream kept running' (*'Xi Shui Chang Liu, Leng Er Bu Duan'*) to describe the future state of Sino–British relations. For an official British view of the commercial relations with China and its obstacles, see P.G.F. Dalton (FO), minute 28 Jan. 1957, FC1151/3, FO371/127353.

Appendix: Items Subject to Embargo for China*

1. Arms, ammunition, and implements of war, including aircraft and engines.
2. Atomic energy materials and equipment.
3. Petroleum Products. Crude petroleum, and refined petroleum products. Naphtha, Mineral Spirits and Solvents.
4. Transportation Materials:
    (a) Internal combustion engines.
    (b) All motor vehicles (including tractors and motor cycles); trailers; and components and spares.
    (c) Rails, locomotives and rolling-stock, and parts thereof.
    (d) Ships and floating docks; including important parts.
    (e) Cables suitable for harbour defence or minesweeping.
    (f) Minesweeping equipment.
    (g) Road and aerodrome construction machinery.
    (h) Cranes.
    (i) Nylon rope and parachute cloth.
    (j) Containers suitable for use in storing or transporting petroleum of capacity of four gallons or more.
5. Metals, Minerals and their Manufactures.
    (a) All classes of iron and steel products (including alloy steels) up to and including the finished stage and including barbed wire and steel wire strand and cable and iron and steel scrap.
    (b) Metals, the following and alloys wholly or mainly thereof including ferro-alloys and scrap:

Aluminum	Copper	Sodium
Antimony	Lead	Strontium
Beryllium	Germanium	Tantalum
Bismuth	Magnesium	Titanium
Cadmium	Molybdenum	Tungsten
Calcium	Nickel	Vanadium
Cobalt		Zinc
Columbium		Zirconium

   (c) Items in the following fields:
    (i) Items used for the production of alloy steels.
    (ii) Low melting-point alloys
    (iii) Metals (and their compounds) used in connection with petroleum warfare and military pyrotechnics.
    (iv) Special abrasives for lens-grinding.
    (v) Compounds constituting potential sources of metals listed under 5 (b) above.

* *Board of Trade Journal*, vol. 160, no. 2844, 23 June 1951, pp. 1321–2

(d) Asbestos and asbestos yarn, textiles and clothing.
(e) Strategic grades of mica.
6. Rubber and Rubber Products.
   (a) Natural Rubber (including latex and scrap).
   (b) Synthetic rubber.
   (c) Oil and fire-resisting rubber hosing and high-pressure hosing.
   (d) Tyres and tubes, other than those for pedal cycles.
7. Chemicals. Chemicals of importance in the production of:
   (a) Chemical warfare preparations.
   (b) Military pyrotechnics.
   (c) Fuels for self-propelling missiles.
   (d) Additives for mineral oils.
   (e) Strategically important plastics.
   (f) Explosives and stabilisers, detonators, initiators and plasticisers for explosives.
   (g) Anti-freeze and de-icing preparations.
   (h) Fluids of use in hydraulically operated mechanisms.
   (i) Materials having application in atomic energy.
   (j) Special steels.
   (k) Tyres and other rubber and synthetic rubber products.
   (l) Refrigerants for use in tanks and submarines.
   (m) Smoke screens and incendiary preparations.
8. Chemicals for use in the exploitation of mineral deposits and ores.
9. Catalysts for use in the manufacture of nitric acid.
10. Chemical and Petroleum Equipment and Plant:
   (a) For the production of poisonous gases.
   (b) For the production of chemicals for explosives, propellants, etc.
   (c) Equipment capable of being used for bacteriological warfare purposes.
   (d) Petroleum refinery equipment.
   (e) Oil well drilling and exploration equipment.
11. Electronic (Including Radio and Radar) Equipment:
   (a) Radar and other radio-location equipment.
   (b) Electronic devices designed or specially suitable for use in warfare.
   (c) Communication equipment including cables.
   (d) Valves and other components specially suitable for use in the above and machinery for making these valves and components.
   (e) Tissues for use in electrical apparatus.
   (f) Other materials having important applications in electronics.
12. Precision and Scientific Instruments.
   (a) Laboratory instruments of importance in research in such strategic fields as Atomic Energy.
   (b) Precision and Scientific instruments capable of being used in the development, production and testing of military equipment.
   (c) Telescopes, binoculars and special optical glass.
13. Other Machinery and Accessories of the following types:
   (a) Metal-working machine tools.
   (b) Specialised types of Rubber Machinery, and Specialised machinery for making tyre fabric.

(c) Diamond tools and industrial diamonds.
(d) Ball and Roller bearings.
(e) Electric generators and Motors.
(f) Compressors for wind tunnels.
(g) Steel Mill Equipment.
(h) Non-ferrous metal concentrating, refining, alloying, rolling and casting equipment.
(i) Portable hand-held power tools.
(j) Welding machines and equipment (including electrodes).
(k) Measuring and testing instruments and machines for use in engineering workshops.
(l) Important abrasives.

Bibliography

PRIMARY SOURCES

Archival Sources

1. *Public Record Office: Kew (London), UK*
Cabinet papers 1949–57 (CAB128, 129, 130, 134)
Board of Trade papers 1939–52 (BT5, 11)
Foreign Office papers 1947–57 (FO371, 800)
Prime Minister's Office: Correspondence and Papers (PREM8, 11)

2. *SOAS, University of London, UK*
China Association:
  Annual Reports, 1949–57
  Bulletins, 1949–56
  British Community Interests Shanghai – Correspondence, 1948–53
  Correspondence with Foreign Office I, 1945–9
  Correspondence with Foreign Office II, (Cresta File) Jan. 1950–July 1956
  Minutes and Circulars, 1949–57
The Papers of John Swire and Sons Ltd: JSS 1–12

3. *Sino–British Trade Council, London, UK*
SBT Committee:
  Working Committee: Agenda and Minutes, 1954–64
  The Orr File (named after Ian C. Orr of FCO)
SBT Council:
  Archival Files on SBTC history 1965–81

4. *The '48' Group, London, UK*
Liaison Committee: Minutes 1954–7
Liaison Committee: Minutes and General Meetings, 1958–63

5. *Hongkong Bank Group Archives, Hong Kong*
Correspondence etc. (GHO154, 164, 170–4)
Shg I (R) 1–870, business letters and agreements
Shg II (R) 1–949, opinions, accounts and closures

6. *Shanghai, China*
The Yee Tsoong Files, Shanghai Academy of Social Sciences
Archives of the China Merchant Steam Navigation Co., Shanghai Ocean
  Shipping Corporation

Printed Primary Sources

China:
Ying Mei Yan Gong Si Zai Hua Qi Yie Zi Liao Hui Bian

(British–American Tobacco Company's Enterprises in China. A Collection of Source Material) 4 volumes, Shanghai Academy of Social Sciences, Institute of Economics (ed.) (Beijing: Zhong Hua Shu Ju, 1983)
Zhong Guo Gong Chan Dang Li Ci Zhong Yao Hui Yi (Major Meetings of the CCP) Zhong Gong Zhong Yang Dang Xiao Jiao Yan Zu (Teaching Group of the CCP Central School of the Party) (Shanghai: Ren Min Chu Ban She, 1982), *vol. I*
Zhong Hua Ren Min Gong He Guo Dui Wai Guan Xi Wen Jian Ji (Collection of Documents on Foreign Relations of the People's Republic of China) 4 volumes, 1949–58 (Beijing: Shi Jie Zhi Shi Chu Ban She (World Knowledge Press), 1959)
Zhong Yang Cai Jing Zheng Ce Fa Ling Hui Bian (Collection of Financial and Economic Decrees of the Central Government) Zheng Wu Yuan Cai Zheng Jing Ji Wei Yuan Hui (Financial and Economic Commission of the Administrative Council) (ed.) vol. 3, 1952
Hong Kong:
Hong Kong Annual Reports, 1949–57 Hong Kong Government Printer, 1949–57 *The Hong Kong Law Reports*, vol. XXXIV, Charles Loseby (ed.) (Hong Kong Government Printer, 1951)
Xiang Gang Yu Zhong Guo   Li Shi Wen Xian Zi Liao Hui Bian (Hong Kong and China: A Collection of Historical Documents and Papers) (Hong Kong: Guang Jiao Jing (Wide Angle) Publishing House, 1984), vol. I
UK:
Annual Statement of the Trade of the United Kingdom with Commonwealth Countries and Foreign Countries (vol. I for each year's series only) 1949–57 (London: H.M. Stationery Office, 1951–59).
Command Papers 1950–54 (Cmd 870B, 8110, 8159, 8366, 8369, 8793, 8938, 9186, 9239)
Parliamentary Debates (Hansard) House of Commons, 1949–57
The Law Reports of Incorporated Council of Law Reporting: House of Lords Judicial Committee of Privy Council and Peerage Cases, London: The Council, 1953
US:
American Foreign Policy, Current Documents, Washington, 1956
Battle Act Report (Mutual Defense Assistance Control Act of 1951) no. 5 (on 1954 revision, added by the 1956 Congressional Hearings, Washington)
Foreign Relations of the United States, Dept. of State, Washington 1944 (6), 1945 (7), 1949 (8–9), 1950 (6–7), 1951 (7), 1952–4 (14–16), 1955–7 (2, 3, 9)

Private Papers

A Study of China's External Debt (with a tentative scheme for the liquidation of the unsecured or insufficiently secured part of the said debt), unsigned, date 20 Feb. 1934, Shanghai Academy of Social Sciences
Butterfield & Swire, 1867–1957, Blue Funnel Bulletin, 1957
113th Annual Report, Council of the Corporation of Foreign Bondholders, 1986
Grantham's Recollections (Sir Alexander, Hong Kong Governor, transcrip-

tion of an interview by D.J. Crozier) Rhodes House, Oxford, n.d.
The Company's 35th Anniversary Commemoration Book, Chinese–Polish
Joint Stock Shipping Company, Shanghai, 1986
Two Decades with People's China, 1952–1972, London Export Corporation,
London, 1972

Newspapers, Periodicals and Miscellaneous Collections

Beijing Library Newspaper Collections, Beijing.
Board of Trade Journal, UK.
Dang Shi Tong Xun (The Party History Circulars) China.
Far Eastern Economic Review, Hong Kong.
Guo Ji Jing Mao Xiao Xi (International Economics and Trade News)
Beijing.
Guo Ji Mao Yi Xiao Xi (International Trade News) Beijing.
Jie Fang Ri Bao (Liberation Daily) Shanghai.
New York Times, New York.
Ren Min Ri Bao (People's Daily) China.
Shi Jie Zhi Shi (World Knowledge) Beijing.
The Economist, UK.
The Manchester Guardian.
The Times, London.
Xin Hua Yue Bao (New China Monthly) China.

Interviews

Berger, Roland, London, 16 December 1986.
Chen, Zengnian, Shanghai, 6 July 1987.
Huan, Xiang, Beijing, 10 and 27 July 1987.
Huang, Hua, Beijing, 3 September 1987.
Marshall, Peter, Liphook, 9 September 1988.
Mi, Rucheng, Beijing, 4 September 1987.
Powell, Christopher, London, 27 January 1989.
Samuel, Herbert G., London, 14 December 1986.
Sloan, S. Gordon, London, 4 January 1989.
Tennant, Sir Peter, Haslemere, 9 September 1988.
Wu, Chengming, Beijing, 9 September 1987.
Officials of the following organisations interviewed prefer to remain anony-
mous:
Bank of England, London.
China Petroleum Corporation, East China Office, Shanghai.
Ministry of Foreign Affairs, Beijing.
Ministry of Foreign Trade and International Economic Relations, Beijing.
Shanghai Foreign Trade Corporation, Head Office, Shanghai.
Shanghai Gas Corporation, Shanghai.
Shanghai Ocean Shipping Corporation, Shanghai.
Shanghai Public Transportation Administration Bureau, Shanghai.
Shanghai Water Corporation, Shanghai.

SECONDARY SOURCES

Books in English

Adler-Karlsson, G., *Western Economic Warfare, 1947–67* (Stockholm: Almqvist & Wilksells Boktryckeri 1968).
Allen, G.C. and Audrey G. Donnithorne, *Western Enterprise in Far Eastern Economic Development: China and Japan* (London: George Allen & Unwin, 1954).
Bank of China, *Chinese Government Foreign Loan Obligations* (Shanghai: Bank of China, 1935).
Barber, Noel, *The Fall of Shanghai* (New York: Coward, Mclann & Geoghegan, 1979).
Barnett, A. Doak, *Communist China: the Early Years, 1949–55* (London: Pall Mall Press, 1964).
Beal, Tim, *A Preliminary Study of Britain's Trade With China Since the War* (University of Edinburgh, 1973–74).
—— *Political Economy of East Asia, No. 4, The China Trade* (Sheffield City Polytechnic, Department of Political Studies, 1982).
—— *Calculating China's Terms of Trade, 1939–1969: Methodological Problems and Strategies* (Glasgow: Department of Marketing, University of Strathclyde, 1984).
Berman, Harold J. and John R. Garson, *United States Export Controls* (New York: Past, Present and Future, 1967).
Blum, Robert M., *Drawing the Line* (New York: W.W. Norton & Company, 1982).
Boardman, Robert, *Britain and the People's Republic of China 1949–1974* (New York: Harper & Row, 1976).
Bullock, Alan, *Ernest Bevin, Foreign Secretary 1945–1951* (London: Heinemann, 1983).
Cairncross, A.K., *Home and Foreign Investment, 1870–1913* (Cambridge University Press, 1953).
Carlson, Ellsworth C., *The Kaiping Mines (1877–1912)* (Cambridge, Mass.: Harvard University Press, East Asian Research Centre, 1957).
Chang, John K., *Industrial Development in Pre-Communist China* (Chicago: Aldine, 1969).
Chang, Kia-Ngau, *The Inflationary Spiral The Experience in China 1939–1950* (Cambridge, Mass.: The Technology Press of MIT; New York: John Wiley and Sons, 1958).
Ch'en, Jerome, *China and the West, Society and Culture 1815–1937* (London: Hutchinson, 1979).
Chen, Ti-Chiang, *The International Law of Recognition* (London: Stevens and Sons, 1951).
Cheng, Nien, *Life and Death in Shanghai* (London: Grafton Books, 1986).
Cheng, Yu-kwei, *Foreign Trade and Industrial Development of China: An Historical and Integrated Analysis Through 1948* (Washington, DC: The University Press of Washington, 1956).
Clabaugh, Samuel F. and Edwin J. Feulner, Jr., *Trading With the Commu-*

nists (Washington, DC: The Center for Strategic Studies, Georgetown University, 1968).

Clifford, Nicholas R., *Retreat from China: British Policy in the Far East, 1937–41* (London: Longmans, 1967).

Cochran, Sherman, *Big Business in China*, (Cambridge, Mass.: Harvard University Press, 1980).

Cole, G.D.H., *The Post-war Conditions of the British Economy* (London: Routledge & Kegan Paul, 1956).

Colin, N. Crisswell, *The Taipans, Hongkong's Merchant Princes* (Hongkong: Oxford University Press, 1981).

Collis, Maurice, *Wayfoong: the Hongkong & Shanghai Banking Corporation Hongkong Bank Group*, 1978.

Deloitte, Haskins and Sells, *Doing Business in the People's Republic of China* (New York: Deloitte, Haskins & Sells, 1983).

DePauw, John W., *US–Chinese Trade Negotiations* (New York: Praeger Publishers, 1981).

Dow, J.C.R., *The Management of the British Economy, 1945–60* (London: Cambridge University Press, 1964).

Doxey, Margaret, *Economic Sanctions and International Enforcement* (London, Oxford, New York: Oxford University Press, 1977).

Drage, Charles, *Taikoo* (London: Constable, 1970).

Earl, Lawrence, *Yangtze Incident* (London: White Lion, 1973).

Eckstein, Alexander, *Communist China's Growth and Foreign Trade* (New York: McGraw Hill, 1966).

—— *China's Economic Revolution* (Cambridge University Press, 1977).

Elvin, Mark, *The Pattern of the Chinese Past, A Social and Economic Interpretation* (Stanford University Press, 1973).

Endacott, G.B., *Government and People in Hongkong 1841–1962* (Hongkong University Press, 1964).

—— *A History of Hong Kong* (Hongkong University Press, 1958).

Fairbank, John K., *The United States and China*, 4th ed. (Cambridge, Mass.: Harvard University Press, 1979).

—— *Trade and Diplomacy on the China Coast* (Cambridge, Mass.: Harvard University Press, 1969).

—— & Albert Feuerwerker (eds) *The Cambridge History of China, vol. 13 'Republican China 1912–1949', Part 2* (Cambridge University Press, 1986).

Feuerwerker, Albert, *The Foreign Establishment in China in the Early Twentieth Century* (Ann Arbor: University of Michigan Centre for Chinese Studies, 1976).

Fieldhouse, D.K. (ed.) *The Theory of Capitalist Imperialism* (London: Longmans, Green & Co, 1967).

Fishel, Wesley R., *The End of Extraterritoriality in China* (Berkeley and LA: University of California Press, 1952).

FitzGerald, C.P., *Mao Tse-tung and China* (Harmondsworth: Penguin Books, 1976).

Fitzsimons, M.A., *The Foreign Policy of the British Labour Government, 1945–1951* (Notre Dame: University of Notre Dame Press, 1953).

Forman, Harrison, *Blunder in Asia* (New York: Didier Publishers, 1950).

Foster, Vivien, *Pearls of Wisdom* (London: Penguin Books, 1987).

Friedman, I.S., *British Relations With China 1931–39* (New York: Institute of Pacific Relations, 1940).

Gittings, John, *The World and China, 1922–1972* (London: Eyre Methuen, 1974).

Gluckstein, Ygael, *Mao's China* (London: George Allen & Unwin, 1957).

Gull, E.M., *British Economic Interests in the Far East* (London: Royal Institute of International Affairs, 1943).

Gurley, John G., *China's Economy and the Maoist Strategy* (New York: Monthly Review Press, 1976).

Hao, Yen-p'ing, *The Comprador in Nineteenth Century China: Bridge Between East and West* (Cambridge, Mass.: Harvard University Press, 1970).

Hinton, Harold C., *China's Turbulent Quest: An Analysis of China's Foreign Relations Since 1949* (New York: Macmillan, 1970).

Holzman, Franklyn D., *International Trade Under Communism – Politics and Economics* (London: Macmillan, 1976).

Hooper, Beverley, *China Stands Up: Ending the Western Presence 1948–1950* (Sydney: Allen & Unwin Australia, 1986).

Hou, Chi-ming, *Foreign Investment and Economic Development in China, 1840–1937* (Cambridge, Mass.: Harvard University Press, 1965).

Howe, Christopher (ed.) *Shanghai, Revolution and Development in an Asian Metropolis* (Cambridge University Press, 1981).

Hoyle, Mark S.W. (ed.) *Cases and Materials on the Law of International Trade* (London: Laucreate-Thomson Press, 1983).

Hsiao, Liang-lin, *Chinese Foreign Trade Statistics 1864–1949* (Cambridge, Mass.: Harvard University Press, East Asian Research Center, 1974).

Hsin, Ying, *The Foreign Trade of Communist China* (Hong Kong: The Union Research Institute, 1954).

Hsü, Immanuel C.Y., *The Rise of Modern China*, 3rd ed. (New York: Oxford University Press, 1983).

Hsü, Ti-hsin, *An Analysis of China's Economy in the Transitional Period*, revised ed. (Beijing, 1959).

Hsueh, Mu-chiao, Su Hsing and Lin Tse-li, *The Socialist Transformation of the National Economy in China* (Beijing: Foreign Languages Press, 1960).

Hughes, T.J. and D.E.T. Luard, *The Economic Development of Communist China, 1948–1958* (London: Oxford University Press, 1959).

International Economic Conference in Moscow (Moscow: Foreign Languages Publishing House, 1952).

Jardine, Matheson and Co. Ltd, *'Jardine' and the Ewo Interests* (New York, 1947).

Jardine, Matheson & Co. *An Historical Sketch* (Hong Kong, 1960).

Jones, F.C., *Shanghai and Tientsin* (London: Oxford University Press, 1940).

Keswick, M. (ed.) *150 Years of Jardine, Matheson & Co: The Thistle and Jade*, (London, 1982).

Khrushchev, Nikita, *Khrushchev Remembers* (London: Sphere Books, 1971).

Kim, Samuel S. (ed.) *China and the World: China's Foreign Policy in the Post-Mao Era* (Boulder and London: Westview Press, 1984).

King, Frank H.H., *The History of The Hongkong and Shanghai Banking*

Corporation: vol. I: *The Hongkong Bank in Late Imperial China 1864–1902 – On Even keel* (Cambridge University Press, 1987).

Kuhlmann, Wilhelm, *China's Foreign Debt 1865–1982* (Hannover: Freiberg Druck, 1983).

Lawrance, Alan, *China's Foreign Relations Since 1949* (London and Boston: Routledge & Kegan Paul, 1975).

LeFevour, Edward T., *Western Enterprise in Late Ch'ing China: A Selective Survey of Jardine, Matheson & Co.'s Operations, 1842–1895* (Cambridge, Mass.: Harvard University Press, 1968).

Li, Victor H. (ed.) *Law and Politics in China's Foreign Trade* (Seattle, University of Washington Press, 1977).

Lieberthal, Kenneth G., *Revolution and Tradition in Tientsin, 1949–1952* (Stanford University Press, 1980).

Loeber, D.A. (comp. and ed.) *East-West Trade: A Sourcebook on the International Economic Relations of Socialist Countries and Their Legal Aspects*, 3 volumes (New York: Oceana Publications, 1976).

Lowe, Peter C., *Britain in the Far East: A Survey from 1819 to the Present* (London: Longmans, 1981).

—— *The Origins of the Korean War* (London: Longmans, 1986).

Luard, Evan,*Britain and China* (London: Chatto & Windus, 1962).

Lucas-Phillips, C.E., *Escape of the Amethyst* (London: Heinemann, 1957).

MacFarquhar, Roderick and John K. Fairbank (eds) *The Cambridge History of China*, vol. 14 *The People's Republic of China 1949–1965* (Cambridge University Press, 1987).

Mah, Feng-Hwa, *The Foreign Trade of Mainland China* (Edinburgh University Press, 1972).

Mao, Zedong, *Selected Works of Mao Tse-tung*, 5 volumes (Beijing: Foreign Languages Press, 1961–77).

Medlicott, W.N., *Economic Warfare*, 2 volumes (London: H.M. Stationery Office, 1952 and 1957).

Medvedev, Roy, *China and the Superpowers* (translated by Harold Shukman) (Oxford: Basil Blackwell, 1986).

Metzger, Stanley D., *Law of International Trade, Documents and Readings*, 2 volumes (Washington DC: Lerners Law Book Company, 1966).

Mikesell, R.F. and J.N. Behrman, *Financing Free World Trade With the Sino–Soviet Bloc* (Princeton University Press, 1958).

Moser, Michael J. (ed.) *Foreign Trade, Investment and the Law in the People's Republic of China* (Hong Kong, Oxford, New York: Oxford University Press, 1987).

Ovendale, Ritchie, *The English-Speaking Alliance, Britain, the United States, the Dominions and the Cold War* (London: George Allen and Unwin, 1985).

—— (ed.) *The Foreign Policy of the British Labour Governments, 1945–1951* (Leicester: London University Press, 1984).

Pannikkar, K.M., *In Two Chinas, Memoirs of a Diplomat* (London: Allen & Unwin, 1955).

Perkins, Dwight (ed.) *China's Modern Economy in Historical Perspective* (Stanford University Press, 1975).

Pfeffer, Richard M., *Understanding Business Contracts in China 1949–1963*

(Cambridge, Mass.: East Asian Research Centre, Harvard University Press, 1973).

Platt, D.C.M., *Business Imperialism, 1840–1930: An Inquiry Based on British Experience in Latin America* (Oxford: Clarendon Press, 1977).

Porter, B.E., *Britain and the Rise of Communist China: A Study of British Attitudes 1945–1954* (London: Oxford University Press, 1967).

Reardon-Anderson, J., *Yenan and the Great Powers: The Origins of Communist Foreign Policy 1944–46* (New York: Columbia University Press, 1980).

Remer, Carl F., *Foreign Investments in China* (New York: Macmillan, 1933).

Ren Jianxin et al., *Legal Aspects of Foreign Investment in the People's Republic of China* (Hong Kong: China Trade Translation Co., 1988).

Renwick, Robin, *Economic Sanctions* (Cambridge, Mass.: Harvard University Center for International Affairs, 1981).

Rooke, Barbara E. (ed.) *The Collected Works of Samuel Taylor Coleridge, The Friend* (I) (London: Routledge & Kegan Paul, 1969).

Rosenau, James N. (ed.) *International Politics and Foreign Policy* (New York: The Free Press, 1969).

Tai, En-sai, *Treaty Ports in China: A Study in Diplomacy* (New York: Columbia University Printing Office, 1918).

Shai, Aron, *Britain and China, 1941–47* (London: Macmillan Press, 1984).

Sit, Victor F.S. (ed.) *Commercial Laws and Business Regulations of the People's Republic of China 1949–1983* (London: Macmillan, 1983).

Strang, William,*The Foreign Office* (London: George Allen and Unwin, 1955).

Teng, S.Y. and J.K. Fairbank, *China's Response to the West: A Documentary Survey 1839–1923* (Cambridge, Mass.: Harvard University Press, 1954).

Thompson, T.N., *China's Nationalization of Foreign Firms: The Politics of Hostage Capitalism, 1949–57* (Baltimore, Ma.: University of Maryland School of Law, 1979).

Trevelyan, Humphrey, *Worlds Apart: China 1953–5, Soviet Union 1962–5* (London: Macmillan London, 1971).

Tucker, Nancy Bernkopf, *Patterns in the Dust: Chinese–American Relations and the Recognition Controversy 1949–1950* (New York: Columbia University Press, 1983).

Tung, William L., *China and the Foreign Powers: The Impact of and Reaction to Unequal Treaties* (Dobbs Ferry, NY: Oceana Publications, 1970).

Vincent, John C., *The Extraterritorial System in China: Final Phase* (Cambridge, Mass.: Harvard University Press, East Asian Research Center, 1970).

Vogel, Ezra F., *Canton Under Communism: Programs and Politics in a Provincial Capital 1949–1968* (New York: Harper & Row, 1971).

Wallace, William, *The Foreign Policy Process in Britain* (London: The Royal Institute of International Affairs, 1975).

Wilczynski, J., *The Economics and Politics of East–West Trade* (London: Macmillan, 1969).

Wiles, Peter J.D., *Communist International Economics* (Oxford: Basil Blackwell & Mott, 1968).

Williams, F., *A Prime Minister Remembers: The War and Post-War Memoirs of the Rt. Hon. Earl Attlee* (London: Heinemann, 1961).
Willoughby, Westel W., *Foreign Rights and Interests in China*, revised edn, 2 volumes (Baltimore: John Hopkins Press, 1927).
Wright, S.F., *China's Struggle for Tariff Autonomy, 1843–1938* (Shanghai: Kelly & Walsh, 1938).
Yahuda, M.B., *China's Role in World Affairs* (London: Croom Helm, 1978).

Articles and Unpublished Theses in English

Baster, A.S.J., 'Origins of British Exchange Banks in China', *Economic History*, Jan. 1934.
Chen, Chin-Yuen, 'American Economic Policy Towards Communist China, 1950–1970', unpublished Ph.D. thesis, Columbia University, 1972.
Chen, F.S., 'Foreign Banking in China', M.Sc (Econ.) thesis at London University, 1937.
Chiu, Hsu-yao, 'The Development of Foreign Trade of China and Her Trade with the U.K.', unpublished Ph.D. thesis, University of Birmingham, 1952.
Chuthasmit, Suchati, 'The Experience of the U.S. and Its Allies in Controlling Trade with the Red Bloc, 1948–1960', unpublished Ph.D. thesis at the Fletcher School of Law and Diplomacy, Tufts University, 1961.
Dernberger, Robert F., 'The Role of the Foreigner in China's Economic Development 1840–1949' in Dwight H. Perkins (ed.) *China's Modern Economy in Historical Perspective* (Stanford University Press, 1975).
Dockrill, M.L., 'The Foreign Office, Anglo–American Relation and the Korean War, June 1950–June 1951', *International Affairs*, 62, 3, 1986, pp. 459–476.
Dulles, John F., 'Our Policies Toward Communism in China,' *U.S. Department of State*, Bulletin 37 (15 July 1957) pp. 91–5
Esherick, Joseph, 'Harvard on China: The Apologetics of Imperialism', *Bulletin of Concerned Asian Scholars*, 4, 4, 1972.
Green, O.M., 'The British in China', *World Review*, July 1952.
Gupta, Karunker, 'How Did the Korean War Begin?', *China Quarterly*, VIII 1972.
Heuser, D.B.G., 'Yugoslavia in Western Cold War Policies, 1948–1953', unpublished D.Phil thesis Oxon., 1987.
Kim, Gye-Dong, 'Western Intervention in Korea 1950–1954', unpublished D.Phil thesis Oxon., 1988.
Lee, Luke T. and John B. McCobb, Jr., 'U.S.Trade Embargo on China, 1949–1970: Legal Status and Future Prospects', *Journal of International Law & Politics* (New York University) 4:1–28, Spring 1971.
Murphy, Rhoads, 'The Treaty Port and China's Modernization: What Went Wrong?' *Michigan Papers on Chinese Studies*, 1970.
Oakeshott, Robert, 'The Strategic Embargo: An Obstacle to East-West Trade', *World Today*, 19:240–247, June 1963.
Osgood, T.K., 'East-West Trade Controls and Economic Warfare', unpublished Ph.D. thesis at Yale University, 1957.
Peffer, Nathaniel, 'China in Reappraisal: Menace to American Security?',

Political Science Quarterly, 71 (Dec. 1956), pp. 481–515.
—— 'Should U.S. Ease China Trade Embargo?', *Foreign Policy Bulletin*, 35 (15 March 1956), pp. 100–102.
Porter, Patrick G., 'Origins of the American Tobacco Company', *Business History Review*, 43.1 Spring 1969.
Shai, Aron 'Imperialism Imprisoned: the Closure of British Firms in the P.R.C.', *The English Historical Review*, 1, 1989, no. 410, pp. 88–109.
Strange, Susan, 'The Strategic Trade Embargoes: Sense or Nonsense?', *Yearbook of World Affairs*, 1958, pp. 55–73.
Tang, James T.H., 'Diplomatic Relations With a Revolutionary Power: Britain's Experience with China, 1949–1954', unpublished Ph.D. thesis at LSE, University of London, 1987.
Tsang, Steve Y.S., 'Hong Kong Constitutional Development, 1949–52', unpublished D.Phil thesis Oxon., 1986.
Watt, D.C., 'Britain and the Cold War in the Far East, 1945–1958' in Nagai and A. Iriye (eds) *The Origins of the Cold War in Asia* (University of Tokyo Press, 1977).
Weiss, Laurance, 'Storm Around the Cradle: The Korean War and the Early Years of the PRC, 1949–53', unpublished Ph.D. thesis at Columbia University, 1981.
Yasuhara, Yoko, 'Japan, Communist China, and Export Controls in Asia, 1948–52', *Diplomatic History*, vol. 10, no. 1, Winter 1986.
Zhang, Zhongli, 'The Development of Foreign Enterprises in Old China and Its Characteristics – The Case of the British–American Tobacco Company', in SASS Editorial Board, *SASS Papers* (Publishing House of Shanghai Academy of Social Sciences, 1986) pp. 132–73.

Books in Chinese

Chen, Zhen *et al.*, (comp.), *Zhong Guo Jin Dai Gong Yie Shi Liao* (Historical Materials on Modern Chinese Industry) vol. II: *Di Guo Zhu Yi Dui Zhong Guo Gong Kuang Shi Yie De Qin Lue He Long Duan* (Imperialist Aggression Against and Monopolisation of China's Industries and Mines) (Beijing: San Lian Shu Dian, 1958).
Da Gong Bao (*Ta Kung Pao*), *Ren Min Shou Ce* (People's Handbook) (Shanghai: Ta Kung Pao She, 1950).
Gao, Pingshu & Ding Yushan, *Wai Ren Zai Hua Tou Zi Zhi Guo Qu Yu Xian Zai* (Foreign Investments in China Past and Present) (Beijing: Zhong Hua Shu Ju, 1947).
Guo, Shihao, *Jiu Zhong Guo Kai Luan Mei Kuang Gong Ren Zhuang Kuang* (Conditions of Workers in Old China's Kailan Mines) (Beijing: Ren Min Chu Ban She, 1985).
Han, Nianlong *et al.* (eds) *Dang Dai Zhong Guo Wai Jiao* (China Today: Diplomacy) (Beijing: Zhong Guo She Hui Ke Xue Chu Ban She [Chinese Social Sciences Press], 1987).
Hei Long Jiang Ren Min Chu Ban She, *Dong Bei Jie Fang Qu Cai Zheng Jing Ji Shi Gao* (A Draft History of the Finance and Economy of the Northeast Liberated Area) Harbin, 1987.
Hu, Hua (ed.) *Zhong Guo She Hui Zhu Yi Ge Ming He Jian She Shi Jiang Yi*

(History of China's Socialist Revolution and Construction: A Textbook for Teaching Purposes) (Beijing: Zhong Guo Ren Min Dai Xui Chu Ban She, 1985).

Hu, Sheng, *Di Guo Zhu Yi Yu Zhong Guo Zheng Zhi* (Imperialism and Chinese Politics) (Beijing: Ren Min Chu Ban She, 1955).

Huang, Yiping (ed.) *Zhong Guo Jin Dai Jing Ji Shi Lun Wen Xuan Ji* (A Collection of Essays on the Economic History of Modern China) (Shanghai: Hua Dong Shi Fan Dai Xui Chu Ban She, 1979).

Jin, Licheng *et al.* (eds) *Shang Hai Gang Shi: Xian Dai Bu Fen* (History of the Shanghai Port: Modern period) (Beijing: Ren Min Jiao Tong Chu Ban She, 1986).

Lan, Yiqiong, *Jie Kai Di Guo Zhu Yi Zai Jiu Zhong Guo Tou Zi De Hei Mu* (Unveil the Medusa of Imperialist Countries' Investment in Old China) (Shanghai: Ren Min Chu Ban She, 1962).

Li, Enji, *Ai Li Yuan Meng Ying Lu* (Dreams and Shadows of the Hardoons Garden) Beijing: San Lian Shu Dian, 1984).

Liu, Binglin, *Jin Dai Zhong Guo Wai Zhai Shi Gao* (A Draft History of Modern China's Foreign Debt) (Beijing: San Lian Shu Dian, 1962).

Liu, Dajun, *Wai Ren Zai Hua Tou Zi Tong Ji* (Statistics of Foreign Investments in China) (Shanghai: Zhong Guo Tai Ping Yang Xue Hui, 1932).

Liu Shaoqi, *Liu Shao Qi Xuan Ji* (Selected Works of Liu Shaoqi) 2 volumes (Beijing: Ren Min Chu Ban She, 1981 and 1985).

Mao, Zedong, *Mao Ze Dong Shu Xin Xuan Ji* (Selected Letters of Mao Zedong) (Beijing: Ren Min Chu Ban She, 1983).

Mi, Rucheng, *Di Guo Zhu Yi Yu Zhong Guo Tie Lu* [Imperialism and China's Railways) *1847–1949* (Shanghai: Ren Min Chu Ban She, 1980).

Nie, Baozhang, *Zhong Guo Mai Ban Zi Chan Jie Ji De Fa Sheng* (Origins of China's Compradore Bourgeois Class) (Beijing: Zhong Guo She Hui Ke Xue Chu Ban She, 1979).

Shanghai Academy of Social Sciences, Editing Board, *Shang Hai Jing Ji* (Shanghai's Economy) *Vol: I: 1949–82*, vol. II: *1983–85* (Shanghai: Ren Min Chu Ban She, 1983 and 1986).

Shang Hai Gang Shi Hua Editing Board, *Shang Hai Gang Shi Hua* (Historical Accounts of the Shanghai Port) (Shanghai: Ren Min Chu Ban She, 1979).

Shang Hai Wai Mao Shi Hua Editing Board, *Shang Hai Wai Mao Shi Hua* (Historical Accounts of Shanghai's Foreign Trade) (Shanghai: Ren Min Chu Ban She, 1976).

Sun, Jian, *Zhong Hua Ren Min Gong He Guo Jing Ji Shi Gao* (A Draft Economic History of the PRC) *1949–1957* (Changchun: Ji Lin Ren Min Chu Ban She, 1980).

Sun, Yutang (comp.) *Zhong Guo Jin Dai Gong Ye Zi Liao* (Historical Materials on Modern Chinese Industry) vol. I, (Beijing: Ke Xue Chu Ban She, 1957)

Wai Jiao Xue Yuan (Foreign Affairs College) (ed.) *Zhong Hua Ren Min Gong He Guo Dui Wai Guan Xi Shi* (History of the Foreign Relations of the PRC) (Beijing, 1964).

Wai Mao Qi Ye Jing Li Chang Zhang Guo Jia Tong Kao Jiao Cai Bian Xie Zu (Editing Board for Compiling Textbooks for National General

Examinations of Senior Managers and Executives of Foreign Trade Corporations), *Dui Wai Mao Yi Li Lun Yu Shi Wu Gai Lun* (A Survey of Theories and Practices of Foreign Trade) (Beijing: Dui Wai Mao Yi Jiao Yu Chu Ban She, 1985).

Wan, Xinping and Pu Wenqi, *Tian Jin Shi Hua* (Historical Accounts of Tianjin) (Shanghai: Ren Min Chu Ban She, 1986).

Wang, Bingnan, *Zhong Mei Hui Tan Jiu Nien Hui Gu* (Nine Years of Sino–US Talks Recalled) (Beijing: Shi Jie Zhi Shi Chu Ban She, 1985).

Wang, Haibo (ed.) *Xin Zhong Guo Gong Ye Jing Ji Shi* (History of Industrial Economy in New China) (Beijing: Jing Ji Guan Li Chu Ban She [Economic Management Press], 1986).

Wang, Jingyu (comp.) *Zhong Guo Jin Dai Gong Ye Shi Zi Liao* (Source Materials on the Industrial History of Modern China) vol. II, (Beijing: Ke Xui Chu Ban She, 1957).

Wei, Lin et al. (eds) *Di Er Ci Shi Jie Da Zhan Hou Guo Ji Guan Xi Da Shi Ji* (Chronicle of Major Events in International Relations After the Second World War) *1945–1979* (Beijing: She Hui Ke Xue Chu Ban She, 1983).

Wei, Zichu, *Di Guo Zhu Yi Yu Kai Luan Mei Kuang* (Imperialism and the Kailan Mines) (Shanghai: Ren Min Chu Ban She, 1954).

——(ed.) *Ying Guo Zai Hua Qi Ye Ji Qi Li Run* (British Enterprises in China and Their Profits) (Beijing: Re Min Chu Ban She, 1951).

Wu, Chengming, *Di Guo Zhu Yi Zai Jiu Zhong Guo De Tou Zi* (Investments of Imperialist Countries in Old China) (Beijing: Ren Min Chu Ban She, 1958).

Wu, Xiuquan, *Zai Wai Jiao Bu Ba Nien De Jing Li* (Eight Years in the Foreign Ministry) (Beijing: Shi Jie Zhi Shi Chu Ban She, 1983).

Xu, Dixin et al. (eds) *Zhong Guo Zi Ben Zhu Yi Gong Shang Ye De She Hui Zhu Yi Gai Zao* (Socialist Transformation of Capitalist Industry and Commerce in China) 2nd ed. (Beijing: Ren Min Chu Ban She, 1978).

Xu, Gongsu and Qiu Jinzhang (eds) *Shang Hai Gong Gong Zu Jie Shi Gao* (Collection of Essays on the History of the Shanghai International Settlement) (Shanghai: Ren Min Chu Ban She, 1986).

Xue, Shixiao, *Zhong Guo Mei Kuang Gong Ren Yun Dong Shi* (History of the Miners' Movement in China) (Zhengzhou: He Nan Ren Min Chu Ban She, 1986).

Xue, Tiandong and Hu Dun-ai, *Xiang Gang Yu Nei Di Mao Yi* (Hong Kong's Trade with Mainland China) (Beijing: Zhong Guo Dui Wai Jing Ji Mao Yi Chu Ban She, 1984).

Yang, Qinliang and Song Ning (eds) *Gong Chan Gou Ji He Zhong Guo Ge Ming Jiao Xue Can Kao Zi Liao* (Comintern and the Chinese Revolution: Background Documents for Teaching Purposes) (Beijing: Zhong Guo Ren Min Da Xue Chu Ban She, 1984).

Yao, Xiangao (ed.) *Zhong Guo Jin Dai Dui Wai Wai Mao Shi Zi Liao* (History of Foreign Trade in Modern China: Background Documents) *1840–1895*, vol. II (Beijing: Zhong Hua Shu Ju, 1962).

Yu, Zhenzhou et al. (eds) *Zhong Gong Dang Shi Jiao Xue Can Kao Zi Liao* (Background Documents on the History of the CCP; A Collection for Teaching Purposes) (Beijing: Zhong Guo Ren Min Da Xue Chu Ban She, 1980).

Zhang, Zhongli and Chen Zengnian, *Sha Xun Ji Tuan Zai Jiu Zhong Guo* (The Sassoons Group in Old China) (Beijing: Ren Min Chu Ban She, 1985).

Zhao, Shumin, *Zhong Guo Hai Guan Shi* (History of China's Maritime Customs) (Taipei: Zhong Yang Wen Wu Gong Ying She, 1982).

Zhong Guo Dui Wai Jing Ji Mao Yi Nian Jian Bian Ji Wei Yuan Hui (Editing Board), *Chinese Yearbook of Foreign Trade and Economic Relations* (Beijing: Zhong Guo Dui Wai Jing Jo Mao Yi Chu Ban She, 1984).

Zhong Guo Ren Min Da Xue (Chinese People's University) *Zhong Guo She Hui Zhu Yi Ge Ming He Jian She Shi Jiao Xue Yan Jiu* (Teaching and Research in History of Socialist Revolution and Construction in China) (Beijing: Zhong Guo Ren Min Da Xue Chu Ban She, 1985).

Zhong Guo Yin Hang Zong Guan Li Chu Jing Ji Yan Jiu Shi (The Research Department, Bank of China) (ed.) *Zhong Guo Wai Zhai Hui Bian* (Chinese Government's Foreign Loan Obligations) (Shanghai, 1935).

Zhong Hua Ren Min Gong He Guo Wai Jiao Bu (Foreign Ministry of the People's Republic of China) (ed.) *Zhong Guo Wai Jiao Gai Lan* (A Survey of China's Diplomatic Relations) (Beijing: Shi Jie Zhi Shi Chu Ban She, 1987).

Zhou, Enlai, *Zhou En Lai Xuan Ji* (Selected Works of Zhou Enlai) 2 volumes (Beijing: Ren Min Chu Ban She, 1980 and 1984).

Zhou, Gengsheng, *Guo Ji Fa* (International Law) 2 volumes, (Beijing: Shang Wu Yin Shu Guan, 1983).

Zi, Zhongyun, *Mei Guo Dui Hua Zheng Ce De Yuan Qi He Fa Zhan* (Origins and Development of the US Policy Towards China) *1945–1950* (Chongqing: Chong Qing Chu Ban She, 1987).

Articles in Chinese

Gao, Pingshu, 'Ying Guo De Jing Ji Kun Nan He Fa Zhan Dong Xi Fang Mao Yi' (Britain's Economic Difficulties and the Development of East–West Trade), *Shi Jie Zhi Shi* (World Knowledge) 1954, 12:22–3.

Geng, Biao, 'Hui Yi Xin Zhong Guo Jie Chu De Wai Jiao Jia Zhang Han Fu Tong Zhi' (In memory of New China's Outstanding Diplomat, Comrade Zhang Hanfu) *Ren Min Ri Bao* (People's Daily) 3 Sept. 1987, p. 5.

Hao, Shuyun, 'Ying Guo Si Shi Ba Jia Ji Tuan Qing Kuang Jian Jie' (A Brief Introduction to the British '48' Group) *Guo Ji Mao Yi Xiao Xi* (International Trade News) *Supplement*, 17 Sept. 1982.

Kang, Maozhao, 'Hong Dong Yi Shi De Ying Jian Chang Jiang Shi Jian' (The British Warship Incident on the Yangtze Which Stirred Public Opinion) *Shi Jie Zhi Shi* (World Knowledge), 1988, 8:25–6, 10:22–3, 11:22–5.

Su, Chao, 'Zhan Wang Zhong Ying Guan Xi' (An Overview of Sino–British Relations), *Shi Jie Zhi Shi* (World Knowledge) 1954, 17:10–11.

Xie, Yao, 'Ying Guo De Dui Wai Mao Yi Wei Ji He Ying Mei Mao Dun De Jian Rui Hua' (Crisis in Britain's Foreign Trade and Intensification of Anglo–American Contradictions) *Shi Jie Zhi Shi* (World Knowledge) 1953, 12:9–11.

Xu, Ziqing, 'Lun Zhong Ying Mao Yi Wen Ti' (On the Question of Sino–British Trade) *Shi Jie Zhi Shi* (World Knowledge) 1952, 30:5–6.

Index